P9-DHM-993

"*The Profit Zone* is so insightful that most managers will pray that their competitors never read it."

—Richard D'Aveni, Amos Tuck School of Business, Dartmouth College; author of *Hypercompetition*

"*The Profit Zone* is by far the best, most informative, and most instructive business book I've read in over a decade."

—David L. Sliney, president, Lamco Ventures, I.L.C.

"*The Profit Zone* could safely come with a guarantee that it would increase a company's profit if management read it and acted on it."

—Philip Kotler, Kellogg School, Northwestern University

"This important and meaningful book is must reading for anyone responsible for business strategy formulation. Slywotzky and Morrison's strategic approach is woven through a range of real-world examples that reinforce the power of creative business design and ongoing reinvention."

—Richard L. Keyser, chairman and chief executive officer, W. W. Grainger, Inc.

"Adrian Slywotzky and David Morrison show how to achieve profitable results by developing superior insight into customers and adapting a company's business design to stay ahead of customer needs, rather than attempting to do more of what you've always done faster and better. *The Profit Zone* gives the reader confidence that these ideas work through clear and detailed examples."

—Samuel J. Palmisano, general manager of the IBM Personal Computer Company

The
PROFIT ZONE

*How Strategic Business Design
Will Lead You to Tomorrow's Profits*

ADRIAN J. SLYWOTZKY
and
DAVID J. MORRISON

with Bob Andelman

THREE RIVERS PRESS

NEW YORK

Also by Adrian J. Slywotzky and David J. Morrison

Profit Patterns
How Digital Is Your Business?

and by Adrian J. Slywotzky

Value Migrations

Copyright © 2001 by Mercer Management Consulting, Inc.

All rights reserved. No part of this book may be reproduced or transmitted in any form or by any means, electronic or mechanical, including photocopying, recording, or by any information storage and retrieval system, without permission in writing from the publisher.

Published by Three Rivers Press, New York, New York.
Member of the Crown Publishing Group, a division of Random House, Inc.

www.randomhouse.com

THREE RIVERS PRESS and the tugboat design are registered trademarks of Random House, Inc.

Originally published in hardcover by Times Business in 1997.

Printed in the United States of America

Library of Congress Cataloging-in-Publication Data

Slywotzky, Adrian J.
    The profit zone: how strategic business design will lead you to tomorrow's profits / Adrian J. Slywotzky and David J. Morrison, with Bob Andelman.
    Includes index.
    1. Success in business.   2. Corporate profits.   3. Competition.
I. Morrison, David. J.   II. Andelman, Bob.   III. Title.
HF5386.S6363   1998
658.15'5—dc21   97-27496

ISBN: 0-8129-3304-4

10 9 8 7 6 5 4 3 2 1

First Paperback Edition

Contents

Preface to the Paperback Edition

IN THE YEARS since the original publication of *The Profit Zone*, the quest for profitability has become more important than ever. The hype of the Internet, the free flow of excess venture capital, and the strength of the equity markets collaborated to create many foolish business models. These facts have increased the need for the discipline of business design reinvention, which we introduced in this book. A high price is being paid by companies and investors that fail to master this discipline or fail to apply its basics to their businesses.

Just looking at one industry, it has become increasingly obvious that traditional product-centric, manufacturing-based business growth is dead. We've recently experienced a time of turmoil in the stock markets, triggered in part by unrealistic expectations from the dot-coms. This turmoil has forced millions of managers and investors to recognize the failure of many companies to develop plans for long-term, sustainable growth. Yet even before the recent market meltdown, once-great product-based companies were already stumbling. In just months, firms like Gillette, Polaroid, Lucent, Procter & Gamble, Maytag, and many others lost between forty and one hundred percent of their market value.

The collapse of the high-tech sector ratified the sense of gloom. The apparent strength of that sector during most of the 1990s was really little more than a series of bottle rockets—sizzling, dizzying ascents followed by equally spectacular crashes to earth. Most had products that played to the market's endless excitement for low-cost digital bandwidth, but had business designs that were neither profitable nor sustainable. (Intel, IBM, Cisco, and Microsoft seem to represent exceptions—great businesses with long-term prospects built on a high-tech base. Are there any others? We're hard put to name them.) This short-lived tech era was simply a replay of the bankrupt, unworkable strategy of "Grow first and profit later," which people have tried to practice for decades, without success. The Japanese tried to grow their product-centric, manufacturing-led economy into profitability during the 1980s. They spent the 1990s paying for that mistake. The similar attempt by the "Asian Tigers" ended in the collapse of 1997.

In short, the No-Profit Zones whose existence we warned about in *The Profit Zone* have spread and multiplied globally, engulfing thousands of companies in arenas from consumer packaged goods to automobiles to telecommunications to the Internet.

Now, we're looking forward to the real possibility that the next decade will be a sustained period of low profit and low growth for all of the thousands of businesses that don't understand where tomorrow's profit will come from and how to reinvent their obsolete business designs accordingly.

Major economic trends are involved, of course. The current slowdown has made it impossible to ignore the structural weaknesses of many poorly designed companies. But this doesn't mean that businesses are helpless, or that there's no effective, proactive strategy for business leaders to pursue in a time of recession. In fact, there's no question that real, sustainable profitability and growth can be achieved, even in a highly challenging business climate like the one we face today. One need only look at a company like IBM—a remarkable example of a major company that has successfully transformed its disadvantageous hardware business model to fit the profitability demands of a new economic landscape. Dozens of smaller companies have achieved similar turnarounds in almost every conceivable business arena. It can be done.

The first step for any business leader is to ask the crucial questions:

- How does profitability happen in my business today?
- How will it happen in the foreseeable future?
- Who will be my most valuable customers?
- How will their critical priorities evolve?
- How must I reinvent my business design to take advantage of the new paths to profitable customer-centric growth?

Though the same questions must be faced by every business, the answers will vary widely. In *The Profit Zone*, we offer our analysis of the experiences of some of the great businesses of the recent past as a guide for discovering the answers that will work for your company today and tomorrow.

ADRIAN SLYWOTZKY
DAVID MORRISON
Boston, Massachusetts
October, 2001

PART ONE

Succeeding in the Changing
World of Business

ONE

MARKET SHARE IS DEAD

THE NUMBER one problem in business today is *profitability*. Where will you be *allowed* to make a profit in your industry? Where is the profit zone today? Where will it be tomorrow?

The profit zone is the area of your economic neighborhood where you are allowed to earn a profit. To reach and operate in the profit zone is the goal of every company.

You've been told how to get there. "Get high market share and the profit will follow." "Get high growth and your profits will expand." As a manager, you were schooled in how the pursuit of market share and growth automatically places you on a direct route to business success.

However, these formerly direct roads have become mazes riddled with traps, wrong turns, and dead ends. Many large companies, after taking the turn toward market share and volume growth, have only hit a profitless wall.

* * *

Market share was the grand old metric, the guiding light, the compass of the product-centric age. Companies focused on improving their product and building economies of scale. This product-centric thinking led to the battle cry: "Get more market share and the profit will follow."

In the past decade, some disturbing examples began to subvert the widespread faith in market share as the ultimate goal and guarantor of business success. Consider the experience of IBM, DEC, GM, Ford, United Airlines, US Steel, Kodak, Sears, and Kmart. All achieved leading market share positions: number one or number two in their industries. Yet all these market share leaders saw their profitability begin to erode during the 1980s. Their dominant share positions did not protect them. As profitability began to be detached from market share, shareholders began to suffer. Despite their strong market position, these market share leaders significantly underperformed the S&P 500 from 1985 to 1995.

Several of these companies have recently initiated radical changes in their business design. Their new focus on profit, not just market share, has led to dramatic rebounds in value. As a result, many other traditional market share leaders have been encouraged to reconsider the assumptions on which their business design is built.

As you think about your own business, ask yourself: Am I managing for market share, or for profit? Is the market share I own profitable and alive, or is it profitless and dead?

There are countless businesses with high market share but low profitability and low shareholder value. The Japanese have a lock on the memory chip market. USAir once dominated air travel in the eastern United States. Philips is a leader in consumer electronics. None of these companies has experienced significant value growth.

Nor are these isolated cases. The list goes on:

- *A&P had a high share of grocery sales.*
- *Intel had a high share of memory chips.*
- *WordPerfect had a high share of word processor software.*
- *DEC had a high share of minicomputers.*
- *Kmart had a high share of the urban discount business.*

Each company was a market share triumph and a profitability disaster. In a broad cross-section of high market share situations, the right economic response has been: "So what?"

Many companies simply hoped that profitability would return. Some managers inside the companies suspected that it would not, but were hesitant to bring that suspicion to the surface and open up a debate. How could they possibly argue against a high market share position?

Other managers, in their private, honest moments, *knew* that the profit would never come back but were hesitant to confront the issue openly, fearing that the organization's morale would plummet.

Intel was an exception. It was the one company on the above list that confronted the issue head-on. It had high market share in memory chips in 1985, but Intel's managers recognized that its market share was dead, valueless, and profitless. The 1980s game was over; it was time to build the company's next business design.

Companies like Intel force us to think harder about—or to completely rethink—market share as a predictor of profitability.

AM I MANAGING FOR VOLUME GROWTH OR VALUE GROWTH?

"Be in high-growth markets." In the old economic order, in the age of market share, volume growth was a guarantor of success. Growth was what we were taught to pursue. It created higher profits for all, including market share laggards, companies with poor business designs, and companies that were poorly managed. A rising tide raised all boats. One manager articulated the classic view: "There are no management problems that volume growth can't solve. Even if we manage poorly, rising revenue helps cover the mistakes we made."

This maxim, too, has been shaken. Industry growth and a company's value (stock price) growth no longer have a one-to-one correlation. Fast-growing industries such as PC manufacturing, consumer electronics, telecommunications, and software have each produced scores of terminally unprofitable companies. By contrast, no-growth or low-growth industries have produced some of the most successful companies in the world. Coca-Cola achieved significant value growth in the low-growth beverage industry, as did General Electric (GE) in a collection of low-growth manufacturing industries, and Swatch in the low-growth watchmaking industry.

The two most valuable ideas in the old economic order, market share and growth, have become the two most dangerous ideas in the new order. To apply these ideas appropriately (and safely), you must understand the rise of no-profit zones in the economy.

NO-PROFIT ZONES

Companies used to be able to command a premium price by simply showing up. There were relatively few players in any competitive arena, and customers held little power. Over the past two decades, however, advances in industrial technology, innovation in business design, increases in global competition, and tremendous improvements in information technology have altered the game. In the face of intense competition, companies in many industries have leveraged efficiency gains and competed for market share by lowering price.

Simultaneously, information has become more accessible to customers, allowing them to conveniently shop for the best deals and the best prices. This forces all contenders to match price reductions or lose customers to a lower-priced competitor. It creates no-profit zones. In the old world, the rule was: Every industry makes money, and the market share leaders make the most money. There have always been one or two exceptions, such as agriculture or passenger rail travel, but they were few and far between.

In the past decade, the rule was broken. Today, no-profit zones are everywhere, and they are growing. The map of the economy is covered with more and larger patches of unprofitability. No-profit zones come in various forms. They can be a part of the value chain (e.g., distribution in computing); they can be a customer segment (e.g., the Medicaid segment in healthcare, or the grocery segment in carbonated beverages); they can be an entire industry (e.g., environmental remediation); they can be individual customers (e.g., Wal-Mart or other large, powerful buyers); or they can be entire business models (e.g., hub-and-spoke airlines, or integrated steel mills).

No-profit zones are the black holes of the business universe. In a physical black hole, light waves go in, but never come back out. In an economic black hole, investment dollars go in, but the profit dollars never come back out.

Paradoxically, the devout pursuit of market share may be the single greatest creator of no-profit zones in the economy.

Imagine an industry with ten competitors. By definition, their market shares add up to 100 percent. Read their strategic plans. They *all* plan to *increase* market share. Not by a little, but by a lot.

Add up the 5-year market share objectives, and you get a number that adds up to 150 to 170 percent of market share.

This, of course, cannot happen. It doesn't make sense; but even as you read this, it is going on around you—perhaps in your own industry or in your own company.

The vigorous pursuit of market share and the rise in customer power have driven profit from many activities and products, and even from entire industries. More and more no-profit zones have been created. Still, many companies continue to pursue a market share and volume growth strategy, trying to get a bigger piece of a pie that is losing all of its value.

A senior manager at an equipment manufacturer captured perfectly the spirit of market share myopia that dominated the thought processes, and the business press, in the age of market share:

> We are all focused on market share, on units, units, units. Units sold vs. competitors'. Units sold this quarter vs. same quarter last year. We focus on every single point, or fraction of a point, of market share gained, or lost.
>
> And it's not just our management team. It's our competitors' management teams. And it's the periodicals that follow our industry. The market share tables come out and we all follow them as closely as NBA standings.

All too often, the vigorous pursuit of market share is done at the expense of business design innovation. However, market share leadership in a no-profit zone, or high market share with the wrong business design, is more of a curse than a blessing.

GROWTH, WITH THE WRONG BUSINESS DESIGN, DESTROYS VALUE FASTER

It is easy to understand the trap of market share and growth in a no-profit zone. It is more difficult to understand how growth in a thriving industry can be dangerous. Growth is important, but *how growth is achieved* is much more important.

There are three curses of growth. First, high growth with a bad business design destroys value faster. Witness the value destruction occurring in so many high-tech, high-growth industries today. Growth is attractive, but growth carries high risk, especially when the business design is wrong.

Second, besides being riskier, high growth is much harder to manage. The euphoria of being in a high-growth environment blocks out the reality that growth creates a much higher *management* challenge.

An aerospace industry executive explained:

> Managing in a downturn is hard, but managing high growth intelligently is much harder. You're tempted to overbuild capacity, add infrastructure, headcount, lots of fixed cost. Then when the growth waters recede, you're stuck in a no-profit zone with lots of resources and lots of red ink. It's a great way to destroy shareholder value. Businesses do it all the time.

The third curse of growth arises when a business grows by stretching its business design to serve customers that the business design was not intended to serve. To make up for the mismatch, the company is forced to lower prices or expand its scope into areas where it is not operationally efficient. Both of these actions depress profitability. Once again, the end result is a no-profit zone.

No-profit zones are emerging every day. Activities that were once valuable turn profitless. Value migrates toward activities that are more important to customers—activities where profit is possible.

Yesterday's profit zones are becoming, with increasing frequency, today's no-profit zones.

REINVENTORS

In the past decade, several business leaders have emerged who have figured out, or intuitively understood, how the rules of the game have changed. Their record of value growth is all the more remarkable when compared to the growth prospects of their industries and the lagging value performance of the market share leaders.

These reinventors think differently; they see things differently; they act differently. They start with the customer and work their way back. They start with the profit question ("Where will I be allowed to make a profit?") and work their way back. They are constantly focused on how the profit zone is shifting. Where is it today? Where will it be tomorrow?

A decade ahead of their peers, the reinventors saw the move from the old product-centric, market share world to the new customer-centric and profit-centric environment. They were not alone; the investment community also understood that the sands were shifting. It downgraded the "old order" market share stocks and reallocated its investment dollars to the "new order" reinventor companies. The old order companies concentrated on market share and yesterday's profit zone. The new order companies reinvented their business design every five years to stay relevant to customers and to move into new profit zones. Several hundred billions of dollars of value shifted from companies that had dominated yesterday's profit zone to those that were finding or creating the profit zones of tomorrow.

LONG LIVE MARKET SHARE

Ironically, the reinventors all created high market share for their companies, but their way of thinking about market share was diametrically opposed to the logic of the conventional approach.

The sequence of the conventional approach was:

1. *Gain market share.*
2. *Profitability will follow.*

The reinventors' logic was:

1. *What's most important to the customer?*
2. *Where can we make a profit?*
3. *How can we gain market share in that space?*

This difference in sequence reflects two very different ways of thinking. The conventional approach was market share-centric. The reinventors' approach is customer-centric and profit-centric.

Reading about *how* the reinventors created a record of sustained value growth can help you to learn a different way of thinking. You will gain an expanded repertoire of strategic and tactical moves that you can use to create the next profit zone in your industry. The reinventors' experience can help you to understand:

- *What specific business design moves can manufacturers with disappearing margins adapt from GE's business design in order to reestablish a path of profit growth?*
- *What principles of business design did Nicholas Hayek apply to build a 20 percent profit growth business for Swatch in what appeared to be a terminal no-profit zone?*
- *What are the three changes in its business design that allowed Coca-Cola to grow its value from $10 billion to $150 billion?*
- *What two specific profit models did Disney use to grow the company's profit from $100 million to $3 billion in less than a decade?*
- *How did Intel repeatedly change its business design to grow its value from $3 billion to $100 billion in the past 20 years?*

Part Two of this book answers these questions and provides insight into how these and other reinventors systematically built customer-centric and profit-centric business designs to create value for shareholders. Each example highlights the strategic and organizational challenges that each leader faced and the innovative moves that were made in response. Like many innovators in other arenas, the reinventors have been able to see things that others couldn't (or wouldn't) see. You can learn to see those things by studying their success.

INNOVATION IN BUSINESS DESIGN

Each of the questions listed above asks how a major company fundamentally redefined itself and the way it does business—how it reinvented its business design. We all know intuitively what a business design is, but it helps to be explicit about the key strategic dimensions that define a company's business design.

A company's business design is composed of four strategic elements: (1) customer selection, (2) value capture, (3) strategic control, and (4) scope. If the business is to succeed, it must be designed in such a way that its key elements are aligned with customers' most important priorities. It must be *designed* for profitability. And, its elements must be tested for consistency with each other, to ensure that the business design functions as a coherent and mutually reinforcing whole.

The customer selection dimension of a business design describes the company's chosen customer set. A business has the opportunity to choose and to segment its customers based on the customer set to which it is best suited, or the one it is best able to serve. A business may change the customers it chooses to serve as value migrates to a new customer set or new customer segments. This can be a wrenching change for an organization. Moving away from customers is among the most difficult decisions a company can make. But it is critical. It is as important for you to ask yourself, "Whom do I choose *not* to have as my customer?" as it is to ask, "Whom do I choose to be my customer?"

The value capture dimension of a business design describes how the company gets rewarded for the value it creates for its customers. Traditionally, companies have captured value through product sales or service fees. Product-centric thinking limits itself to these traditional means of capturing value. Today, reinventor companies employ a more extensive repertoire of value capture mechanisms than they ever have before: financing, ancillary products, solutions, downstream participation in the value chain, value sharing, licensing, and many others. They get rewarded for the value they deliver to customers in highly innovative ways.

The strategic control of a business design refers to the company's ability to protect its profit stream. It answers the questions: "Why should a customer buy from me? Why *must* a customer buy from me?" There are at least ten different ways to create a strategic control point for a business (see Chapter 3). Strength of strategic control is a critical element in successful business design innovation.

The scope of a business design refers to the company's activities and its product and service offerings. Companies increase or decrease their scope constantly. The key question for business designers is: "What changes in scope do I need to make to remain customer-relevant, to generate high profits, and to create strategic control?"

EXHIBIT I.I *The Dimensions of Business Design*

Dimension	Key Issue	Key Questions
1. Customer Selection	Which customers do I want to serve?	To which customers can I add real value? Which customers will *allow* me to profit? Which customers do I *not* want to serve?
2. Value Capture	How do I make a profit?	How do I capture, as profit, a portion of the value I created for customers? What is my profit model?
3. Differentiation/ Strategic Control	How do I protect my profit stream?	Why do my chosen customers buy from me? What makes my value proposition unique/differentiated vs. other competitors'? What strategic control points can counterbalance customer or competitor power?
4. Scope	What activities do I perform?	What products, services, and solutions do I want to sell? Which activities or functions do I want to perform in-house? Which ones do I want to subcontract, outsource, or work with a business partner to provide?

Exhibit 1.1 profiles the four strategic dimensions of a company's business design. Each dimension is linked to all the others. For example, which customers I choose depends in part on which customers will allow me to make a profit. How I make a profit depends in part on the scope of activities I perform. Decisions about differentiation and strategic control depend on who the customers are and the scope of activities the firm is capable of. Decisions about scope should support decisions about what customers to serve, how to create profit, and how to create strategic control.

When these choices match customer priorities and are internally consistent and mutually reinforcing, they can produce an extraordinarily powerful business design for the company. The reinventors have achieved an extraordinary level of excellence in the design choices they have made.

Great business design is just like great product design. Extraordinary achievement in product design is a combination of superb engineering and great imagination. Similarly, great business design is a combination of superb *knowledge* about customers and profit ("You can't intuit the facts"), together with great strategic imagination. The reinventors' unique skill is strategic creativity: constantly reversing traditional assumptions, developing new options, and making more inspired choices.

To ensure long-term viability, a company's business design must be reinvented as customers' needs and priorities change and as value migrates away from the industry's traditional business designs. Just as products become technologically obsolete, business designs become economically obsolete. Over time, because of the competitive nature of business, most business designs are no longer allowed to make a profit. Their profit zone has moved. If a company hopes to create value for shareholders and wants to continue operating in its profit zone, it must reinvent its business design every five years, or even sooner.

THE NEXT TURN OF THE WHEEL

The reinventors know that the game is *never* over. For each company, the ground is shifting and the profit zone is moving once again. Intel faces the K6-chip challenge from Advanced Micro Devices (AMD). Coca-Cola faces a newly focused Pepsi. Microsoft faces the Internet. Disney faces accelerating imitation from Time Warner.

Similar types of challenges face the other reinventors. Unless their business designs are reinvented, their profits will start to bleed away. More importantly, their customers are changing. For every customer group, yesterday's magic is turning into today's commodity.

Lew Platt, CEO of Hewlett-Packard, has an invaluable perspective on reinventing: "The single biggest problem in business is staying with your previously successful business model . . . one year too long."

Whether you think of it as "paranoia" à la Andrew Grove ("Only the paranoid survive"), or as staying with the old formula too long, the message is identical: When customers move, the profit zone moves. You must reinvent your business design to move with them.

This is not news to the reinventors. Most have created a new architecture for their business model every five to seven years. But having done it successfully in the past is no guarantee that the next design will work. Each design has to be right for the customers and right on the economics. Each reinvention takes incredible concentration and hard thought. The case examples developed in Part Two are provided to help you through the process.

CRACKING THE CODE ON PROFITABILITY

Roberto Goizueta, CEO of Coca-Cola, likes to say: "You can think through a problem so hard that you develop a sweat." The problem to think about that way is *profitability*. Where is it today? How does it really happen? Where will it be tomorrow?

If organizations don't answer these questions correctly, much of their efforts will be wasted.

Where is the profit? In yesterday's world, the answer was: with the player who has the highest market share. In today's world, the answer is: with the player who has the best business model, a model *designed* for customer relevance and high profitability.

Thinking about profitability isn't easy, for several reasons. First, the profit zone, the arena in which high profit is possible, keeps changing and keeps moving. The customer doesn't stand still, and the business design must respond (see Chapter 2). Second, there are at least twenty-two different ways that high profit happens—twenty-two different models that explain and quantify the mechanism by which profit occurs (see Chapter 3). Third, most organizations use two or three of these profit models. Understanding which ones to apply in which circumstances requires careful thought and considerable organizational persistence.

In this new economic order, characterized not by equilibrium but by fluidity, customers and profit zones always shift. To reinvent its business design and stay a step ahead of these shifts, a company must move beyond product-centric thinking to a customer-centric approach. Market share thinking must yield to a profit-centric approach. The ideas behind customer-centric and profit-centric thinking are critical to success in the new world of business. We will spend the next two chapters developing these two ideas.

TWO

CUSTOMER-CENTRIC BUSINESS DESIGN

THIRTY YEARS ago, the customer didn't matter. That sounds heretical, but it is true. In the postwar business landscape of the 1950s and 60s, customer demand outstripped capacity. It was a supplier's world, and large monolithic companies ruled. These sellers were in the economy's driver's seat.

Today, in contrast, the number of customer options is dwarfed only by the amount of information available about each option. There has been a secular shift in power from the supplier to the customer. Highly competitive markets and abundant information have placed the customer at the center of the business universe. In this new environment, successful businesses are those that employ customer-centric thinking to identify customer priorities and construct business designs to match them.

WHAT IS CUSTOMER-CENTRIC THINKING?

Let's begin with what customer-centric thinking isn't. It isn't traditional, conventional market research—mountains of data, hundreds of tables, and no actionable insight. Nor is it traditional customer satisfaction research, an important but backward-looking measurement of how yesterday's decision makers rated us on what was important in yesterday's business model.

Conventional market research tries to measure everything. Strategic, customer-centric thinking deciphers the puzzle of the customer's top two or three priorities with enough insight to have a good chance of matching those priorities profitably.

To create a strategic and dynamic perspective on the customer, one must have a clear and compelling point of view on one question:

Exactly how is the customer changing?

Write this question down. It is your single most powerful management weapon. The answer to this question does not come from conventional market research or traditional customer satisfaction analysis. It comes from a powerful desire to crack the code of shifting customer priorities by doing complex, demanding, street-level detective work.

Typical market research explores quickly and measures profusely. It is often too removed from the customer to be of help; a firm hires a market research company to conduct a survey that asks customers a limited set of multiple-choice questions. Answers are then aggregated and cut a number of different ways to reveal "true" customer preferences. Such research may ask the wrong questions or not probe deeply enough. In contrast, customer-centric thinking needs to look at the customers' problems through the customers' eyes, not through the eyes of a market researcher. The customer-centric thinker spends time talking to customers rather than reading market research reports. The conversations yield an understanding of the customer's problems directly from the customer's perspective—a far cry from getting this information filtered through a large and cumbersome report.

Successful entrepreneurs live at the opposite end of the spectrum from conventional market research. The entrepreneur's customer exploration process is alive, pulsating, interactive; filled with energy, missteps, miscues, errors, insights, and aha!s. Successful entrepreneurs act on those insights and design their businesses around what they have learned. Through direct contact with the customer, the entrepreneur is able to identify solutions to the customers' problems that unlock the customers' enthusiasm, budgets, and loyalty.

Customer-centric thinking is not a colorless, odorless, bloodless process. It is messy, nonlinear, and confusing—but it is essential. Customer-centric thinking asks: So what? Who cares?

WHY IS CUSTOMER-CENTRIC THINKING SO HARD?

Customer-centric thinking is not easy for managers in business today, for two reasons. First, because managers—particularly those at the senior executive level, whose careers span two decades or longer—were trained in a product-centric world. They were trained to continually focus on improving their products, increasing their market share, and growing their revenues. They became senior managers because they functioned well in this world.

Second, customer-centric thinking is difficult because of what happens when companies succeed. Over time, a company's center of gravity moves. As Exhibit 2.1 indicates, during the entrepreneurial phase, the center of gravity of a company's thinking resides with the customers. A small business *must* focus intensely on the customers or it will fail. As the company grows, the center of gravity begins to

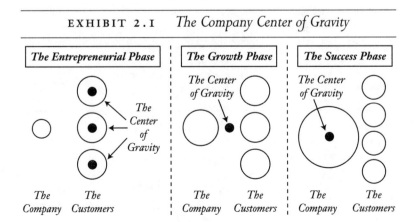

EXHIBIT 2.1   *The Company Center of Gravity*

shift in small, subtle degrees. It moves away from the customers and toward the company itself. In the success phase, the company grows ever bigger and the center of gravity moves more toward the company and away from the customers. Finally, it is in the company, which is now focused on itself. A company focused on itself—its internal budgets, internal resource concerns, and internal politics—will have a great deal of difficulty with customer-centric thinking.

REVERSE THE VALUE CHAIN

To begin customer-centric thinking, managers must reverse the traditional value chain (Exhibit 2.2). The traditional value chain begins with the company's core competencies, its assets. It then moves to inputs and other raw materials, to an offering, to the channels, and then finally to the customer. This value chain begins with the assets and then finds ways to make those assets into a product or a service that will fit into the template of what's important to the customer. This entire thought process needs to be reversed.

EXHIBIT 2.2   *The Value Chain*

The Traditional Value Chain
Start with Assets, Core Competencies

Assets/ Core Competencies	Inputs, Raw Material	Product/ Service Offering	Channels	The Customer

The Modern Value Chain
Start with the Customer

Customer Priorities	Channels	Offering	Inputs, Raw Material	Assets/ Core Competencies

Customer-centric thinking begins first with the customer and then moves, ultimately, to the assets and core competencies. Customer-centric thinking focuses on the customers' needs and priorities and identifies options through which these needs and priorities can be met in the best way possible. It literally reverses the value chain so that the customer is the first link in the chain and everything else follows—everything else is driven by the customer. Managers should think of: (1) what their customers' needs and priorities are; (2) what channels can satisfy those needs and priorities; (3) the service and products best suited to flow through those channels; (4) the inputs and raw materials required to create the products and services; and, (5) the assets and core competencies essential to the inputs and raw materials.

RESTRUCTURE MANAGEMENT'S TIME

Cracking the code on your customers' needs and priorities can't be accomplished within your office.

The key information needed is "out there" in the market: in the customer's office, or factories and warehouses, or operational systems. This reality points directly to a radical restructuring of senior management's time.

In the old economic order, most of the information you needed to succeed came from inside your company and inside your industry. Today, the key information you need comes from outside your company (the customer base and the edge of the competitive radar screen) and outside your industry (great business designs, already developed by others, that can solve the strategic problems your company faces).

Unfortunately, a recent survey indicated that senior managers still spend 70 percent of their time "on the inside." And the 30 percent of their time dedicated to "outside" activities is fragmented among suppliers, security analysts, journalists, charities, other boards, and customers. In the old economic order, this distribution of energy made sense. In a value migration world, it doesn't.

With value rapidly flowing from old business models to new business designs with more customer relevance, you must reverse the inside/outside ratio. Spend most of your time "outside," with customers. Don't spend your time with customers who like you. Seek out the customers who are the most demanding, the angriest, and the most insightful about tomorrow.

Finally, don't go into these customer dialogues asking yourself, "What do I need to know?" Ask the right questions, such as: "What am I afraid to find out?" The answer to this second question will give you the best clues about how to change your business design to win tomorrow's customers and to capture tomorrow's profits.

Mastering the art of honest and persistent customer dialogue will always open new opportunities for profit growth. It will also create enormous frustration among your competitors. As an example, an executive at a GE competitor summarized the difference between his firm (a major materials supplier) and GE:

Our senior managers' time looks like this:

Schedule A
9:00	Internal Meeting
10:00	Internal Meeting
11:00	Internal Meeting
12:00	Lunch
2:00	Internal Meeting

The problem is that Jack Welch's schedule looks like this:

Schedule B
9:00	Customer Meeting
10:00	Customer Meeting
11:00	Customer Meeting
12:00	Lunch (with customer)
2:00	Customer Meeting

Schedule B trumps Schedule A every time. With direct access to a constantly shifting data stream, successful managers get the critical information they need. They figure out the customer's number-one priority and build a customer-centric business design around it—one that will score highest on the customer's most important decision criteria.

CRACK THE CODE ON
CUSTOMER PRIORITIES

The value of any product or service is the result of its ability to meet a customer's priorities. Customer priorities are, in simple terms, the things that are so important to customers that they will pay a premium for them or, when they can't get them, they will switch suppliers.

Customer priorities have a variety of different elements, from purchase criteria to systems economics (Exhibit 2.3).

Each of these dimensions contributes to a customer's priorities when considering a supplier. To understand the customer, the manager must be asking the right questions of the right person. Within an industrial customer, there is rarely one buyer or one source of influence. There are many, and they are scattered throughout the customer's organizational pyramid.

The challenge in strategic customer analysis lies not only in understanding multiple levels within an organization, but in using various methodologies to put together a mosaic of the real picture. The structure of a customer's needs, behavior, decision-making process, price sensitivities, and preferences is as complex as any molecule. In

---

EXHIBIT 2.3 *The Modern Value Chain*

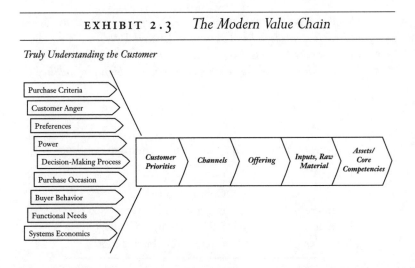

Truly Understanding the Customer

molecular science, researchers use X-ray crystallography (taking pictures from many angles) to determine the true structure of the molecule. In customer science, the same approach is needed.

And although the picture in X-ray crystallography is never perfect or complete, a working sense of a molecule's structure can be created. So, too, in deciphering the structure of the customer, interviews, economic analysis, surveys, focus groups, trade-off analyses, and a rich array of other methods all give a *partial* reading. Integrating them is even harder and trickier than creating the pieces, but that's where the value and the insight are found.

Consider the descriptives in Exhibit 2.4. Which ones describe the customers served by your company or your industry?

An understanding of how your customers feel, and why, offers you a major opportunity to find clues about changing priorities and future profit growth opportunities. Many organizations, blinded by their traditional way of doing business, fail to stay on top of their customers' key priorities. As one senior executive recently put it, "We don't see things as *they* are, we see things as *we* are." As a result, in many industries, customers are bored, angry, and disinterested. The industry is populated by very similar business designs that compete in the same way and are product-focused rather than customer-centric. This type of situation presents great opportunities for entrepreneurs and newcomers to:

- *Decipher what customer priorities are being ignored (a clear link to the words in the left-hand column in Exhibit 2.4).*
- *Invent a new business design that responds to those priorities.*
- *Create a new profit zone with extraordinarily high profitability.*

EXHIBIT 2.4 *Customers' Responses*

Bored	Enthusiastic
Angry	Committed to you
Disinterested	Eager to talk to you
Distant	Excited about your offering
Arm's-length contact	Interested in buying more

The entrepreneur or newcomer doesn't have to come from outside the industry. Your company could play that role. The key is to understand your customers' priorities.

The reinventors profiled in this book are masters at customer-centric thinking. They identified the changes in their customers' priorities and reinvented their businesses with those changes in mind. Nicolas Hayek, head of SMH, the Swiss watchmaking company, understood that a growing set of consumers would buy watches based on taste and emotion, rather than on prestige. Roberto Goizueta understood that, in many situations, Coca-Cola's customers' priority is not price but availability and that the key customer in the system is the bottler, whose actions determine how available the product will be. Charles Schwab broke away from the traditional "customer as sales target" mentality when he saw that investors had varying desires for guidance and a high distaste for pressure selling. Michael Eisner at Disney saw that customers were willing to pay more money for toys and other products related to Disney movies. Jack Welch saw that GE's customers saw less value in the product and more value in the services and financing. And Bill Gates saw where customer priorities were shifting in the computer industry time and time again—from languages to operating systems to applications to communications to the Internet. These and other examples, such as Intel's unique perspective on customer power and ASEA Brown Boveri's (ABB) devotion to being best at serving several distinct customer groups, are discussed in Part Two.

SILENT PRIORITIES: CRACK THE CODE ON SYSTEMS ECONOMICS

Even putting the right questions to the right people will not always provide a manager with enough information, because not all of a customer's needs are articulated. Every customer has a broad set of needs—some spoken, others silent.

Managers are challenged to get a clear read on the spoken needs, but they must apply a considerable degree of rigorous creativity to reach the *silent* needs. Customers are not always able to communicate their entire range of needs; some remain silent, poorly defined, or poorly articulated because companies are organized in silos, and the different silos don't speak to or share information with one another. In today's business landscape, it becomes the supplier's job to identify these silent needs, define them, and give them a voice in the supplier's decision-making process.

One of the most powerful tools for ferreting out those silent, unarticulated, and, at times, unknown priorities is analysis of the customer's systems economics (Exhibit 2.5), regardless of whether you are dealing with an industrial buyer, a family, or an individual customer.

A customer's systems economics includes the amount paid for the product or service; the costs to use, store, and dispose of it; the time consumed in the purchase transaction and the usage pattern; and the amount of hassle that has to be tolerated or paid out throughout the entire process. In short, it is the dollars, hours, and hassle the customer will "pay" for buying and using the product or service. It is the "big box" of the customer's economics that grows out of the "little box" of your products.

Most customers don't know their own systems economics. They can sense and feel it, but they don't know it. The auto industry,

EXHIBIT 2.5   *Systems Economics*

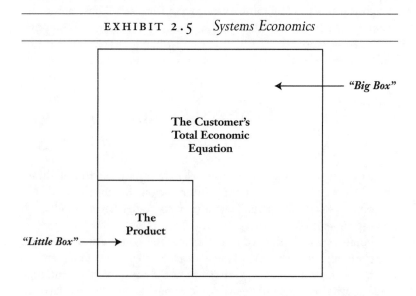

until very recently, didn't know the full systems economics of an instrument panel, a door, or a front-end system. Most families do not know their household systems economics for buying and maintaining transportation. For many, it would be quite a surprising number.

The fact that most customers don't know their own true systems economics is wonderful news for suppliers. Therein lies great opportunity for profit gain.

Disney streamlined the hassle out of the family vacation. Intel made it easy for its industrial customers to apply its chips. Microsoft gave the customer standards, ease of use, and a world-beating basket of applications. All these suppliers were rewarded beyond anyone's imagination.

Really knowing the customer's systems economics brings another enormous benefit to suppliers. It puts them in a legitimate position to answer the question:

How can we really add value to the customer?

One answer to this question led to the reinvention of an entire industry. During the 1980s, $8 billion worth of paper business forms were sold in the United States each year. The priorities of purchasing agents, who were responsible for buying forms, reflected the economics of their positions: meeting budgets, time constraints, and meeting minimum quality standards. Successful forms companies were those that offered high-quality, low-cost forms and quick delivery.

In the early 1990s, executives at large forms-consuming customers—insurers, banks, and hospitals—began searching for ways to reduce company expenses. After looking at the entire form-related system, they realized that the cost of a form was the tip of the iceberg. For every dollar spent on a paper form, the organization spent $20 filling it out, copying it, routing it, amending it, storing it, and throwing it out.

This realization elevated the issue of record-keeping systems on each organization's agenda, and decision making began moving from purchasing agents to senior management. Customer priorities changed radically. Saving a nickel on a dollar's worth of paper forms was no longer enough. Rather, the customer now said, "Help my organization—which uses 20,000 different types of paper forms—to transition from paper to an electronic forms system so that we can lower our total systems costs from $20 to $10."

Forms companies that adapted to meet this new customer priority created enormous value for customers and for themselves. Those that did not found themselves supplying an irrelevant product to indifferent customers.

To get an accurate analysis of a customer's systems economics and changing priorities, managers should exploit every tool at their disposal. Incumbent companies have the advantage of easy access to the customer, but it is their most underutilized asset. Start-ups like Microsoft scratched and clawed their way to their first customers. Incumbents like IBM and DEC had easy access to any customer or prospect in the marketplace, but it was a powerful advantage that they did not use.

The few companies that do use their access rarely take the critical next step: creating a privileged and often proprietary information flow from major customers—or, more importantly, from a truly market-representative cross-section of customers—to themselves. In today's ultradynamic business landscape, this information flow could be one of a company's most priceless assets. It is an enduring paradox that so few major organizations gather and systematize strategic customer information and convert it into an unmatched understanding of what the customer's true priorities will be.

EXPAND THE CUSTOMER FIELD OF VISION

Deciphering the secret code of changing customer priorities is the most difficult task in business. There is no single method to crack the code, nor is there any one customer in the buying organization—whether an industrial buyer or a family—who provides the entire answer.

In the old economic order, the focus was on the immediate customer. Today, business no longer has the luxury of thinking about just the immediate customer. To find and keep customers, our perspective has to be radically expanded. In a value migration world, our vision must include two, three, or even four customers along the value chain. So, for example, a component supplier must understand the economic motivations of the manufacturer who buys the components, the distributor who takes the manufacturer's products to sell, and the end-use consumer.

This phenomenon stretches across all industries today. Business book publishers, for example, must understand booksellers, *and* corporations that buy books, *and* the individual readers within those companies. Hotel managers must understand travel agents, *and* corporations that have offsite meetings, *and* the human resources people who organize the corporate offsites, *and* the people at the company that will be attending the offsite.

Expanding the customer field of vision is critical to smart business design. It opens the mind to new possibilities and to profitable innovation in the area of customer selection. Given three or four potential customers, who is the *most* important? On whom should a business design be most sharply focused? Innovation in customer selection has been a key factor in several of the reinventors' most brilliant business design achievements.

GO BEYOND EPISODIC
TO CONTINUOUS

Traditional market research models try to measure customers over time by periodically asking them a set of questions and measuring change. The frequency of these probes varies by market, but change is measured as point-to-point. Strategic customer analysis demands moving beyond this episodic approach to creating a continuous dialogue with the market's most important customers.

Creating a continuous flow of customer information into and throughout your organization can provide management with much greater sensitivity to new competitive business designs that are suddenly appealing to buyers, and to the changing decision-making environment within the customer. Businesses that lack this level of continuous communication are too often left surprised when the orders do not come in at the end of the quarter because the customer has chosen the competitor.

Episodic market research results in backward-looking insight. Continuous customer interaction yields real-time insight and a glimpse into tomorrow.

ANTICIPATE CHANGING PRIORITIES

The key question for customer-centric business design is not what a customer's priorities are today—that game is already over—but what a customer's priorities will be tomorrow. Answering that question requires wrestling with the future or even indulging in a certain degree of prophecy or at least of anticipation. The odds of relevant discovery rise dramatically when three things happen:

1. *The information comes from the relevant sources at* multiple *levels of the customer's organization.*
2. *The questions asked are nonstandard, creative, and challenging (e.g., "What am I afraid of finding out?"). Even the most diligent multilevel, multiangle, and multizone analysis will fail without the right questions.*
3. *There is a balance between understanding the next opportunity and recognizing the financial, political, accounting, and organizational barriers that stand in the way of capturing it.*

Predicting the future at 100 percent accuracy is impossible. That's why the 60–70 percent that can be anticipated is so critical. A tiny subset of the customer base, no more than 2 or 3 percent of the total, can help to do that. These are not the "leading-edge customers," the ones who are the most sophisticated and technologically advanced. Sometimes they represent the future; more often however, they do not. They tend to remain a small specialty segment rather than predictive of the broader market.

Instead of the leading-edge customers, we are looking for "future-defining customers," those whose issues, practices, and solutions today represent what the median of marketplace behavior will be tomorrow.

BUILD THE NEXT BUSINESS DESIGN

Equipped with an understanding of what your customer's priorities will be tomorrow, you can begin the process of building your company's next business design. Two examples, one historical and one contemporary, illustrate shifting customer priorities at work and the huge fortunes that are lost and gained in the process—fortunes that migrate to those who "get" what the priority is and away from those who "don't"; fortunes that migrate to those who build the next business design and away from those that don't.

*   *   *

From 1900 to 1920, the customer's number-one priority in the automotive business was basic, reliable transportation. "Give me a car that works and that I can afford," the customer said. "I hear you loud and clear," said Henry Ford, who built the Model T. More importantly, Ford built a vertically superintegrated business design that produced the Model T at an incredibly high volume, with a high reliability rate and a low cost. Customers responded. By 1920, an estimated 22 million cars had been sold. The car was so reliable that most older Model Ts were still on the road.

Ford's market share went from nothing to 55 percent. It became the undisputed leader of the automotive industry.

In the 1920s, the customer changed profoundly. The customer got rich—or at least richer, a great deal richer. The priority of the new car buyer was no longer "basic transportation, reliable and cheap." The new, revised customer, 1920s edition, said, "Give me color, give me style, give me choice. I have more money to spend, and, in fact, I'm willing to spend beyond what I have, so give me financing as well."

Alfred Sloan heard this; Henry Ford did not.

Sloan invented the variable-price-and-product pyramid (Chevrolet, Pontiac, Oldsmobile, Buick, Cadillac), as well as auto financing and a divisionalized, functionalized business design that produced and sold his heterogeneous product set efficiently and effectively.

Within a few years after 1920, Ford's market share plummeted from 55 percent to 12 percent. It lost its automotive leadership for more than the next half century.

*   *   *

During the 1980s, application software companies ruled the PC market because the customer's number-one priority was personal productivity software. Any good application that increased productivity was a sure winner and generated oceans of profit for its developers. But in the late 1980s, customer priorities began to shift from single applications to bundled suites in which multiple applications shared the same look and feel and worked smoothly together. The product-centric business designs of most application companies—those that assumed that a good product alone brought profits—were unable to change and keep up with shifting customer priorities. Lotus was one of the few to "get it," and began to outperform its single-product competitors by changing its business design to offer integrated suites to customers.

By the early 1990s, customer priorities began to shift to communications on the network. E-mail and groupware became the new keys to productivity improvement. Customer priorities were defining a new profit zone again; a new business design was required.

Some at Lotus wanted to stay the course as only a shrink-wrap applications business. They were mesmerized by its past profitability. But as the profit zone shifted, that was becoming a loser's game. Ultimately, Lotus "got it" again. It went after Novell, the leader in network computing. When that deal fell through, Lotus funded the development of Notes and acquired cc:Mail, driving the success of these products with a new business design based on a direct specialist sales force, a value-added reseller (VAR) channel, consulting services, and alliances. Responding to shifting customer priorities, Lotus bet its long-term value on a business design centered on the future of communications products.

As a consequence, Lotus is the only desktop applications company other than Microsoft to have made it into the next phase of the industry. Did IBM pay $3.5 billion for the shrink-wrap business design from the old glory days at Lotus? No. It paid for the value created by Lotus in the previous 4 or 5 years, the value inherent in a business design capable of capturing the next cycle of value growth in the industry.

The skill of customer-centric business design begins with the single most important insight about the customer and works its way back from that insight to craft the right business design. Equipped with a genuinely customer-centric point of view, managers will always make different decisions about scope. Their first question will not be about core competency, but about customer relevance. They will drive the company to do those things that customers need, want, and are willing to pay for.

As is shown in a rapidly growing number of cases, the customer-centric approach will fundamentally change the company's offering and value-chain activities. The offering will change from products (which are abundant) to solutions (which are difficult to create). The company's activities goal will change from "Do everything" or "Do what we do well" to "Do what matters to the customer" and "Do what you are *best* at." Outsource the rest, or find business partners to provide it with you.

The key driver will be customer relevance, rather than a focus on what a company knows how to do. If a skill is relevant to the customer and is not currently offered, the company must develop it, or hire it, or acquire it, or license it, or find a business partner who will provide it.

Finally, scope will change as smart companies aggressively shift their offerings from high physical content to high knowledge content. Knowledge content is harder to create and is often more highly valued by customers. It is how value will be created in the future.

As a business manager in the new world of business, customer-centric thinking will be your most powerful tool. But it is not enough. Customer-centric thinking that is unaccompanied by profit-centric thinking is ultimately sterile. Doing great things for the customer is necessary but not sufficient. Profits don't come as easily as they once did. You must design an explicit plan and mechanism for how profits will occur. Intentionally, explicitly, and proactively, you must think about what future actions will make profit possible, and what exactly your profit model will be.

THREE

HOW PROFIT HAPPENS

WHAT ARE the ten most profitable companies you know? Why are they so profitable? Are the reasons the same?

Everyone knows that profitability is important. Earnings reports and price/earnings ratios are daily reminders of its prominence. Many companies, however, do not operate on a common understanding of how profitability works in their business.

In the product-centric world of the past, profit was an outcome of a strong market share. Companies focused on one goal: Sell more, to anyone willing to buy. Companies generated revenue on each unit sold. How the company profited from those sales was all but taken for granted. Today, profit is not generated merely from the products a company sells, and profit cannot be taken for granted. Today, profit is an outcome of smart business design. In fact, the value recapture dimension of a business design—the "How do I get paid?" dimension—is one of its most critical components. Without a clear understanding of how profit happens and how businesses must be designed to capture it, there will not be any profit.

Articulating and designing the profit model is now a critical strategic skill. The profit models described in this chapter illustrate that there are many different ways of solving the "profit-by-design" problem. Don't make another major investment until you have satisfied yourself that the company knows exactly how it will make money and what tactical actions will be required to do so consistently.

Profitability is an extraordinarily complex phenomenon. How and why profitability occurs varies significantly from one industry or company to another. There are at least twenty-two models/patterns of profitability that explain how profit happens in various businesses.

More will be discovered in the next few years. And, in certain businesses, the interplay of two or more of these models explains how profit really happens in the business.

A review of these different models shows how different the mechanisms of profitability can be. It also reveals the central role of the customer—in terms of acquisition cost, buying behavior, price sensitivity, bargaining power, and so on—in the mechanism of action of each model.

PROFIT-CENTRIC BUSINESS DESIGN

One of the most productive questions you can ask your organization today is: What is our profit model? How do we make money?

In the past, profit-centric thinking was not a key part of the strategy process because it didn't need to be. The classic rules of strategy said: "Gain market share and profits will follow." Empirically, this was an accurate rule-of-thumb for most industries. The driver, the central issue in strategy, wasn't profit—it was market share. The sequence was as follows: Create or gain competitive advantage. Then competitive advantage will gain market share. The gain in market share will make the company increasingly profitable.

In the past decade, the classic rules of strategy broke down. The close correlation between market share leadership and superior profitability collapsed. Recall some of the examples from Chapter 1: IBM, GM, Sears, Kodak, US Steel, United Airlines. The actual list is quite long. Market share leaders? Yes. Profitable? No.

What happened? Why did these market share leaders fail to earn sustainable profits from their position? The rules changed. Rapid technological change and enormous influxes of venture capital lowered barriers to entry and cost-to-serve in many industries. In the new environment, enormous market share with the wrong business model is a liability, not an advantage. In the new profit-centric world, massive market share doesn't matter. What matters is understanding where you can make a profit in your industry. Within that potentially profitable zone, is your business model closely matched to what customers want and are willing to pay? Is your business model cost-effective enough to be profitable?

In the classic product-centric age, the key question was: "How can I gain market share, increase unit volume, and gain scale economies?" In the new age of rapidly shifting market value that commenced in the mid to late 1980s, the questions are different:

- *"Where will I be allowed to make a profit in this industry?"*
- *"How should I design my business model so that it will be profitable?"*

Eleven profitability models are described here. Each model has different business patterns and strategies that you can use to move your company into the profit zone.

1. Customer Development/ Customer Solutions Profit

Companies that implement a customer development model invest heavily to understand their customers' economics and find ways to make them more favorable. They reach the profit zone by first probing how their customers buy and use their products and then finding ways—beyond merely selling the products—to help the customers in the difficult, expensive, or time-consuming areas of their process. The method by which customers are developed explains the companies' profitability.

One company that implements the customer development model is Factset, a financial information services provider. Factset's strategy was front-end-loading investment in the customer. Factset spent prodigiously in the early part of the customer development cycle, so it would understand its customers' businesses. Next, it tailored its own products as closely as possible to the customers' circumstances, and then wove its products deeply into the fabric of the customers' operations. Early cash flow was negative, but within a few months, it turned sharply positive. Customer relationship maintenance costs were low, and continuity rates were extremely high. Customer selection and front-end-loaded customer investment were the means of creating customer continuity, which was the key driver of profit.

Other successful firms that have applied the discipline of the customer development model include Nordstrom, the United States Auto Association (USAA), Intuit, Northwestern Life, and Leo Burnett, all of which have achieved significantly higher customer continuity than their competitors and, as a result, higher levels of sustained profitability.

In Chapters 4 and 5, we will further examine how General Electric, Madden Communications, Cardboard Box Inc., and Sandoz Pharmaceuticals have successfully implemented a customer solutions model.

2. Product Pyramid Profit

Unlike the customer development model, where customer economics is the most important factor, in a product pyramid profit model, customer preferences of style, color, price, and so on, are of utmost importance. The variations in customer income and preferences make it possible to build product pyramids. They exist in markets as diverse as watchmaking, automotive sales, and credit cards. At the base are low-priced, high-volume products. At the apex are high-priced, low-volume products.

The profit is concentrated at the top of the product pyramid, but the base of each pyramid plays a critical strategic role in the system. Astute business designers, such as Swatch or Mattel, make certain to build a "firewall" brand at the bottom of the pyramid: a strong, low-priced brand that is produced at a profit, however slim. The purpose of this brand is to deter competitor entry, thereby protecting the enormous profit margins at the top of the pyramid.

For example, Mattel produces a low-end Barbie doll so that (1) no uncontested space is left open for competitors and (2) profits from the $200 special-edition Barbie doll at the top of the product pyramid are protected. Similarly, Swiss watchmaker SMH developed a Swatch brand that is ultra-low-priced, yet designed to be profitable. This has limited the ability of competitors to build the position needed to attack the ultra-high-end brands in the SMH system (Blancpain, Omega, Longines, Rado), where most of the profits are. (Seiko recently announced that it will de-emphasize investment in watches and will enter the network systems business to compete with Cisco! Better Cisco than SMH.)

When a firewall brand isn't built, competitors have the opportunity to come in at the bottom and then work their way toward the top, where the profits are. Witness the history of the U.S. automotive market from 1965 to 1995. Japanese competitors first occupied the base with cars designed to be profitable, even at low price levels. They then moved up (Honda's Acura, Toyota's Lexus, Nissan's Infiniti) to where the higher profits were.

Think about what would have happened if Ford and GM had decided to build a "designed to be profitable" sub-Chevy brand in the late 1960s. Japanese growth would have been much slower, and Japan's entry into the top-of-the-pyramid, high-profit positions would have been delayed for a decade or longer.

Chapter 6 explores the development of the product pyramid profit model at SMH.

3. MULTICOMPONENT SYSTEM PROFIT

In some businesses, there are several components of the production and selling system, and each component has radically different profit characteristics. Failure to maximize participation in the highest-profit components depresses the profitability of the entire system. On the other hand, full participation in the less profitable components is required to win the market for the most profitable components. (See Exhibit 3.1.)

In carbonated beverages, for example, the components are grocery, fountain, and vending. Price realizations are: grocery, 2 cents per ounce; fountain, 4 cents per ounce; vending, 6 cents per ounce. The profit zone is in fountain and vending, but, in order to win in those areas, a company needs a strong brand. Brands are developed and maintained through the mass-market, low-profit grocery segment. Even though grocery is low profit, it is an essential part of maintaining position in the profit zone. One fights to maintain share and brand position in low-margin grocery; one maximizes vending penetration to maximize profitability. Coca-Cola learned and applied this brilliantly.

EXHIBIT 3.1   *Multicomponent Systems*

Industry	Base Component	Profit Components
Soft drinks	Grocery	Fountain, vending
Personal computers	PC box	Options, accessories, financing
Consumer electronics retailing	VCR, TV, stereo	Maintenance service agreements
Coffee	Grocery	Cafés, kiosks
Cars	New car sales	Insurance, financing, services
Manufacturing	Goods	Financing, services

Similarly, in coffee, the components are grocery, cafés, and kiosks. Grocery is low margin, cafés are high margin, and kiosks are even higher still. Procter & Gamble, Nestlé, and General Foods play against each other in grocery and break even. Starbuck's plays in cafés and kiosks and enjoys extraordinary returns.

In a multicomponent system, if the business design does not include an aggressive focus on the high-profit components, it is incomplete and far less profitable than it could potentially be.

Chapter 7 details the steps that Roberto Goizueta took to reinvent Coca-Cola and establish a highly profitable multicomponent model.

4. SWITCHBOARD PROFIT

Some markets are characterized by multiple sellers communicating to multiple buyers. High transaction costs are incurred by both. Often, there is an opportunity to create a high-value intermediary that concentrates these multiple communication pathways through one point, or one channel, by creating a "switchboard." The switchboard reduces the costs (both financial expenditures and personal aggravation) of both buyers and sellers, in exchange for a fee to the switchboard operator. Examples include Schwab's

OneSource, Softbank's combination of trade publications and trade shows, and Auto-by-Tel.

A powerful aspect of the switchboard profit model is that it builds on itself. The more sellers and buyers who join, the more valuable the system becomes. Communication and transaction costs continue to decline for buyers and sellers. The switchboard operator controls the information flow, and even a modest charge per transaction becomes extremely profitable as volume increases.

The switchboard profit models used by Charles Schwab and Company are discussed in Chapter 8.

5. Time Profit

In business, speed is usually important. Often, a first-mover advantage allows an innovator to generate excess returns before imitators begin to erode margins. The time profit model is designed to take advantage of this phenomenon. In this model, profit derives from uniqueness. Price premiums exist, but only until imitation erases them.

The reality of this pattern is that prices are high and profits are abundant—there is a profit zone—but only for a short period of time. Constant innovation is the only way to remain in the profit zone. As value migrates away from its most recent innovation, a company must introduce the next one, in order to reenter the profit zone.

This profit model is at the core of Intel's success, which is why the entire Intel business design is geared for speed. High speed means high profit. Moderate speed means break even. Low speed means oblivion. Andrew Grove understands that perfectly, and he manages Intel accordingly (see Chapter 9).

6. Blockbuster Profit

If understanding the time profit model is essential for companies in industries where innovation is highly valued, then understanding blockbuster profit is essential for pharmaceutical companies, publishers, film studios, music companies, and software firms, which have large R&D and launch costs, and finite product cycles.

When the cost to develop a new product is fixed (and, usually, high) and marginal costs of manufacturing after development are low, the best way to maximize profits is to improve the chances that the product will achieve very high volume levels. With these economics, it is better to be the dominant leader in a few products than to support average positions in many products. Costs are roughly the same for all products developed, but returns for those that achieve meaningful scale are much, much larger. For example, the most powerful driver of profitability in the pharmaceutical industry is ownership of blockbuster products. Product scale—in this case, measured by the total sales of the top five products in the firm's product line—drives profitability.

This example illustrates another important aspect of the profit model of a business: the model changes. In the pharmaceutical industry, the profit model in the 1970s was relative market share by product category. At that time, development and launch costs per product were about one-third as high as they are today. Consequently, absolute product scale was much less important. What mattered was leadership in the categories in which the company competed.

Today, category leadership is no longer enough. The average cost of development and launch has risen to $300 million per product, and the average economic life of a product has shrunk to less than 10 years. Leadership in small categories won't recover the large investments required. Profitability and competitiveness hinge on product scale. A number-two or number-three product with $1.6 billion in sales will generate more resources for reinvestment than several $200 million products that lead their markets. Relative market share in a category has been replaced by product scale as the dominant profit model in the business.

Beyond pharmaceuticals, the product scale profit model has broad applicability to any activity where development costs are high and product revenues are highly variable. Other industries affected by the product scale profit model include technology-intensive industries as well as books, music, and films. An outstanding practitioner of this model is Disney (see Chapter 10), which not only created blockbuster profits, but also used its blockbuster films as the foundation for creating a profit multiplier system.

7. Profit Multiplier Model

A profit multiplier model reaps gains, over and over again, from the same product, character, trademark, capability, or service. The best example of a profit multiplier model is Disney. Think about how many different ways Disney packages the same characters. Mickey, Minnie, Hercules, et al. appear in movies, videos, and books; on clothes, watches, and lunch boxes; at theme parks; and in stores that feature them. No matter what form they take, these characters are generating returns for Disney. No one in the company works harder than the characters themselves.

Profit multiplier models can be powerful engines for businesses that have strong consumer brands. Once the investment (often, huge) in creating a brand has been made, the creator may give the brand license across a broad array of products. The appeal of this model, however, must be weighed against the risks of taking a brand to places where it does not have authority with the customer. Disney keeps control over where Mickey is applied and is careful not to put him in places that may threaten his value. Brands are valuable, but fragile, assets.

Chapter 10 highlights how Disney's reinvention created a profit multiplier model that, to date, has not been effectively imitated.

8. Entrepreneurial Profit

Many determinants of profitability are economic. Some are organizational. As organizations succeed and grow, they become more formalized, more bureaucratic, more careful, more remote from customers, and slower to act. Diseconomies of scale begin to work, overshadowing the cost advantages of size. Overhead grows, decision-making slows. Direct feedback from customers is reduced, filtered, and often ignored.

The demon of affordability goes to work. Because the company is successful and profitable, it can afford many things that really aren't necessary for doing a good job for customers. Unnecessary expenses grow and will eventually consume tomorrow's profits.

The consequences of these forces? Customer relevance declines, and the expense structure grows. The company is vulnerable to entrepreneurs who are in direct contact with customers or proactively solicit feedback, and who remain frugal because they have no cushion of affordability to support unnecessary expenses. These twin forces of direct customer contact and extreme frugality create the potential for enormous profitability.

Most large companies do not have a business design that permits them to harness these twin forces of the entrepreneurial condition, but some have found ways of doing so. ABB has broken itself down into 5,000 profit centers that have direct customer contact and direct profit responsibility. Softbank has divided itself into profit centers of as few as ten people, again with direct customer contact, and with a five-day cash flow metric.

The most determined application of the entrepreneurial profit model is Thermo Electron, which preempts the profit-destroying effects of size by constantly spinning out new companies. Managers of the spin-outs are put in direct, uncushioned contact with customers and are made responsible for profit and directly accountable to shareholders.

This structure focuses the mind like no other. It also unleashes a powerful new force: upside motivation. The managers of the spin-outs own stock in the spin-out company. They create their own upside. If they perform well, the stock will rise and they can be enormously rewarded. Unlike many corporate division managers, they cannot blame the "parent company" or "headquarters" or "corporate politics." At a Thermo Electron spin-out, the energy typically devoted to these types of complaints is transmuted into getting the next order at the best possible profit.

Entrepreneurs hate to compete against Thermo Electron. They'd much rather compete against a larger, slower, more insulated player. It is easier to compete against employees than against owners. The power of this model is detailed in Chapter 11.

9. Specialization Profit

All businesses start off being very good at something. They begin by offering a specialist's expertise. But as they grow, they often move beyond their specialization. They take on more and more activities at which they are mediocre. Revenues grow; profitability declines.

On the other hand, growth through *sequenced* specialization can be extraordinarily profitable. Electronic Data Systems (EDS), for example, grew through sequenced specialization—mastering the intricacies and economics of computer solutions for many vertical segments (health care, insurance, manufacturing, banking), but doing so sequentially, not simultaneously. In each vertical segment, EDS establishes expertise that is unmatched—it becomes a specialist—and it rolls that expertise across the entire segment. Then it moves on to another segment.

Even though EDS became very large, it remained a group of specialists. The profitability of this approach can be compelling. In 1994, EDS earned 13 percent margins in its computer services business. IBM, its major competitor, broke even.

The magic of ABB's global business design (see Chapter 12) also comes from specialization. ABB's system enables each of the engineering firms within its network to specialize with greater intensity, rather than trying to be all things to all customers. Profit margins have multiplied (from 2 percent to 10 percent or higher) as a result.

10. Installed Base Profit

One of the most powerful profit mechanisms in business is the installed base profit model (Exhibit 3.2). The supplier creates an extensive installed base of users, who then buy the supplier's brand of consumables or follow-on products.

The installed base profit model can be extremely lucrative—if the follow-on market can be controlled. This type of control is strongest if the installed base allows creation of a standard. In setting a standard, a company effectively creates the largest installed base possible by enticing all customers in an industry to use its product. The company is then able to manage the follow-on market by being the preferred supplier of follow-on products and services.

This was a key component of Bill Gates's thinking, from his very first business move. Microsoft's strategy was to price low, set the standard, achieve ubiquity, and then harvest the profits from

EXHIBIT 3.2   *The Installed Base Profit Model*

Installed Base	Follow-On
Razors	Blades
Elevators	Service contracts
Software	Upgrades
Water purification systems	Treatment chemicals
Personal copiers	Toner cartridges
Cameras	Film

upgrade/revision revenue. Gates operated with a crystal-clear understanding of exactly how profit happened in the business (see Chapter 13).

11. DE FACTO STANDARD PROFIT

Installed base profits provide a protected, highly profitable annuity stream. The installed base becomes a critical element of another high-profit model when it allows the owner to establish a de facto standard. The standard then drives customer and competitive behavior for an entire industry.

The most striking characteristic of a de facto standard business is increasing returns to scale. In this type of business, numerous players, from original equipment manufacturers (OEMs) to applications developers to users, are drawn into the gravitational orbit of the standard holder. The more players that enter the system, the more valuable the system becomes. As a consequence, the holder of the standard can experience increasing returns as the value of the system grows.

Microsoft has been able to convert its installed base position into a de facto standard that is a very powerful economic engine. Oracle has created a similar upward spiral of activity around its de facto standard in relational databases. American Airlines' SABRE system is the de facto standard for airline reservations, earning American significant returns. Entire industries are restructured around de facto standards, leaving behind competitors who lost the standards battle (e.g., Apple and Sybase) and saw their margins erode over time. The power of this model is illustrated in detail in the analysis of Microsoft in Chapter 13.

OTHER WAYS OF MAKING MONEY

Numerous profit models are used by companies today. We have highlighted these eleven because they have been used successfully by reinventors and will be discussed in subsequent chapters. Many other profit models can define how a firm makes money: relative market share, experience curve, transaction scale, local leadership, capacity utilization within a supply–demand cycle, structural control of key points in the value chain, and others. Learning the full

---

EXHIBIT 3.3 *Profit Models and Their Practitioners**

Profit Model	Leading Practitioners
1. Customer Solutions Profit	• GE, USAA, Nordstrom, ABB, Nalco, HP
2. Product Pyramid Profit	• SMH (Swatch), Mattel
3. Multicomponent Profit	• Coca-Cola, Mirage Resorts
4. Switchboard Profit	• Schwab, USAA, Auto-by-Tel, CAA
5. Time Profit	• Intel, Bankers Trust, Sony
6. Blockbuster Profit	• Merck, Disney, NBC
7. Profit-Multiplier Model	• Disney, Virgin, Honda
8. Entrepreneurial Profit	• Thermo-Electron, ABB, 3M
9. Specialization Profit	• ABB, EDS, Wallace
10. Installed Base Profit	• Microsoft, Otis Elevator, Gillette, GE
11. De Facto Standard Profit	• Microsoft, Oracle
12. Brand Profit	• Intel, Coca-Cola, Nike
13. Specialty Product Profit	• Hercules, Merck, 3M, Great Lakes Chemical
14. Local Leadership Profit	• Starbuck's, Wal-Mart
15. Transaction Scale Profit	• Morgan Stanley, British Airways
16. Value Chain Position Profit	• Intel, Blockbuster Video, Republic Industries
17. Cycle Profit	• Toyota, Dow Chemical
18. After-Sale Profit	• GE, Softbank (Kingston)
19. New Product Profit	• Compaq, Chrysler
20. Relative Market Share Profit	• Procter & Gamble, Philip Morris
21. Experience Curve Profit	• Milliken, Emerson Electric
22. Low-Cost Business Design Profit	• Nucor, Southwest Air, Dell

* For further explanation of each model, see the Appendix to Chapter 3.

range of available models is an important step for any management team trying to set strategic direction. It will greatly increase the productivity of managerial decision making. Exhibit 3.3 summarizes the models and their leading practitioners. These are the innovators, the companies in the profit zone. For further discussion of these models, see the appendix to this chapter.

ORGANIZATIONAL CULTURE: THE PSYCHOLOGY OF PROFITABILITY

Even if profitability is allowed in an industry and the profit model is understood, there are still significant differences in performance, depending on the norms, expectations, and culture that have been created within the organization.

In a recent interview, the head of a large sales organization lamented how a lack of frugality was accepted as the norm in her company.

"We're not very careful about our dollars," she said. "We stay in the best hotels, the annual sales meeting is in a fancy Florida resort, we eat well, we don't buy our airline tickets far enough in advance to save on the fare. We've come to think that this is how it's meant to be."

She described the very human, organizational consequences of several years of corporate life in the land of illusion, the land of the "perpetual profit zone."

Once formed, these organizational habits are extremely hard to break. As the profit zone moves, they can prove fatal.

The chief executive officer of a small specialty coffee roaster recognizes this, and his expense approach reflects this fear. His is a healthy company, generating $50 million in revenues, 20 percent pretax margins, and 25 percent annual growth. It is not a capital-intensive business, and there is ample cushion for a little luxury.

"We hold our annual sales meeting near the office, we rent a high school gym, and our people stay at the local Quality Inn," he says. "We can afford to be more lavish, but once you start walking down that path, it will kill you.

"My head of manufacturing is a genius at jerry-rigging," the CEO adds. "He buys used equipment, never new. He spends hours modifying it to fit our operation and to run more efficiently. He hates to pay new equipment prices, or to pay full price for supplies. He never does."

The CEO's pride in these stories and the sense of a deeply held philosophy, a set of values that he unceasingly communicates to the organization, are as important as his words.

"The day I start getting ostentatious," he says, "this company will have to battle an unnecessary internal challenge. There are more than enough customer, distributor, and competitor challenges out there. We aren't good enough to fight those and internal challenges as well."

Wal-Mart employees double up in budget hotels when they travel. They constantly search for suppliers who offer better value. Like the coffee company, they live by the same values and ideas. In Wal-Mart's case, however, the entrepreneur's frugality was preserved even after achieving $100 billion of revenue.

It is a rare company, and a rare leader, that can leave the land of illusion and return to entrepreneurial principles. The company must then recreate—or, in many cases, create for the first time—the psychology of profitability as a central element in the organization's culture. A $200 million chemical company provides one example.

The company's profit model once was defined by protected technology. Commodity products, with 25 percent gross margins, filled its plants. Specialty, patent-protected chemicals generated 20 percent of the revenue, but with 70 percent gross margins, they generated all of the profit in the business. By the late 1980s, the patents on all of the specialties had expired. Technology depletion exhausted all the possibilities for new inventions. In 1987, the profit model underwent a transition to a pure experience curve profit model. The firm had become a commodity company. The single most important rule was low-cost wins.

It took management eight months to change the corporate culture by weaning the organization away from its accustomed luxuries. It held meetings, gave presentations, and engaged in education and constant communication about the new economics. Eight months of hard work established a new psychology: profitability was no longer taken for granted. It depended on how aggressively the organization focused on resource-conserving programs, and programs to improve quality, in order to both differentiate its products and save resources.

"Profitability is a game of inches" was the theme. The things done at the margin have a huge impact. They determine the difference between profit and loss.

The transition was effective. It drove return on sales up from a negative 4 percent to a positive 6 percent and kept it there. The same psychology could have been created 5 years earlier, but, until the crunch came, it wasn't pursued.

The impact of organizational focus on frugality and pricing opportunity is not always this dramatic. The accumulation of hundreds of culturally induced behavioral changes will sometimes add only two to three points to profit. But when these two to three points are reinvested in R&D for new products, for lower-cost processes, or for service to the customers, the impact is multiplied tenfold. Whatever the profit model that drives the firm's earnings, the overlay of organizational culture plays a critical role in either subtracting or adding two to three points of profit to the outcome. When properly reinvested, the two to three points of incremental profit have a remarkable impact on building capability, reducing commoditization, and enhancing long-term viability.

CUSTOMER PROFITABILITY

Although a fanatical focus on an entrepreneurial cost model can be a powerful lever, an organization's psychology of profitability must extend beyond the cost line. Each of the profit models described above is founded on a fundamental understanding of the customer. Each is customer-centric in its own particular way. As an organization translates a profit model into action, it must execute effectively at the level of the individual customer—where profit is ultimately created.

For the profit model to work, a company must invest in developing a detailed understanding of how profit happens at this level. Only then is the financial profile of the customer revealed. Ask three basic questions about your customers:

1. *Who are the most profitable customers?*
2. *Within that group, which customers have the highest profit growth potential?*
3. *What mix and level of investments are needed to meet those customers' needs efficiently and enable profit growth to occur?*

In many companies, this profitability analysis has revealed that 10 to 15 percent of the customer base is unprofitable, consisting of buyers who absorb the company's resources and do not provide a return. In some cases, the proportion of unprofitable customers is even higher.

Calculating the customer profitability profile has a great liberating effect for an organization. It uncorks countless decisions that should have been made long ago. What price increases should be implemented, and to whom? What accounts should receive greater, or lower, levels of service? Which types of customers should we acquire and develop and which should we avoid—or even channel to our competitors? How should we change our customer development process in order to increase the chances of profitability at the account level?

Customer profitability analysis provides the basis for a more highly focused, laserlike investment process. Laser-guided investment—or disinvestment—creates windfall returns and provides management with the financial flexibility to act strategically.

ASSET INTENSITY

This customer investment mentality is at the core of another element of the psychology of profitability: asset intensity. A company's asset intensity is determined by its ratio of assets to sales. The higher the asset intensity, the greater the drag on the profit engine. Even the most powerful profit engine can be neutralized by a business design that is unnecessarily asset-intensive. Asset intensity absorbs the profit and leaves no cash flow for the shareholders.

An understanding of customer profitability allows an organization to rationalize investment, to focus on those skills and activities that are most important to customers, and to avoid investment in things that only burden the organization with charges for capital employed. The reinventors know this acutely, and fight for it vigorously. Consider Coca-Cola's asset intensity (see Chapter 7) or Disney's (see Chapter 10). Smart business designers use every means available—from operating improvements to financial engineering—to drive down the asset intensity of their business design.

PROTECTING YOUR PROFITABILITY: CREATING A STRATEGIC CONTROL POINT FOR YOUR BUSINESS

While a company is developing a powerful business design to generate profit growth, it must simultaneously search for and develop the strategic control points in its industry. The purpose of a strategic control point is to protect the profit stream that the business design has created against the corrosive effects of competition and customer power. A business design without a strategic control point is like a ship with a hole in its hull. It will sink much sooner than it has to.

Strategic control has always been an important part of business strategy; today, it is critical. The rapid growth of customer power in the past decade and a half has forced strategic control to the top of the priority list. Many laws protect customers against powerful suppliers, but no laws really protect suppliers against powerful customers. The job of a strategic control point is to redress that imbalance.

There are many types of strategic control points: brand, patent, copyright, 2-year product development lead, 20 percent cost advantage, control of distribution, control of supply, owning customer information flow, a unique organizational culture, value chain control. Each control point is designed to keep a company in the profit zone and to prevent competitors from stealing away the profitability.

In each industry, different types of strategic control points are viable. Brand is not applicable to every market. Value chain control may be impossible or irrelevant. Therefore, the first task in determining how to build strategic control is to identify the relevant hierarchy of control points. Exhibit 3.4 provides one such hierarchy. This specific hierarchy might not work in your industry (or might require significant modification), but it illustrates that not all strategic control points have equal profit-protecting power.

EXHIBIT 3.4   *Strategic Control Point Index*

Profit-Protecting Power	Index	Strategic Control Point	Example(s)
High	10	Own the standard	Microsoft, Oracle
	9	Manage the value chain	Intel, Coke
	8	String of superdominant positions	Coke, internationally
	7	Own the customer relationship	GE, EDS
Medium	6	Brand, copyright	Countless
	5	Two-year product development lead	Intel
Low	4	One-year product development lead	Few
	3	Commodity with 10 to 20 percent cost advantage	Nucor, SW Air
None	2	Commodity with cost parity	Countless
	1	Commodity with cost disadvantage	Countless

Every good business design has at least one strategic control point. The best business designs have two or more. Intel, for example, has a 2-year lead, value chain control, and a brand. Coca-Cola has a brand, a low-cost logistics system, value chain management, and a string of superdominant positions (a market share that is three, four, or five times competitors' share) around the world.

GE has a low-cost position, and it owns the customer relationship in the many cases where it provides a full package of services and solutions to its customers.

Disney owns the customer relationship in family vacations, plus a set of copyrights and a unique organizational culture that competitors have yet to copy.

Microsoft owns the standard, a string of superdominant positions (in multiple product categories), and a brand.

A final note. Although they use different words, all security analysts look for the strategic control points that protect the profit stream of the business. Why? Because one of their most important criteria for evaluating stocks is *predictability*. The greater the strategic control, the greater the predictability; and the greater the predictability, the higher the valuation. Creating a strategic control point is critical to enabling a company to achieve sustained value growth.

What's the Value of My Business Design?

Profit-centric business designs create value for shareholders. How much value? How effectively is that profit model reflected in the market value of the company? The simple model shown in Exhibit 3.5 helps us to shape the answers to these questions.

The examples highlighted in the exhibit—Coca-Cola, Procter & Gamble, and US Airways—illustrate how a business design is translated into market value for investors. Across industries, the drivers of value are the same: return on sales, profit growth, asset intensity, and strategic control.

Coca-Cola has margins of 26 percent. Its profits are projected to grow at 17 percent annually, its asset-to-sales ratio is 0.7, and its strategic control index is 9. This consistently strong performance leads Coca-Cola's business design to be rewarded by investors with a 7.0 market value-to-sales ratio.

Procter & Gamble has 9 percent margins, 16 percent projected profit growth, a 0.6 asset-to-sales ratio, and a strategic control index of 4. Investors value the company at three times revenue—a strong valuation, but less attractive than Coke.

US Airways has 7 percent margins, 2 percent projected profit growth, an asset-to-sales ratio of 1.0, and a strategic control index

EXHIBIT 3.5   *What's the Value of My Business Design?*

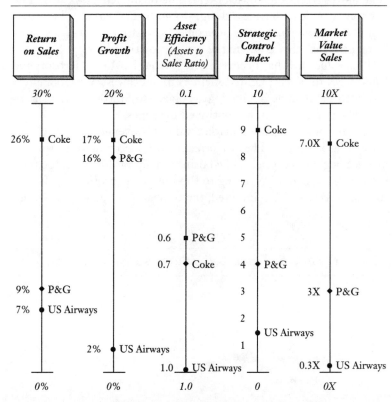

Note: Return on Sales = EBIT/Sales; Profit Growth = projected earnings growth via Value Line & analyst reports; Asset Efficiency = (Assets – Cash & Equivalents – Accounts Payable)/Sales; Market Value/Sales = (Shares Outstanding × Share Price)/Sales.

Source: Compustat, Value Line, Company Reports, CDI Estimates.

of 1.5. These metrics lead investors to value the company at a market value-to-revenue ratio of 0.3.

These four metrics are excellent proxies for the quantitative and qualitative judgments that investors make every day. Their predictive power is quite high. As business designs are crafted, these become the metrics of value creation that management can use to evaluate alternatives. They become the measurements of success on an ongoing basis.

In value migration, customers move from A to B, and the profit zone moves from A to B with them. The incumbent stays at A. The newcomer builds a business design to go to B. Market value shifts from the incumbent to the newcomer. Investors endorse the newcomer, because that is where the profit growth will be.

This value shift has occurred often: from IBM to Microsoft and Intel; USX to Nucor; United Airlines to Southwest Air; Computervision to Parametric Technology; Folgers to Starbuck's; Kmart to Wal-Mart. The list can be continued for pages.

When your company's market value-to-revenue ratio declines, something is wrong. The performance on one or more of the key metrics begins to degrade. The business design is losing its focus on the customer, and it is starting to slip out of the profit zone. Unless the business model is reinvented, the company's value will fall lower.

EXHIBIT 3.6   *Coca-Cola's Business Design Reinvention*

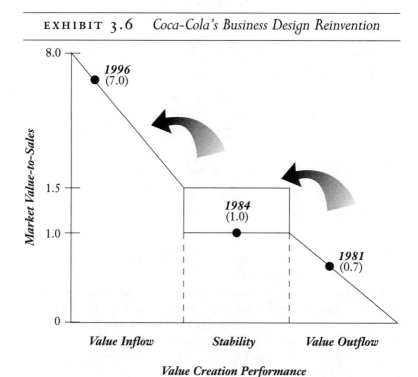

Value Creation Performance

The market value-to-revenue ratio is only one indicator. We all know the others. We work harder and harder, and the results are more and more elusive. Customers leave, profit margins decline. Whether we measure numbers or feelings, we know it is time to change the business design.

Reinventing the business design by using customer-centric and profit-centric principles has great rewards. Customers return. Profits grow. Employee morale rebounds.

The market value-to-revenue ratio goes up by a lot. Coca-Cola, one of the leading reinventors, saw its market value-to-revenue ratio soar as it improved its performance on the four driving metrics (Exhibit 3.6).

In Part Two, we will observe how the reinventors went through this process—repeatedly.

APPENDIX TO CHAPTER THREE: TWENTY-TWO PROFIT MODELS

1. Customer Solutions Profit

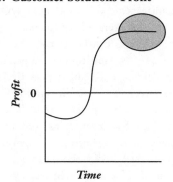

Invest to know the customer, create a solution, develop the relationship. This causes losses early in the relationship, and significant profits thereafter. Outstanding practitioners include GE (from hardware to services and solutions), USAA (financial services), and Nordstrom (retailing services).

2. Product Pyramid Profit

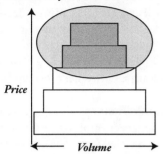

In a product pyramid profit model, meeting customer preferences of style, color, price, etc., is of utmost importance. It is exactly the variations in customer income and preferences that make it possible to build a product pyramid. At the base are low-price, high-volume products. At the apex are high-price, low-volume products.

Most of the profit is concentrated at the top of the pyramid, but the base of the pyramid plays a critical strategic role in creating a "firewall" at the bottom. The firewall brand creates a barrier to competitors, and protects the rich profitability at the top of the structure.

3. Multicomponent Profit

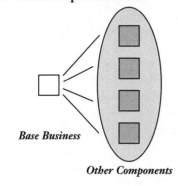

In this profit model, there are multiple components within a system, and several of the components represent a disproportionate share of the profits. Multicomponent profit models apply to industries as diverse as beverages (the profit is in fountain and vending), hotels (the base business has low margins, the corporate meeting business is highly profitable), bookstores (the bookstore itself is asset-intensive, low margin; the institutional business from corporations, book clubs, and other sources is high profit, low asset intensity.)

4. Switchboard Profit

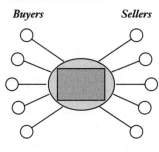

Buyers　　　　*Sellers*

Some markets are characterized by multiple sellers communicating with multiple buyers, with high costs incurred by both. In many cases, there is an opportunity to create a high-value intermediary that concentrates these multiple communication pathways through one point, one channel, by creating a switchboard. The switchboard reduces the costs to both buyers and sellers.

A powerful component of the switchboard model is that it builds on itself; the more buyers and sellers that join, the more valuable it becomes.

5. Time Profit

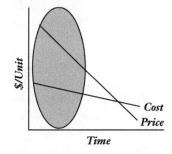

Many times in business there is a first mover advantage that allows the innovator to generate excess returns before imitators begin to erode margins. The time profit model is designed to take advantage of this phenomenon. In this model, profit derives from uniqueness. Price premiums exist, but only until imitation erases them.

A good example of a successful Time Profit model is Intel, which is always two steps ahead of its competition. Other industries in which time profit is critical include consumer electronics and innovation in financial instruments.

The key point in a time profit model is not, as many believe, time to market; rather it is creating and maintaining a 2-year lead over the next competitor, because all the profits happen in the first few quarters after launch.

6. Blockbuster Profit

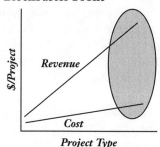

In certain industries (pharmaceuticals, music, film making, publishing), the key economic activity is project-based.

Within these industries, the cost per type of project may vary by 5x, and the revenues generated may vary by 50x. For example, the cost to develop a drug varies from $50 million to $300 million; the cumulative revenue varies from $500 million to $15 billion. The cost to develop a film varies from $10 million to $100 million; the revenue varies from $10 million to $500 million. All of the profit is concentrated in the blockbuster projects, where revenue realization is so powerful that it pays the development costs many times over.

7. Profit Multiplier Model

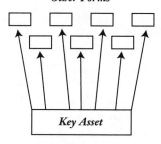

A profit multiplier model reaps gains from the same product, character, trademark, or service, over and over again. The best example of a profit multiplier model is Disney. Think about how many different ways Disney packages the same characters. Mickey, Minnie, The Little Mermaid, et al. appear in movies, in videos, in books, on clothes, on watches, on lunch boxes, at theme parks, and in stores that feature them. No matter what form they take, these characters are generating returns for Disney. No one in the company works harder than the characters themselves.

Profit multiplier models can be a powerful engine for businesses that have strong consumer brands. Once the investment in creating a brand has been made (often, a huge investment), the consumer may give the brand license across a broad array of products. The appeal of this model, however, must be weighed against the risks of taking a brand to places where it does not have authority with the customer. Disney keeps control over where Mickey is applied and is careful not to put him in places that may threaten his value. Brands are valuable, but fragile, assets.

8. Entrepreneurial Profit

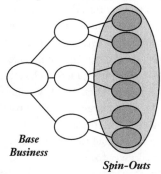

Base Business

Spin-Outs

As companies grow, diseconomies of scale take effect: overhead grows, unnecessary expenses grow, decision making slows, customers become remote.

To counteract these forces, some companies have organized themselves into very small profit centers (e.g., ABB, Softbank) to maximize accountability and maintain closeness to the customer.

In the extreme case, Thermo-Electron spins out subsidiary companies to maintain closeness to the customer and accountability for profits and share price. This model also unleashes the powerful force of upside motivation: the managers of the spin-out company own stock in that company, and if they perform well they can experience extraordinary rewards.

9. Specialization Profit

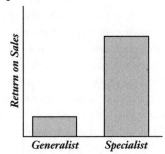

Return on Sales

Generalist   **Specialist**

In many industries, specialists are *several times* more profitable than generalists. The specialists' superior profitability derives from a multitude of factors, including lower cost, higher quality, stronger reputation, shorter selling cycle, and better price realization.

Specialization is not limited to products. For example, Home Depot specializes in a customer segment—the Do-It-Yourselfer. Home Depot's success results from its focus on meeting the needs of that particular group.

10. Installed Base Profit

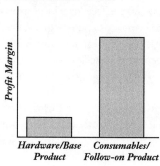

Profit Margin

Hardware/Base
Product

Consumables/
Follow-on Product

In many installed base businesses, the profit or initial product sales are slim, but the margins on follow-on products are extremely attractive. Businesses of this genre include copiers, printers, razors, elevators, and many others. The key point is to build the largest installed base to enable the highly attractive follow-on revenue and the profitability that derives from it.

11. De Facto Standard Profit

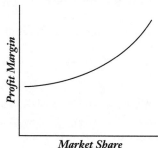

Profit Margin

Market Share

The most striking characteristic of a de facto standard business is increasing returns to scale. In this type of business, numerous players, from OEMs to developers to users, are drawn into the gravitational orbit of the de facto standard holder. The more players that enter the system, the more valuable the system becomes (as in the case of network economics, the more users there are, the more valuable the network becomes). As a consequence, the holder of the standard can experience *increasing* returns as the value of the system grows. Examples include Microsoft, Oracle, and American Airlines' SABRE system. The flip side is also at work. The companies that lose the battle to establish a standard (e.g., Apple or Sybase), experience diminishing margins over time.

12. Brand Profit

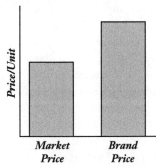

Over a period of years, a brand-building company expends significant marketing investment in order to build awareness, recognition, trust, and credibility.

These "intangibles" are reinforced by the customers' experience with the service or product. They are rendered tangible by the price premium that customers are happy to pay. This price, which may be significantly higher than that for functionally comparable products, often explains 100 percent of the brandholder's profitability.

13. Specialty Product Profit

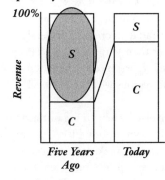

When a firm introduces a new product, it enjoys a premium on that product. (The "S" denotes specialization; the "C" denotes commodity.)

Specialty products enjoy a greater portion of the profits until competitors begin their imitations.

Industries characterized by the specialty product profit model include pharmaceuticals and specialty chemicals. The product cycle can vary from 8 to 15 years. Over time, the proportion of specialty revenue decreases, due to patent expirations, competition, etc. That is why the key task in maximizing profitability is astute selection of R&D projects to generate tomorrow's products. Outstanding practitioners include Merck, Hercules, and 3M.

14. Local Leadership Profit

Local Market Share

For many businesses, the economics of the company are almost entirely local. Examples include home health care companies, grocery stores, and many branches of retailing.

A leading home health care company in the United States illustrates the mechanism of profitability at work in these settings. A review of the company's cost structure indicates that the great majority of elements in the cost structure are local in nature. What matters is local leadership, not national scale. When the profitability of its 300 branches was charted as a function of local strength, what emerged was the pattern seen here.

As the company reflected on which customers to invest in, and in which cities it should concentrate that investment, it became clear that a sequential investment policy, driving branch offices toward the leadership asymptote, would generate the highest returns for the business.

A similar dynamic was at work in the classic case of A&P in the 1960s. A&P sought and achieved national leadership in the grocery business. Winn Dixie, on the other hand, concentrated on creating leadership in the Southeast. Despite being much larger than Winn Dixie, A&P's profitability was significantly lower, because it represented a collection of relatively weak local positions, especially in regions with strong local competitors like Winn Dixie.

The A&P case illustrates the risks involved when an organization is not working with an accurate model of its own profitability. Not only did A&P seek national share, it also systematically weakened its local positions. It undertook a major study of store-level profitability and then, city by city, began closing down its least profitable stores! By doing so, it weakened its own local market share position, thereby suffering the consequences of impaired local economics in purchasing, communication, logistics, etc. Instead of building, local share diminished, working in a direction exactly opposite of what was required by its true profit model. The very effective implementation of the wrong strategy led to a financial weakening that ultimately resulted in the sale of the company to Tenglemann, a West German grocery company.

Despite Sam Walton's homespun demeanor, few business leaders understood the fundamental economics of their company's profit model as clearly as he did. He knew that local leadership, to the point of absolute dominance, mattered above all else. Local leadership reduced logistic costs, advertising costs, recruiting costs, etc. He was not seduced into the notion of stringing out a necklace of Wal-Marts across the country. Rather, his approach was more akin to carpet bombing, county by county by county. This grasp of the primacy of local economics for his business, and highly disciplined execution in accordance with the terms of that model, gave Walton several points of margin advantage over competitors, both proximate and remote. The profitability difference provided the resources to support a 20 percent-plus growth rate over three decades. In his method, profitability supports growth, not the other way around. The retailing landscape is littered with experimental business designs that tried growing their way to profitability. It just doesn't work.

A latter day example of disciplined execution in accordance with the requirements of the "local economics" profit model is Starbuck's. Rather than spreading itself over acreage that it couldn't manage profitably, Starbuck's conquered Seattle first, then Chicago, then Vancouver. Starbuck's understood that its economics were local—logistics, word of mouth, recruiting. It exploited those economies to grow *profitably*, not just grow.

15. Transaction Scale Profit

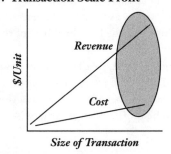

Size of Transaction

Certain industries are transaction-based. In many of these arenas, as the size of the transaction goes up, the cost to perform or deliver a transaction does not rise as quickly as the revenue received. All the profit is concentrated in the big deals. Examples include investment banking, real estate, and long-haul air travel.

Transaction scale businesses reward those who control the largest transactions. Customer selection—investing in those customers with the largest deals—is key.

In these businesses—typified by investment banking, real estate, commercial lending, long-distance haulage, long-distance travel, etc.—costs do not rise as rapidly as fees as a function of transaction size. Inevitably, gross margins on smaller-scale transactions are small. On megatransactions, the gross margins can be as high as 90 percent.

In this type of business, the experience curve matters little—perhaps not at all—and relative market share is not as important as the ability to tap into and control the flow of the largest deals. Two equal market shares—one composed of a hundred small deals, the other of five or six big ones—will not produce equivalent levels of profitability. The latter will be several times more profitable than the former.

An outstanding example of the transaction scale profit model is Morgan Stanley in the early 1970s. Morgan Stanley's phenomenal profitability during that period was not driven by total market share in investment banking, but by its dominant share of the Fortune 100. The Fortune 100 generated the largest-scale financial transactions. The costs incurred by Morgan Stanley to manage a $100 million financing were not dramatically greater than the costs of a $5 million financing. The difference in fees was enormous. Little wonder that Morgan Stanley's most aggressive rivals competed so fiercely to capture a higher portion of the Fortune 100 business. That's where all the profit was. In the venture world, several funds have worked their way into a position where they have access to the best and biggest deals.

The economic characteristics of large-scale securities transactions apply to transportation as well. Long hauls are more profitable than short hauls. Long flights are more profitable than short ones. Why? The actual costs (per mile) don't increase as rapidly as revenues. Carriers who succeed in concentrating their activity in the long-haul part of the industry can do much better than their peers.

In the low- or no-profit landscape of air travel, British Airways has worked hard to bias its business toward long-haul routes. Its relative focus on long-distance routes has enabled it to benefit from transaction scale profitability, and has allowed it to be profitable in an otherwise bleak economic environment.

16. Value Chain Position Profit

In many industries, profit concentrates itself in certain parts of the value chain and is absent in others. In PC computing, the profit is concentrated in microprocessors and software. In chemicals, it is in manufacturing, not in distribution. In general merchandise, it is in distribution, not in manufacturing. In automotive, it is in downstream activities such as financial services and extended warranty, not in assembly or distribution.

17. Cycle Profit

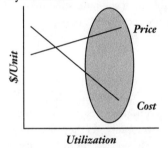

Many industries are characterized by distinct and powerfully cyclical behavior: chemicals, steel, industrial equipment. The profitability of the firm is a function of the cycle. Tell me the capacity utilization, and I'll be able to tell you what the profitability is.

In a cycle profit model, some companies play much better than others. Toyota, recognizing how intimately bound to the cycle it is, constantly strives to lower its breakeven profit, to achieve greater relative profitability. It can't control the cycle, but it works to maximize its position within the cycle's grip.

A cycle profit model can also be optimized on the revenue side. Dow Chemical, for example, has mastered the skill of pricing within the cycle. As capacity tightens, it leads price increases; as capacity loosens, it lags price declines.

Profit levels will be set by the cycle, but managerial actions can create a cost or pricing edge that has a major influence on the firm's profitability.

18. After-Sale Profit

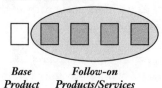

Base Product   **Follow-on Products/Services**

In some industries, such as manufacturing and airlines, it is not the sale of the product or service that generates the profit, but the after-sale financing or service of the product. Companies in industries in which the profit has migrated away from a product may have to move downstream to find annuity value streams.

GE is an excellent example of a company that has used the after-sale profit model to its advantage. GE has developed financing and servicing in its airplane engines and locomotives divisions to capture even more value from its customers.

Although the after-sale profit model is similar to installed base profit, it is fundamentally different because companies without an installed base can take advantage of the after-sale model. For example, Softbank, through its Kingston subsidiary, has no installed base in computers but makes significant profits selling add-on memory products to PC users.

19. New Product Profit

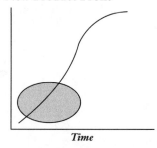

Time

New product profits are a function of newness and growth. New, high-margin products are introduced, and grow rapidly. As they mature, profits fall. A classic example is the PC business. Desktop PCs are mature and profitless. Laptops (in the middle of the S-curve) are still profitable. Servers (at the bottom of the S-curve) are immensely profitable (most of Compaq's profitability is explained by its lead in servers).

Other industries subject to the new product profit model include cars, copiers, industrial equipment, and instrumentation. In these businesses, the product cycle may vary from 3 to 7 years. The key to winning is being prepared to shift investment to create undisputed leadership in the next-generation product, the one that most closely matches the customer's most important current priorities.

20. Relative Market Share Profit

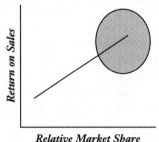

Return on Sales

Relative Market Share

In many industries, companies with high market shares tend to be more profitable because large companies have pricing advantages and cost economies due to greater manufacturing experience and volume purchasing ability. Advertising and fixed costs are also reduced with more sales dollars. Relative market share refers to a company's market share in relation to its competitors. The greater it is, the greater the profitability.

21. Experience Curve Profit

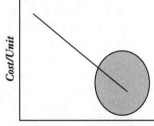

Cost/Unit

Cumulative Experience

As a firm becomes more experienced at manufacturing a product or delivering a service, its price per transaction decreases. A firm that specializes in the delivery of a particular product or service and has more experience in those transactions will be more profitable than a firm without that experience.

22. Low-Cost Business Design Profit

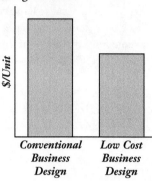

$/Unit

Conventional Business Design

Low Cost Business Design

You can always trump cumulative experience. Many have. You can trump cumulative experience with a low-cost business design, which makes the incumbent's cumulative experience irrelevant. Nucor did this in steel (the minimill model trumped the integrated mill); Southwest Air, in air travel (the point-to-point model trumped hub-and-spoke); Dell, in computing (direct marketing trumped a feet-on-the-street sales force and multilevel distribution channels).

The player focused on building cumulative experience to gain lowest cost is always vulnerable to the player who creates a low-cost position through design. High experience with the wrong business model doesn't get you very far.

PART TWO

---

*The Reinventors and How
They Succeeded*

JACK WELCH

The Customer Solutions Business Design

- *Do my products have high market share, but low profits?*

- *Is my organization pushing products or creating customer solutions?*

- *Should I be shifting my mix from manufacturing to services and knowledge-based activities?*

- *Is there a feasible way to transition my organization to tomorrow's high-profit activities?*

HERE'S A story all the business magazines missed: A mid-size company bought $500,000 worth of personal computers from General Electric (GE). What makes that news? Well, for starters, General Electric doesn't make computers! Why didn't the firm buy its computers directly from the manufacturer? Because the manufacturer only sells computers, a commodity product available from dozens of manufacturers. In contrast, GE sold the company the computers—plus options, accessories, service contracts, and financing. The company works with its clients electronically, and its computer network must be up 24 hours a day, 7 days a week, 52 weeks a year. The firm will need computer support services. And financing provides cash generation, better matching of revenues and expenses, and a 3-year technology upgrade path. GE saw this set of needs and met them. It provided a solution.

GE is at the forefront of a business design that provides a profitable answer to the question many executives who manufacture products are asking themselves: "How can I make a profit by making and selling my product?" Manufacturing computer boxes is, or is rapidly becoming, a profitless activity, as is manufacturing cars, consumer electronics, and countless other categories of product or hardware businesses. In fact, manufacturing is under the constant threat of unprofitability, as powerful customers and rapid imitators work in concert to evaporate yesterday's profit pool and to turn formerly profitable activities into the no-profit zones of tomorrow.

Is all manufacturing a no-profit zone where great effort is expended but the returns are elusive? The answer is both yes and no (Exhibit 4.1). Yes, if your business design focuses only on "the box"—the product. No, if you approach the box as GE did: as one part of a strategic business system that regards customer problems as new opportunities for entering the profit zone.

However, most manufacturers still rely on the same business model that they used two decades ago. They presume their customers are the same; they produce the same set of products; they still try to

---

EXHIBIT 4.1   *GE's Business Design: "Sell the Solution, Not Just the Box"*

Sell the Box, or ...

... Sell the Whole Solution

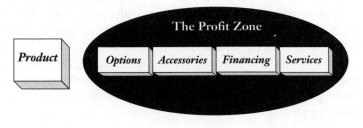

differentiate themselves with the same quality and price messages; and they still rely on sale of their products as their only value capture mechanism. Most importantly, these manufacturing companies only create value for customers with their *products*—they all have product-centric business designs. If every company in a given industry maintains the same product-centric business design, they all compete in the same way and provide the same offering to their customers. The only way a company can differentiate itself and its products in this environment is by establishing itself as a cost or quality leader. And if all players within an industry pursue cost and quality leadership, the industry becomes a no-profit zone.

With no more value left in existing manufactured products, manufacturers who still play the market share game will see profits decrease as revenues increase. This, in turn, will prevent them from creating value for shareholders. This pattern is being played out in dozens of manufacturing-based markets.

Over the course of his tenure as the CEO of General Electric, Jack Welch has reinvented GE's business design three times, each time moving further away from the traditional product-centric manufacturing model. From his first profit-centric "Be No. 1 or No. 2" business model, to a second profit-centric business model, "Work-Out," to GE's current profit- and customer-centric business design, "Solutions Selling," Welch has consistently responded to the needs and priorities of GE's customers. As a result, GE's market value grew from $13 billion when Welch began as CEO in 1981 to $162 billion at the end of 1996 (Exhibit 4.2).

Welch generated $150 billion in shareholder value because of his customer-centric and profit-centric approach to business. He recognized early in his career that customer needs and priorities would change and, as a result, that the profit zone within his industries would shift. To keep moving GE into that profit zone, Welch recognized that he must constantly reinvent GE's business model.

Welch reinvented GE's business model in stages. He made GE healthy in its fundamental businesses before he developed a more sophisticated business design. To do so, he made GE a leader in each of its businesses and dramatically cut costs. These profit-centric moves gave GE the industry leadership and installed base position it needed so that Welch could then move GE to its next generation business design.

EXHIBIT 4.2   *GE's Market Value Growth*

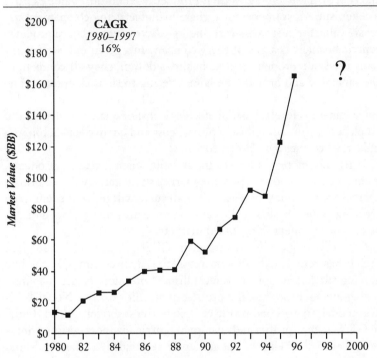

At each business model reinvention, Welch invented, developed, and applied ideas that drove change. Welch confronted institutional memory and created intense, challenging work environments. He faced enormous resistance from co-workers, customers, and competitors. Welch overcame these obstacles by developing each business concept, promoting it, rallying the organization behind it, then following it through until GE—its employees, customers, and even its competitors—saw its value and believed in it. And Welch ensured that GE will continue to use an ideas-driven business design by investing in GE's business school in Crotonville, New York. That's how GE became America's preeminent applied-knowledge company.

Welch found a way of making money in manufacturing. He crafted a business model that leverages GE's greatest assets—its customer relationships and its installed base position—and generates even more value for GE's shareholders. And it appears that GE is well positioned to continue growing its value. At a time when many manufacturers feel manufacturing is becoming a large-scale, no-profit zone, GE is making money in a broad cross section of manufacturing industries.

BE NO. 1 OR NO. 2

When Welch took the helm of GE in 1981, it was a large, incredibly diverse manufacturing organization producing a range of products from light bulbs to jet engines to locomotives to plastic resin. This diversity of product offerings reflected the growth strategies of many manufacturers over the previous decade. Successful manufacturing companies acquired or merged with other manufacturing companies because they sought greater success and could simultaneously spread their risk across a number of different industries with a variety of product lines. When much of the value these manufacturing companies created for their customers resided within the products they sold, such growth strategies made sense. Produce the best product, develop a strong distribution system, sell the product well, and you create value. If a company sought more value, it increased the number of products it sold.

Many companies stopped there. Not GE under Welch. He saw that companies created more value not merely by increasing the number of products sold, but by increasing the profit per product sold. And, at that time, the best way of increasing the profit per product sold was by becoming the market share leader. Market share leaders in the 1970s and 1980s enjoyed superior profitability because of greater economies of scale, greater manufacturing experience, and volume purchasing ability. Furthermore, the market share leader can become an industry standard, so it can price higher and still sell to risk-averse customers. Market share leadership was the profit zone in 1981.

Profit-centric thinking focused Welch on the benefits of market share leadership. So Welch reinvented GE's 1970s conglomerate business design using one overarching idea: Be No. 1 or No. 2—or Get Out! This idea stated in the clearest and most direct manner possible that GE would only invest in businesses that were leaders in their industries. Often, selling the weak businesses to eager owners who were better positioned to manage them was a smarter idea. GE could use the resources from the sale to build a stronger position in other businesses, or to fund better opportunities. Thus the edict: Improve or leave. And do it now.

Yet, although Welch saw that this idea could be a powerful profit growth engine, he knew that leading the diverse collection of GE's businesses in a company-wide effort would be a huge challenge. It would require an extremely simple and actionable message, one that could be understood, repeated, and implemented. Achieving real change, Welch believed, would require constant communication, tireless reinforcement, and a set of implementable actions—often difficult and strongly resisted—proving commitment to the message.

After the excitement of launching the Be No. 1 or No. 2 model came the long trek through a dark valley of resistance, characterized by tough decisions, few visible results, and a sincere belief by many within the organization that "this too shall pass." Counterarguments to Welch's plan were, on the whole, reasonable. One can imagine the objections of the division heads:

"But Jack, be reasonable. The guy who's running a No. 4 or No. 5 business—which, by the way, was No. 6 when he inherited it—can't be blamed. He's doing a great job, in fact. The business brought in $100 million in revenues last year. We should keep him, we should keep that business."

After all, the goal of attaining only No. 1 or No. 2 market position could easily be interpreted as overly simplistic and arbitrary. Any reasonable person would have relented and softened his position.

But Jack Welch was not a reasonable person—at least, not when he was trying to change an organization as large and as successful as GE. For 2 years, he held firm to this position, and, in 1983, the results began to evidence themselves in the company's improved financial results. Be No. 1 or No. 2 became more broadly and more actively supported within GE, it even became a source of internal pride. To the increasingly profit-centric GE managers, Be No. 1 or No. 2 was the tough-minded, realistic, and strategic principle for which General Electric stood.

The principal profit-centric tenet of Be No. 1 or No. 2 was that it was a means to an end, a strategic step toward a stronger company, not an end in and of itself. Be No. 1 or No. 2 was merely one profit-centric business model, a model that would be reinvented as the customer changed.

And customers did change. Customers became more powerful. GE was selling a large portion of its products to customers like Ford, Wal-Mart, GM, and Boeing. In a world where a few customers had become responsible for a large part of the seller's revenues and profits, the customers used their growing power to force down prices. In their race toward market share leadership, manufacturers cut prices to unprofitable levels. Market share leadership was no longer enough to be profitable. The profit zone had begun to shift. To remain profitable, GE needed a new idea and a new business design.

WORK-OUT

By the mid-1980s, it was clear to Welch and other forward-looking managers that winning the market share game was not enough. The relationship between market share and profitability was eroding. In some industries, the downward price spiral was leading to the creation of enormous no-profit zones. In many cases, an inverse relationship between share and profit began to emerge. In industries as diverse as cars, coffee, and structural steel, the smallest players became the most profitable, and the largest players became the least profitable. High market share without high productivity was a losing hand.

Welch knew GE could become significantly more productive than it had been in the mid-1980s. He could see it in the numbers. GE's productivity improvements were a disappointing 2 percent per year through the early 1980s. As customer power put pressure on price negotiations across many GE businesses, GE had to change the focus of the Be No. 1 or No. 2 business design—from market share to high-productivity market share. Welch's idea for accomplishing this transformation was the program that became known as Work-Out—literally: Take work out of the process.

The program's primary focus was to bring together employees who were closest to actual work processes. Workers described and mapped out methods currently being used by the business, then identified unnecessary steps that could be eliminated. Work-Out sidestepped or attacked head-on bureaucratic obstacles. Proposals were formulated on the spot. Recommendations were made to managers that day. They decided "Yes" or "No"—on the spot—and then the process moved on.

The informality of Work-Out boosted employee involvement and participation, improved communication, and gave employees a sense of personal control. This shift represented a profound change in the organizational dimension of the GE business model—from command and control to a new perspective on the role and potential contribution of GE's employees. It was a major talent-unlocking mechanism. Welch, by minimizing hierarchical constraints and increasing genuine employee engagement, increased productivity spectacularly. This was the only guarantee that leading market share positions would translate into highly profitable businesses.

Formally kicked-off in October 1988, the Work-Out program expanded exponentially throughout the corporate culture. It became a semicontrolled organizational chain reaction. By 1992, more than 200,000 GE employees had participated in Work-Out training, and by 1993, as many as 20,000 GE people were involved in Work-Out programs at any one point in time. The effect on GE was profound. From 1981 to 1986—before Work-Out—GE's annual productivity gains averaged 2 percent. From 1987 to 1991, Work-Out doubled the rate of annual productivity improvement to more than 4 percent.

Welch's genius lay in his early and far-seeing analysis of the situation and his responses to it, not just in the originality of his methods per se. Just as Be No. 1 or No. 2 was Welch's creative and actionable synthesis of a cluster of existing ideas, Work-Out was a creative, internally marketable, GE-branded synthesis of emerging ideas on speed and reengineering that were not formally articulated by business observers until the early 1990s.

Like many of Welch's ideas and actions, Work-Out anticipated by several years what other major U.S. corporations spent the early 1990s doing: creating a more streamlined, more productive corporate configuration. Many companies, when they did get the reengineering fever, made attempts that were often misguided. They concentrated on doggedly streamlining already-obsolete business models rather than reinventing their business design to move into tomorrow's profit zone. By contrast, even as GE was using Work-Out to streamline its current business model, Welch was already at work inventing the next one. GE continued evolving its business model, making it even more customer-centric and profit-centric in its philosophy, structure, and methodology.

SOLUTIONS SELLING

Lawrence Jackson, president of a major automotive supplier (with over $1 billion in sales) warmed to his topic. He had recently been promoted and loved to talk about the deals he had been working on.

"Let me tell you about three different sales pitches that I experienced over the last two months. The first was from a major chemical company that manufactures a broad line of chemicals we use in our process. This man was smooth, polished, professional. He knew the technical specs and characteristics of his products to a 'T.' He went on and on about why his products were so good.

"He was right, of course. His company makes very good products. But then, so do all of my other suppliers. His pitch was that he could be a one-stop shop. Nice concept, but it doesn't do much for me, because my other chemical suppliers have products just as good, and their delivered costs are low. What's the benefit to *me* of a single supplier of a dozen commodity products?

"The second rep was different. He sold plastics. We use a lot of plastic. He, too, was technically solid. And he was passionate about his product and his company, talking about all the new value-added programs they were developing. That was all great, but what did it mean for me? He said, it would create benefits in the future. I said, then come see me in the future.

"The third rep was from GE. Although his job was to sell plastics, he didn't tell me anything about his product. He just asked questions. How much capital do I have tied up in equipment? What are my yield losses in the plant? What are the biggest operational problems I run into at the plant, using my current materials, and process set-ups? How much capital do I have tied up in my trucks and logistical operations?

"We really got talking. As I described the operational problems we faced, we got into some very interesting issues. There were big numbers involved.

"He came back in two weeks. Showed me how GE Capital can reduce my capital intensity and my financing costs. In both plant equipment and logistics. Showed me how we could save on warehouse space. Described an approach for GE engineers to work with my plant people to make changes that would optimize my materials usage.

"Then he went on to talk about global support. We're growing like crazy internationally. He described how GE could support us in our global expansion.

"When I added it all up, he was saving my operation a lot of money. On capital, on financing, on yield losses. Of course, he got my plastics business. Almost all of it. And he's going to get it on a global basis.

"I'm not the only one who's delighted with this approach to doing business. My plant guys love it. They're used to dealing with product pushers. With GE, they're dealing with a group of people who have taken the time to learn their problems, and to help solve them. When it comes to deciding who's going to get our plastics business, it's not even close.

"Also, getting this support on a global basis makes our lives much easier. And given all the scrambling we have to do to serve our own tough customers, the automakers, that kind of support helps us out a lot."

*   *   *

By the early 1990s, it became clear to Welch that even with high market share and high productivity, there was still no assurance of creating sustained profit growth. Success required taking the GE business design to the next level, and making a transition from selling products to providing solutions.

The reason for this change in business design? Changing customer needs and priorities.

Customers were changing in a fundamental way. Over the years, as they purchased more products from their suppliers, they became more sophisticated and more familiar with these products. And as their understanding of the manufacturers' products and technology increased, the technical specifications of the products became less important than the economics of the products for the users. As a result, responsibility for purchasing decisions migrated up the corporate ladder from purchasing agents, technicians, and engineers to administrators and senior executives. Engineers were concerned about the technical details of the manufactured products they purchased: Were these products in accordance with specifications? What were their costs compared to competitors'? Senior executives were more concerned with the system or set of activities in which the products they purchased were used. Senior executives valued the specific product much less than a new approach to an old process that would dramatically reduce the total cost for the process and would improve their company's profitability.

A major new business opportunity was created by this shift, but the traditional, product-centric supplier approach was not well equipped to respond. Taking advantage of this shift meant that manufacturing companies had to change their customer selection from engineers and purchasing agents to senior executives; their scope from products to solutions; their differentiation from price to better systems economics for customers; and their value capture from products to services. In short, manufacturers had to change their entire business design. Welch did this at GE.

To start, as the customer set migrated from engineers to CEOs, Welch changed GE's marketing approach. Rather than rely only on sales reps who marketed products to purchasing agents and engineers, Welch himself engaged in a selling dialogue with the CEOs of GE's customers. Across customer groups as varied as hospitals, retailers, auto manufacturers, and utilities, Welch understood how different CEO-level marketing was from the conventional sales approach. Several moves ahead of the competition, he consciously prepared GE for the new kind of selling required for the solutions-oriented, high-end senior executive customer set. Recognizing that the size and scope of GE's businesses now made the "Vice-President" title of the business heads obsolete (eight of these units are large enough to be listed in the Fortune 500 in their own right), Welch gave the heads new "President and CEO" titles. Now the company had 13 CEOs to call on senior executives.

For Welch's CEO marketing to be effective, he needed a high-level understanding of the forces at work in his customers' industry, including, but not limited to, the concepts of systems economics and revenue enhancement. Welch could not merely sell a product;

he had to place the product in the context of the customer's total economic equation. This systems economics perspective required Welch to move GE beyond the traditional product/sell relationship to a true business partner relationship where value is created for both parties by creating solutions that increase the profitability of both the customer and the supplier.

Welch, and his business heads, became leading practitioners of CEO marketing. They leveraged GE's knowledge of customer usage systems to develop new solutions for customers, and they broadened GE's current customer relationships into more long-term, higher-value relationships. For example, when negotiating with Ford in the mid-1990s, Welch met directly with Ford's CEO, Alex Trotman, and provided Ford with a spectrum of products and related engineering solutions that saved Ford money and improved its profitability. To show GE's commitment to helping Ford, Welch went down to the shop floor and talked directly with Ford's line workers. He asked them what they liked and what they disliked about GE's products and services; what GE could do better; and how he could help. Welch wrote down every comment he heard. When he returned to GE, he called up the managers responsible for different elements of GE's relationship with Ford. Welch told them to develop a program to fix the things that were wrong—immediately. And they did. The result? GE landed the contract with Ford. Moreover, Ford found GE's solutions to be so effective that it agreed to use GE as a major supplier for its European business as well.

Welch was a pioneer in the development of CEO-level marketing. The practice of CEO marketing will rise dramatically in the next decade, as senior management-level business relationships between giant organizations become the norm rather than exception. Because this upper-level interaction requires an increasing sensitivity to customers' systems economics, the consequences of CEO-marketing business designs will be much greater than simply higher-value sales. Such sensitivity brings rising levels of customer responsiveness, increased incentives for anticipating the customer's needs and priorities, and a greater appetite for redefining how the game is played. Traditional product/sell business designs have led to evaporating profitability in many industries, but customer solutions business designs will create a powerful upward spiral for companies that are able to develop the types of solutions that simultaneously create greater value for customers and greater profits for shareholders.

CEO marketing was just one aspect of GE's customer solutions business model. Welch also gradually changed GE's scope and value capture by moving from a product orientation to a services orientation. Again, Welch leveraged GE's installed product base and customer base, and utilized GE's knowledge of customers' systems economics to identify new profit zones and cost-effective business design responses.

One of the greatest lost opportunities in business occurs when companies that possess phenomenal product knowledge do not employ that knowledge in making the transition from product leadership to solutions leadership. During the 1990s, Welch worked to make sure that GE captured all possible value from combining product, maintenance, service, and financing.

In fact, one of GE's greatest business design changes was the aggressive expansion of GE's financial services division, GE Capital, headed since 1986 by Gary Wendt. Welch knew GE's finance business, since it reported directly to him from 1977 to 1981. Its roots were consumer-product-oriented—the financing of GE appliances, for example.

Welch and Wendt brought a larger-scale perspective and appreciation of financial services. Rather than viewing financing as a means to sell more products—the view of most traditional manufacturers—they viewed financing as a core part of the solutions benefits that many customers sought. Value was migrating from manufacturing to financial services. GE moved to where the value would be by aggressively building its financing business. GE Capital bought about 30 insurance, credit-card processing, and other financial companies each year. By the end of 1995, the unit's assets totaled $186 billion, making GE Capital as large as the third largest bank in the United States.

Financing was only part of the enhanced value capture that Welch envisioned in the solutions business design. For example, GE manufactures jet engines, finances their purchase, performs maintenance and overhauls, and provides spare parts. While GE fought tooth and claw against competitors such as Rolls-Royce and the Pratt & Whitney unit of United Technologies to win the market share game for new product sales, in some areas GE's focus on aftermarket services created profit margins in excess of 30 percent. To strengthen its position, GE acquired British Airways' overhaul facilities, and also acquired Greenwich Air Services. This further grew GE's jet engine services division to include service on other manufacturers' equipment.

GE has taken this service-oriented approach into other markets as well. For instance, for years, GE provided hospitals with X-ray machines and scanning devices. As manufacturers cut prices to compete for market share, and as hospitals experienced intensified pressure by managed care organizations to lower costs, most medical equipment started moving into a no-profit zone. In response, GE developed a highly profitable online diagnostic service linked to 11,000 scanning machines across the entire world. The system diagnoses the machines and can even fix problems with the machines remotely. And it creates a new source of profit growth for GE.[1]

GE Capital adroitly extended GE's business model further and further downstream: GE Auto Financial Services is the largest non-captive U.S. auto lessor; GE is the largest equipment management company in the world; GE is the number one player in primary mortgage insurance; GE is the third largest reinsurance company in the world and the largest in the United States. GE is no longer tied to the manufacture of products to define its markets.

Welch understands that the potential for value growth lies in downstream service and financing activities. His concentration on these activities stemmed from a customer-and-economic focus, rather than from a purely product-driven perspective. He redefined the game by seeing the larger economic context around the product.

Welch saw that, for any product on the market, there exists a larger economic context or equation, of which the product itself is only a subset. The product is the catalyst of the profit-producing reaction—it is the trigger that sets things into motion. After the initial purchase, products require maintenance, financing, aftermarket sales of replacement parts, component sales, upgrades, and so on. Often, the revenue associated with these "nonproduct" or "postproduct" dimensions is many times the revenue associated directly with the sale of the product. The disproportion in terms of profitability is even greater. Seeing that the profit zone was moving away from the product and into the downstream activities that the product triggered, Welch changed the scope and value capture mechanisms of GE's business model to take advantage of this migration. Currently, due to careful capture of this postproduct revenue and profitability, 40 percent of GE's overall operating profits derive from services and financing. Furthermore, since the mid-1980s, GE's financial services division, GE Capital, has achieved net income growth at an average rate of 18 percent per year while GE's other businesses, on average, have reached a modest net income growth rate of 4 percent per year.

Despite all of Welch's business design reinventions—making GE's businesses number one or number two across all of its industries; dramatically increasing GE's productivity with Work-Out; and providing customer solutions—Welch still pushed to redeploy GE's assets into high-profit, nonmanufacturing activities, many of which are related to, but not entirely dependent on, the product, "the box." Welch saw that, as a manufacturing company, GE had to find new ways of making a profit, while optimizing its manufacturing activities. True profit-centric business thinking in manufacturing must, inevitably, lead to activities other than manufacturing.

THE APPLIED KNOWLEDGE COMPANY

As CEO of GE, Welch uses ideas to drive GE's business design reinventions. Welch realizes how powerful ideas can be in leading change. Ensuring that GE continues to use ideas as drivers for its business design innovations, Welch has invested heavily in GE's internal business school in Crotonville, New York. Crotonville imprints the process of continual reinvention directly onto the ranks of future GE leaders. Crotonville "students" experiment with new business model ideas. They also collect ideas from within GE that appear effective, develop them, and further disseminate them. Through Crotonville, GE applies knowledge that creates successful new business models.

For example, one GE affiliate became a de facto purchasing cooperative for computer customers—delivering lower prices, gaining share, and retaining a portion of the purchasing economies as profit. The core idea was that, by using the company's natural purchasing power and expanding it by buying on behalf of others, the GE unit could gain share and increase profit concurrently. The idea was brought to Crotonville, where it was packaged and passed along to other parts of GE. In the GE system, profitable ideas are shared more rapidly, and diffusion can be more rapid and comprehensive.

The great value that internal business schools such as Crotonville provide is in testing ideas and techniques across very different industry groups. Typically, though, the richness of a cross-industry perspective is lost because internal business schools draw on company resources, most of which come from within the industry in which the company is involved. But GE itself is nothing if not a cross-industry aggregation of highly dynamic, competitive business models. GE's direct unfiltered access to heterogeneity was historically the chief competitive advantage of

EXHIBIT 4.3   *GE's Business Design Reinvention*

	1981	*1997*	*2002*
Customer Selection	• Consumers • Manufacturers • Engineers	• Consumers • Manufacturers • Senior executives	
Value Capture	• Product sales	• Multi component product, service, solution, and financing	**?**
Differentiation/ Strategic Control	• Brand • Market leader	• Customer solutions • Customer relationships • CEO marketing • 6-Sigma Quality	
Scope	• Manufactured products	• Customer solutions • Financing • Services • Manufactured products	

the traditional idea-makers. Fortunately for them, GE is not going into the business school/consulting business (or is it?). But other corporations are now beginning to grasp the power of the applied knowledge dimension of the GE business model—although they might not understand how many years it takes to build that capability.

Through Crotonville, GE accelerates the process of business design reinvention—and puts itself further ahead of the competition. GE's business design reinventions (see Exhibit 4.3) have created significant value growth (see Exhibit 4.2), moving the company from value outflow, to stability, to value inflow (see Exhibit 4.4). Will the value growth continue? The gathering momentum of the company's 6-sigma quality program, with its goal of virtually eliminating defects by the year 2000, leads most observers to conclude that the value growth will continue well into the next century.

EXHIBIT 4.4   *General Electric Business Design Reinvention*

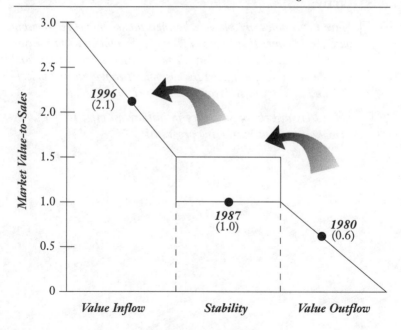

Value Creation Performance

BUILDING A CUSTOMER SOLUTIONS BUSINESS DESIGN
Pilot's Checklist

☑ *Have I fixed the product and maximized my productivity?*

☑ *Have I searched for every opportunity to provide accessories, services, and financing for my hardware customers?*

☑ *Have I translated my organization's knowledge about products and their life-cycle characteristics to create a proprietary advantage in providing services, assessing risk, and making profitable financing decisions?*

☑ *Have I built and quantified an accurate model of my customers' systems economics?*

☑ *Have I created a solution that improves those economics significantly?*

☑ *Have I translated my solutions business into a unique relationship with the customer that creates a flow of information about the customer's business? Does this enable me to understand (better and sooner than anyone else does) the customer's economics and priorities, and what they will become tomorrow?*

☑ *Have I created the opportunity to initiate an effective CEO/senior management marketing program?*

FIVE

THE STORY OF THREE MANAGERS

Reinvention for the Rest of Us

- *Can I change my company's business design even if I'm not the CEO, the owner, or a senior manager?*

- *Can I build a customer solutions business design inside a product-centric company?*

- *Can I get rewarded for doing this successfully?*

REINVENTION IS not just for the giants of industry, nor just for CEOs of large public companies, nor just for senior managers. The principles and techniques of reinventing a company's business design to get it into the industry's profit zone are available to all of us.

These principles and techniques apply with equal force to small companies, to private companies, to divisions of larger companies, and to the middle managers who run them. In fact, the reinventors we will be reading about in the future are already honing their skills at innovative business design today.

The three examples discussed in this chapter—Madden Communications, Cardboard Box, Inc., and Clozaril Patient Management System—illustrate the universal applicability of these management and investor tools.

MADDEN COMMUNICATIONS

As a salesman hired by Chicago-based Madden Graphics in 1975, Jim Donahugh asked his own questions and followed his own instincts. "What can I do to add real value to a customer?" he wondered. "What would be more valuable than just selling the customer a printing job?"

That kind of persistent customer-centric thinking remained with him after Donahugh's ascendancy to president of the commercial printing company.

Madden traces the turning point in its reinvention back to 1988, when it won a contract for printing 100,000 in-store promotional point-of-sale displays for one of America's largest food manufacturers. At a cost of $6 per display, the manufacturer sent every U.S. grocery store a Madden-printed display for use on Labor Day weekend.

"Each kit included multiple die-cut pieces, posters, price cards, shelf-talkers, and danglers," Donahugh says. "It was a printer's dream, a great job. In 1988, that $600,000 job was somewhere in the neighborhood of 10 percent of our total billings for the year. It was a huge chunk of business. Anybody would love to take that order, produce it all, be done with it, and collect the money."

Donahugh visited a grocery store during Labor Day weekend and looked for his company's work. Much to his surprise, he couldn't find it. Thinking that the store might be an exception, he stopped at another grocery store. He didn't find the display there, either. None of the local stores were showing it or even had it in the stockroom. Why, he asked himself, is someone paying us hundreds of thousands of dollars if these things aren't getting into the stores?

Sensing a problem and an opportunity, Donahugh looked into other sales promotion and marketing materials that his client had sent out to the field, and that were not being used by the customer. He met with the senior vice president of sales in the client organization, who said, "Go ahead and figure out what is going on—if you can."

"He gave us some contact points and very quickly we understood—they were overproducing," Donahugh says. "At that point in time, they only had 25,000 active customers in their database, but they ordered 100,000 point-of-sale kits. That was four kits per store! That was unheard of."

Donahugh continued his investigation in a casual way in the months that followed. One executive checked out groceries in Colorado while on vacation; Donahugh did the same in Florida. It sometimes seemed that everybody at Madden had a cousin in the grocery business, because reports came in from all over the country.

"We kept hearing horror stories about entire skids of our customer's displays stacked up for weeks and months at warehouses," Donahugh recalls. "Nobody representing our customers ever did anything about it, so the displays sat around gathering dust until the grocers finally threw them all away."

This was the genesis of Madden Graphics' direct-to-store printing and shipping program, which transformed the company from a me-too commercial printer into a one-of-a-kind, value-added service provider.

A district manager in Minneapolis showed Donahugh his warehouse, stocked with thousands of wasted point-of-sale materials. Six times a year, the manager paid a scavenger service to drop off a three-yard bin container, and warehouse employees threw it all out.

"Why do you do this? Why do you stock this stuff?" Donahugh asked. "Your company ordered something, paid the manufacturer—me—distributed it nationwide, stored it, and now you pay somebody to take it to a dump without it ever reaching the stores. Am I understanding this correctly?"

"Absolutely, that's the way it is," the manager said.

"Why don't you stop this?" an incredulous Donahugh asked.

"Because," the man calmly explained, "if I don't order this much, there is this guy at our corporate headquarters who calls me up and says, 'Your allocated amount for this was 20,000 kits. How come you only ordered 10,000 this time? Aren't you doing your job?'"

The system made little sense to a commonsense thinker like Donahugh. Huge costs, no benefits.

Compiling his findings in a completely unsolicited report, Donahugh went to his client and said, "I have some ideas about how we can better support your executional goals across all of your promotional events." Madden still contracted for the display printing, but, for the first time, it also controlled the value chain by only printing and distributing as many displays as were actually needed. That created value and saved money. Madden took on all those tasks.

Donahugh literally stumbled on this ancillary, value-added business by better understanding how his customer operated and how Madden's products were used by the customer—where they made sense and where they didn't.

When it was successful in one place, Donahugh said, "OK, now I understand this formula; how can I take advantage of it?" He took his display printing and management program on the road and made successful presentations to a leading tobacco manufacturer, a salty snacks company, and a major department store. Madden's 300 employees now focus on fewer than ten accounts, but they represent the number one or number two player in each of the key consumer products categories.

Consistently thinking in this quintessentially customer-centric and profit-centric fashion, Donahugh grew this second-generation printing company from annual revenues of $5 million in 1980 to $10 million in 1990 and $120 million in 1997!

The key insight that made this company so valuable is that printing is a product-centric commodity business that is driven by scale economies and capacity utilization. A successful owner gets the biggest printing press available and runs it 24 hours a day, 7 days a week, because all of the value lies in running off image after image after image. And as long as the press is running fast and the cost of this big capital investment can be amortized over hundreds of millions of copies, the owner does well. If this big expensive equipment is running only 50 or 60 percent of the time, the printer is in deep trouble. In Madden's local market, there was such an endless array of printers that few ran at a profitable level of capacity utilization.

Printers hoped to make money on selling the product—by gaining scale, volume, and market share. For Donahugh, that was exactly the characteristic of the business, but there was no chance of ever getting into a profit zone doing that. As a low-scale player against multi-billion-dollar players, he would never win. Instead, he chose to move from the product to the customers. He understood how and where else he could add value to the customers by understanding what they do, how they use the product, and some of the other related events they face. His action was one or two steps removed from the product, but it affected the product's use and economic value to the customer.

*   *   *

In its new business design, Madden Graphics became Madden Communications, a company that understands how a product is applied in the marketplace rather than one that just fills million-unit orders. This new-generation business model better serves the customer and better understands the customer's systems economics, process, and value chain. A company that does this consistently eventually finds an inner passage and moves from a product-centric business design to a customer-centric business design.

Donahugh began by creating an innovative relationship with his clients' sales, marketing, and product promotion people. He built a business design that not only protected their business but added so much other value that Madden Graphics completely redefined itself. It changed its printing company business model to that of a communications management company, which integrates display construction design, manufacturing, assembly, and distribution of point-of-sale materials. Although not involved in the creative content, Madden is very involved in making sure materials are user-friendly and will work in the trade channel targeted by the customer.

Madden's core activity is still printing, but the Madden people don't really *care* about printing as an end in itself. They care about what it does for their customers and their customers' trade partners, but are not enamored of its technology, presses, and dot structures. Those elements are critical, but they are not the company's end goal. They are vehicles, or enablers.

"We spend most of our time talking about the customers' businesses—how we can add value to them," Donahugh says. "Because if we can add value to them, there will be plenty of work for us. We never say, 'Let's buy a new press that runs 15 percent faster and the world will come to us.' That's looking at the printing industry as if it were a field of dreams: 'Build it and printing customers will come.' Not true! Build it and you will go bankrupt."

*   *   *

Selling the Madden Communications value proposition isn't easy because it is invasive and touches so many people in the customer organization. Conventional printers usually talk to one person in a client's purchasing department, period. Madden people talk to many people in the customer's organization. They have to jump over horizontal and vertical hurdles in most client organizations. It doesn't endear them to everybody, particularly those interested in protecting the status quo, but delivering the value that they believe inherently exists means working effectively with a client's sales force. They also talk to trade development, trade marketing, consumer promotion, and finance personnel, and they spend a great deal of time in the retail channels in which their customers compete.

Madden works hard to overcome the difficulties created by corporate systems and fueled by conventional purchasing practices. How do most corporations solve problems? They chop a task up into its smallest parts. For the point-of-sale displays Madden creates, most clients rely on design agencies, consumer promotions agencies, and their purchasing departments, who typically bid and place the job components separately. Is it any wonder that systems break down?

"That approach," Donahugh says, "is contrary to what we sell. What we sell is a complete integrated solution, where you integrate all those previously separated functions into one streamlined system that compresses time lines and eliminates unnecessary costs and activities. We reduce cost and get the right material to the right people on time, every time, at the lowest total system cost. That total solution is what we sell."

Most commercial printing operations take artwork from clients, print the number ordered, and hand back the completed job. The clients deal with the rest. In a traditional printing business design, printers have no incentive to think beyond that "box." And their clients choose them on the basis of a purely conventional purchasing approach. "Don't get too deep or interested in my organization," is their attitude. "Don't talk to anybody else in my organization but me."

"We take it several steps further," Donahugh says. "We go out with our customer and *their* customer, and see what they need. 'This is what you want? Well, just because you want it, we are happy to give it to you, but let us tell you why you might want to rethink that.'"

In its original survey of the sales reps for its food manufacturing client, Madden found that they spent anywhere from 1 to 3 hours per day moving point-of-sale materials around. Madden's direct-to-store program freed up, conservatively, 7 hours a week per sales rep, times 2,000 sales reps. They can now spend those hours more effectively: visiting stores, talking, listening, and selling products to the store and department managers.

In the course of studying how its clients applied its displays, Madden picked up a few valuable pointers about its own products. Assembly now takes no more than 2 minutes because the display has been redesigned. "We recognized the field sales force's time is valuable," Donahugh says. "So all end-aisle point-of-sale displays can be assembled within 2 minutes of pulling them out of the carton. In the past, the same process took 5 to 10 minutes."

That experience developed out of experiments in Madden's own test lab—an in-house, scale-size grocery store.

"We bring our folks in to see what happens, where the display goes, how it works, and whether it will fit in a congested and crowded end-aisle. We must have a piece that will position correctly and get noticed. Previously, many big floor displays didn't get assembled, let alone get placed."

How much value does Madden gain, based on what it saves clients? By repeatedly demonstrating the program's value, Madden Communications now writes a risk/reward mechanism into contracts for driving down costs. Customers also sign longer contracts (5 years versus 1 or 2 years), giving Madden business it can bank on.

One customer, with whom Madden had developed a direct-to-store relationship in 1989, nonetheless left it in 1993 and went back to bulk printing orders, distribution centers, and salespeople who carried point-of-sale materials one-at-a-time to stores. Giving up an integrated solution proved a costly error in judgment, and the client returned to Madden in early 1997. Why did the client come back? Over four years, 2,000 skids with an approximate value of $2 million were thrown out. This was merchandising material the client had paid for out of cash flow. The skids were warehoused and the merchandising material never made it to the intended destinations.

Under the conventional system, somebody was rewarded for that business, and vendors felt they had done their job because they gave a nice per-unit price. Ultimately, however, this system of false economies failed for everybody.

In recent years, Madden has branched out into packaging sales rep-specific selling information packages and producing interactive CD-ROM sales tools for its customers' field sales reps. The CD-ROMs demonstrate the variety, sizes, dimensions, and types of display and other promotional materials available, so that reps need not carry stock around with them. Automatic ordering from Madden Communications' World Wide Web site is even possible at the touch of a button.

"A field sales rep could actually play this on a laptop computer to show a store manager what the product might look like. And," Donahugh says, "it's fun."

Its deep involvement with its clients' businesses has made Madden very knowledgeable. It develops substantial databases, but the information remains proprietary to the client. What Madden owns is the software it created for maintaining such sophisticated databases.

"We maintain a database that allows us the flexibility to meet their distribution information needs," Donahugh says. "It is the Bible for everything that we do here. Everything is based on that information, so reliability is extremely crucial for us in achieving our objective—getting the right stuff to the right place, on time, and in the right quantities. Database management is nobody's favorite thing. We understand how critical it is.

"We were in manufacturing and we moved into logistics, assembly, and distribution," he says. "Now we are getting into information services. Our entire organization is morphing—again."

*　　*　　*

Under Donahugh, the company has found ways of preempting competition, shielding itself from the open warfare of a thousand printers.

"We were a *relationship* type of organization," Donahugh says. "We developed traditional relationships in the purchasing groups of companies, in the training departments of companies, in a series of jobs. If the relationship guy, the buyer, left, we were really in a pickle. It could be a traumatic event when other people came in and gave work to their own friends."

That's when Donahugh announced to his salespeople: "The game has changed."

He reorganized the salespeople into a salaried staff and eliminated commission positions. The new organization looks and operates more like an advertising agency, right down to the account teams that are devoted to a single food manufacturer or department store. Each includes an account supervisor, account executives, and a customer service group that communicates with the client's headquarters and field operators via toll-free "800" telephone numbers. They are paid well, and there is a big bonus potential for doing the right things.

"We spent a lot of time talking about how we would teach, train, and coach our people in this new approach," Donahugh says. "It came down to three things. No. 1, we really must be experts in our customers' business. No. 2, we must shape the customers' expectations properly. And No. 3, we must communicate well.

"None of that says what we consider obvious: We must still sell printing," he continues. "But the printing business will come, so we changed the game and the compensation structure. In doing that, we changed the type of person we want on the street. We no longer want an experienced printing salesperson who sold a million dollars' worth of work last year. Instead, we grow our own people. We find the brightest young people, the ones who know how to read, write, and think. And we train them."

Madden Communications lets its clients know, up front, that its salespeople are salaried, not paid by commission. Instead of a client–salesperson relationship, the bond is between Madden's organization and the client's organization.

"This is still a relationship business," Donahugh says, "but the relationships are dependent on how we as an organization create value for the customer, and not specifically on an individual. That is a vast difference. And it is difficult. We got laughed out of some buildings because people would say, 'You guys are printers. What do you know about my business?' One customer said, 'The problem with you guys is, we are trying to buy printing and you are trying to help us run our business.'"

Within Madden, resistance to changing the sales compensation structure was not insignificant.

"We have people who still don't get it," Donahugh says. "It is a difficult thing to grasp."

Some people made the change; some didn't and moved on. What's especially remarkable about the company's transition is that Madden was not in distress when Donahugh reinvented its business design. In 1986, when he began the transition, the company was actually having its best year ever.

*   *   *

The idea of getting rid of commissions had its origins in the first substantial deal Donahugh brought in after being hired by the Madden brothers in 1976. Instead of writing him a fat commission check that they couldn't afford, they quenched Donahugh's excitement somewhat by making him a part owner. "It was fine by me," Donahugh says. "The fact is, if you look up 'partner' in the dictionary, there would be a picture of Joe and John. They are wonderful guys. We have all kinds of fun."

"Joe Madden was tough to work for," Donahugh recalls, "because another printing job was not what he wanted. He didn't want salesmen coming in with printing jobs. He wanted salesmen coming in with solutions to customers' problems, salesmen who were thinking about printing differently than traditional printers were thinking about it."

Donahugh has led Madden Communications through a dramatic business design reinvention. Where other printers try to serve as many customers as possible, Madden serves a select group of very profitable accounts. Where other printers focus on printing operations and try to create value for their customers by reducing the cents charged per image produced, Madden provides integrated promotion execution and creates and captures value by shared risk/reward agreements. Most printers have no strategic control point built into their business design, no differentiation versus their competitors. Madden Communications, as shown in Exhibit 5.1, is one of the few printers in the country capable of providing these types of business solutions to its customers.

EXHIBIT 5.1   *Business Design: Traditional Printers vs. Madden*

	Traditional Printers' Business Design	**Madden Communications' Business Design**
Customer Selection	• Many customers	• Few, but profitable, customers
Value Capture	• Gross margin • Cents per image	• Shared risk/reward savings
Differentiation/ Strategic Control	• None	• One of the few printers in the country capable of offering a complete solution, a fully integrated set of services
Scope	• Printing operations	• Fully integrated promotional execution service

On any given day, on any given item, Donahugh's clients can find a lower price than Madden Communications charges, because printing per se is no longer what it sells.

"When somebody says, 'How much is this going to cost?' I say, 'I have no idea.' Ask the brand managers how much they are going to spend and we will evolve into an equilibrium where whatever is right for their business, we can get it done in the most efficient and effective manner and for the least total system cost. What's in it for us? All of the agreements we have with our customers state that we end up with 'incentive' costs. We want to be on the same side as them, so we set up a mechanism that, if we reduce costs and eliminate waste, we get a big bonus, and our customers save money and get a better business result.

"That way," Donahugh says, "if we do the right things the right way, we will be here for the long haul."

CARDBOARD BOX, INC. (CBI)

One of the best profit zone examples comes from Jim Burton (name disguised), a business development manager for Cardboard Box, Inc. (CBI), a major cardboard box manufacturer (name disguised). Jim had a competitive advantage that many managers never get; he actually spent 5 years in the field as a sales executive, and he got to know his customers. Jim described a situation that not only displays the key ideas of customer-centric, profit-centric, and business design thinking, but also shows how a member of middle management can be the catalyst and idea person for moving a company into the profit zone.

Jim's company battled to sell a commodity in a product-centric world. The company sold cardboard boxes to major packaged-goods manufacturers—everything from shipping containers to pizza take-out boxes. A box was a box. The value proposition of their business design was simple: moderate quality, delivery, and competitive price. Value capture was a razor-thin margin negotiated with tough purchasing agents who would change vendors for less than a penny a box. In this world, management focuses on raw material prices, operations, and total cost position. Other than complaining to headquarters about competitive prices, there isn't much a field sales rep can do. Or is there?

Jim's largest customer was a multibillion-dollar food producer who used rugged boxes to ship product to the field. Volume was high, which made the account a great customer from the perspective of manufacturing plant utilization. Volume was also great for Jim, who was on a revenue-based commission plan. Jim's big worry was losing the account—and this was a valid concern. Jim's big competitors were constantly bidding on the opportunity to take away a large portion of his business and his paycheck.

Jim was a friendly and observant sales rep who spent his extra hours at the client's premises, wandering around and understanding the basic process flow on the packaging line. He learned a few things from his questions and observations. He noticed that the packaging process was in disarray. Used boxes were being recycled from the field. Many of these boxes were damaged, and the employee responsible for separating the damaged boxes from the good ones was indifferent to the process. In addition, the packaging line and several thousand square feet of space were flooded with excess packaging material and used boxes. To measure the efficiency of the packaging operation, management used a standard cost system and tracked total costs, including the cost of the boxes. To fix the faulty packaging process, management had placed a capital allocation request to expand the plant.

Jim mentally stepped into his customer's shoes and started to think about what he would value if he were the plant manager. "As plant manager, what should my priorities be? How would I get beyond the obvious immediate needs of price and delivery? What remedies could I propose to create value for the plant manager and help me protect this valuable account?"

Jim had been reading about large information systems outsourcing contracts that lasted 5 to 10 years and aligned the systems integrator as a specialized strategic supplier to a client. He explored the opportunity to apply this thinking to the current situation. He proposed to the plant manager that CBI should sign an attractive fixed-price 5-year outsourcing contract for packaging materials, and should lease a warehouse to ensure just-in-time delivery.

The customer saw the benefits of Jim's approach. The contract would free one full-time employee from the box-sorting task, clear space in the plant, and eliminate the need for expansion capital. The contract pricing equation fit perfectly with the standard costs system, and took one more charge for variances off the plant manager's mind.

The customer was not the only beneficiary. Jim's company had locked in a predictable, high-volume customer. Improving the box sort would create 15 percent savings, and the contract could serve as a test situation that might be applied elsewhere.

This entire customer-centric concept was great, but did it land Jim and CBI in the profit zone? Not immediately. But it gave Jim a partnership relationship with his biggest account, and he now had a new set of fixed-price economics to drive his business design (Exhibit 5.2). Jim began to think about what he could do with this redefined situation, and his thinking led him to the product development staff. Jim explained his new situation, "I've got a major customer that reuses our shipping-grade boxes, and we have an economic incentive to make the boxes last as long as possible. I know this is a big change.

EXHIBIT 5.2   *Cardbox Box, Inc.'s Business Design: Old vs. New*

	CBI's Old Business Design	*CBI's New Business Design*
Customer Selection	• Purchasing agents	• Senior executives
Value Capture	• Product sales	• Product sales • Multiyear inventory management contracts
Differentiation/ Strategic Control	• None	• Five-year contract
Scope	• Boxes/packaging	• Boxes/packaging • Inventory management

The old rules were that the more boxes were destroyed, the more we replaced and the more profit we made. Is there anything Development can do to make the boxes at lower cost or make them last longer?"

Development worked on the problem, and came back to Jim with the following: "We can double the average life expectancy at only 1.2 times the cost." Jim's revenue line was fixed. His cost would go down dramatically. Jim could now see how his new business design would lead his container operation to the profit zone.

He could also see that he would play a significantly increased role in his company in the future.

CLOZARIL PATIENT
MANAGEMENT SYSTEM

Business design thinking permeates organizational thinking far below the CEO level. Anyone who is responsible for a department or product line in an organization can practice it. One product manager who succeeded through business design thinking is Carrie

Smith Cox. In 1988, Cox was a newly appointed product manager at Sandoz, a large pharmaceutical company. One of the products Cox was placed in charge of was Clozaril, an anti-schizophrenia drug designed for the 300,000 "refractory" schizophrenic patients—those who do not respond to other medications. For most refractory patients, Clozaril worked perfectly where no other medication had. However, Clozaril was not a miracle drug for everyone. For every 1,000 patients who received Clozaril, 10 would experience a potentially fatal drop in their white blood cell count. If the white blood cell count began to fall and the patient continued the medication, in 3 weeks the patient would die. There was no way to prescreen which patients would be susceptible to this deadly side effect.

A typical product-centric thinker would have been tempted to go back and reengineer the drug, spending more on research and development—or may have just given up altogether. But not Cox. She was determined to figure out a way to make the drug safe for the patients and profitable for her company. She knew that the drug worked—it had passed a very tough clinical trial required by the Food and Drug Administration (FDA)—but she also knew the dangers. Instead of taking a product-centric approach, Cox took a business design approach and examined the problem from a totally unconventional perspective. The main concern was the safety of the 1 percent of patients who would experience a drop in their white blood cell count. Cox knew that it took 3 weeks for the white blood cell count to fall to fatally low levels. She looked for a way, a system, to determine whether the patient's white blood cell count was dropping.

Cox and her team developed an offering that required measuring a patient's blood count weekly. One week's supply of medication was delivered at a time. A patient who didn't take the test wouldn't receive the next week's supply. It was a fail-safe system. If the count started falling, the drug was discontinued.

It was a breakthrough idea for a pharmaceutical company. The company only manufactured drugs, and this newly proposed offering would require lots of new personnel to visit patients, dispense medication, and draw blood, and a lab to test the blood. Once again, Cox was not deterred. She assembled a team of business partners: a home health care company to visit patients and draw the blood; a national laboratory to test the blood and return results in 24 hours; and a database company to track each patient. Instead of selling a patient a drug that might be fatal and hoping for the best, Cox had developed a highly innovative, highly reliable, safe drug delivery system. The business design she crafted was very different from the product-centric industry standard (Exhibit 5.3).

Still, Cox needed to be sure that the system would work. To test the system, it was rolled out in three local areas first. After all the kinks were worked out in the delivery system, it was expanded to ten centers to make absolutely certain that it worked flawlessly.

EXHIBIT 5.3   *Business Design: Industry Standard vs. Clozaril*

	Industry Standard Business Design	**Clozaril Business Design**
Customer Selection	• Physicians treating chronic schizophrenics	• Physicians treating chronic schizophrenics who agreed to weekly testing
Value Capture	• Product sales	• Product sales • Service sales
Differentiation/ Strategic Control	• Product efficacy	• Product efficacy • System safety
Scope	• Selling the drug	• Sell a comprehensive drug dispensing and patient compliance system: —Weekly blood test —Early warning —One week's supply delivered at a time —Database for tracking, monitoring and record keeping

Finally, the system was rolled out nationally. Even though it had worked in the test centers, those involved held their breath. The first two months went by: No fatalities. After six months: No fatalities. After an entire year without a single fatality, confidence in the system was growing rapidly.

The results, both medical and financial, were impressive. After 5 years, tens of thousands of patients were successfully treated. These patients became functional once again, went back to school, took on jobs, and led normal lives that were impossible before. Observers could not help but be moved by the differences they saw as people slowly transitioned back from movement disorders, incoherence, and mental disease to normal human functioning.

Financially, the system was also a success. Sales grew significantly as tens of thousands of patients were treated. All of this occurred because of Cox's ability to move beyond the traditional product-centric perspective and find other ways to remedy a problem with the product.

Through customer-centric thinking, focusing on the safety of the patient, Cox and her team invented a unique business design that ensured safety, restored normal lives, and achieved high profitability. A focus on designing the business, rather than simply selling the product, had made this extraordinary success possible, for the patients, for the company, for Cox, and for the members of her team.

All three stories in this chapter (Madden, Cardboard Box, Clozaril) took place in the early 1990s, right at the epicenter of the large-scale shift from the old order to the new; from the product-centric world to the new landscape where customer-centric and profit-centric business designs enable companies to create sustained value growth.

The three examples are powerful but not unique. Managers throughout dozens of industries are learning and applying similar ideas. Some are learning the hard way, through trial and error (Group I). Other emerging business designers are learning from each other (Group II).

This book will best serve Group II. We also hope that it helps to convert the trial-and-error designers in Group I to become members of Group II.

REINVENTION FOR
THE REST OF US
Pilot's Checklist

☑ *Have I moved my organization beyond product-centric thinking?*

☑ *Have I developed a clear understanding of my customers' economics?*

☑ *Have I created an offering that improves their economics and my profitability?*

☑ *Have I anticipated all the internal obstacles that stand in the way of creating a new business design?*

☑ *Have I developed effective countermeasures to overcome those obstacles?*

SIX

NICOLAS G. HAYEK

The Product Pyramid Business Design

- *Can I emotionalize my product?*

- *Can I build a product pyramid, from low price point to high?*

- *Can I build a firewall brand to protect the profits in my product pyramid system?*

JOSEPH FERGUSON was flying back to New York from a conference in Switzerland. He'd been away for a week, and it felt great to be traveling homeward. He had planned on working during the flight, but his eye had been seduced by the colorful, glossy in-flight catalog of things for the homeward bound traveler to buy.

There hadn't been enough time to stop and buy gifts for the family. He wondered whether the in-flight magazine might provide some opportunities. His page-turning stopped at the Swatch section in the middle of the magazine. He remembered the "Irony" ads he had seen for the new line of metal Swatches, and it had been impossible to miss the Swatch presence at the Olympics.

He liked the variety and playfulness of the selections, and started figuring out which watch he should get for whom. With a wife and three children (two of whom were teenagers), there was a lot of selecting to do.

When the steward came around to sell, Joe had his selections made. Unfortunately, the oriental motif Sayonara watch he wanted to buy for his teenage daughter wasn't available. He chose another (there were plenty of good options). But he really wanted the Sayonara.

The watches were a great hit with the family. Something for everyone.

One week later, Ferguson was again traveling, this time to Atlanta. On the return trip, his flight was delayed for an hour and a half, and he spent time roaming the shopping area. He spotted the Swatch kiosk and looked at the collection. The Sayonara was there. He was delighted. He bought it. As he started walking to his gate, he was congratulating himself on his purchase. But then he stopped. He couldn't buy a watch just for his oldest daughter. He went back to the kiosk and bought three more.

As with the first set, the watches were a big hit. The designs were different, but equally light-hearted and stylish. He was a hero one more time.

On the Saturday morning after returning from Atlanta, he paged through the in-flight gift magazine from his Swissair flight home from Europe. He had taken the magazine with him for a reason. His father's seventy-fifth birthday was coming up, and he was casting about for gift ideas. The Blancpain watches in the catalog seemed extremely expensive, but incredibly elegant and impressive. He called a couple of stores, and found one that carried the line. Before lunch, he had visited the store, purchased a watch, and had it beautifully wrapped.

He felt happy with the purchase. He knew that his father would love the conservative style, and would know how substantial a gift it was (the watch had carried a four-figure price tag).

When Joe Ferguson bought the Swatches, he generated tens of dollars of gross margin for the manufacturer. When he bought the Blancpain, that transaction generated for the manufacturing company, whoever that was, many times more dollars than all his Swatch purchases combined.

*   *   *

The company that manufactures Blancpain is SMH, the same company that manufactures Swatches. Different brand, different distribution, different purchase occasion; but the same company, led by Nicolas G. Hayek, one of the true originals in business.

Sometimes, the reinvention of a company starts with reinventing an entire industry. That was the task that Hayek, a Swiss engineer and the entrepreneur behind the Swatch watch, set for himself.

Colorful, flamboyant, and unconventional, Hayek enjoys challenging conventional thinking.

Until Hayek launched his fashionable watch line in 1983, most people bought a watch to last a lifetime. The same timepiece was worn with every suit or dress, and few gave it much thought beyond selecting a reliable brand in their price range. Only children wore novelty watches; the most common models bore a likeness of Mickey Mouse. Hayek's leadership of Swatch changed that, and the entire process started with the customers.

Hayek knew customers better than they knew themselves. He *knew* they would respond to the concept of Swatch and all that it represented. He infused Swatch with many new dimensions of meaning. He developed a deep and rich relationship with customers, persuading them to wear different watches for different occasions and purposes. Instead of one watch, his customers have whole collections of Swatches.

From 1983 to 1992, Swatch sold 100 million watches,[1] an incredible feat for any new product. But that was just the first act of Hayek's value play. By 1996, only 4 years later, he had sold his 200 millionth watch![2]

Hayek is a charismatic, irascible businessman and a highly unconventional thinker. But the surface story, the well-known part, is not the whole story, nor the most important part of it.

A LIFETIME OF ASKING QUESTIONS

As a boy, Nicolas Hayek was always asking his family and teachers, "Why do we do things the way we do?"[3] He was born with an innate and incurable curiosity about the way things work and where we come from. He consumed every book he could find on physics, astronomy, the Big Bang, and Einstein's theories of mass and speed.

"Where do we come from? Nobody knows," he says, chuckling at the fruitlessness of his own unquenchable thirst for knowledge. "You finish by believing in God because there is no explanation."

Hayek was trained in mathematics, physics, and chemistry at the University of Lyon; the mental processes and organization learned in those disciplines served him well throughout his career.

A combination of family and financial factors conspired against his plan to study nuclear physics in the United States. Hayek's father-in-law became ill and unable to work. He ran a foundry that made railroad brake shoes, and equipment for the foundry industry. He asked his son-in-law, already a father of two, to run his ten-employee company in his absence. Lacking enough money to go to the United States anyway, Hayek accepted the job.

Almost 3 years later, the company was quite successful under Hayek's aggressive management.

"My father-in-law owned the company but he didn't own the premises, the equipment, the machines, or the furnaces," Hayek says. "All this was not his. He was paying rent every year. He could have been thrown out anytime. I increased production and made so much profit that I purchased the building and equipment for him."

But when his father-in-law, a draftsman, finally returned to work, he was less than enthused about the way Hayek had revolutionized the business, profits notwithstanding. So Hayek left, borrowed $3,000 from a bank (using his furniture and personal belongings as collateral), and started Hayek Engineering Inc., a consulting company in Zurich.

One of his first small jobs caught the attention of German industrialists. Pretty soon, Hayek was what he himself calls "a secret weapon" in postwar German industry. When American companies moved in, they also hired the bright young man with the radical outlook on problem solving. Over the years, his clients included Nestlé, Volkswagen AG, USSteel, AEG-Telefunken, Deere & Company, Digital Equipment Corporation, and Alfa-Romeo. The Swiss government later gave Hayek assignments as well.

"I became very well known in Europe as the guy who tells you the truth," Hayek says.

THE FIXER

As an engineering and industrial consultant, Nicolas Hayek had studied the business designs of many companies and whole industries, but he had never run one, other than his father-in-law's foundry, and his own consulting firm. His engineering consulting firm was action-oriented—more effective than conventional consultants in making change happen.

In the early 1980's, he was called on by the world of Swiss watchmaking. Hayek's advantage was that he was not part of the watchmaking industry. Consequently, the content of what he saw was not defined by decades of experience; his vision was not bent out of shape by decades of extraordinary success. He was a pilgrim in a new land—looking at the problem through a fresh pair of eyes.

As he analyzed the strategic landscape of the industry, Hayek saw the problems he would have to overcome. The Swiss had been devastated by competition from the Japanese. And he anticipated the battles ahead if he wanted to rebuild an industry that didn't want to be rebuilt. Watchmakers wanted to be more efficient and streamlined. They didn't want innovation. To Hayek, it looked like a dead end.

But for every dead end, there must be an opening, an alleyway that would lead to a large-scale new opportunity. Where was it in watchmaking?

His search for the opening led him away from the traditional realities of craftsmanship, technology, production, assets, and distributor relationships, and toward the softer, less "objective" realities of customer behavior, customer preference, and customer emotion. In the Swiss view, craftsmanship was the be-all and end-all. Hayek found that perspective too limiting for modern competition.

Hayek spent a long time studying and listening hard to the market, searching constantly for the empty spaces and what they meant. Before him, all the business models ticking away in the watchmaking industry shared several characteristics: They provided customers with functionality or luxury, and they focused on making watches, not marketing them.

The clues he was looking for were not just in the world of digital technology or low-cost manufacturing systems; they were in the world of fashion and style, where creative organizations grew strongly in the early 1980s and thrived by sensing and catering to the shifting patterns of consumer style. Some of these unusual companies succeeded in shaping those tastes and styles, moving them a little faster along a direction that they had already taken.

Hayek started with customer issues, not production. He didn't worry at first about making a cheaper watch. Instead, he asked what the customer wanted from a watch. Fun? Style? Spirit? All of the above?

That's when he began his campaign to emotionalize the watch, to make it not only a high quality product, but also a zestful, entertaining fashion accessory, like earrings or ties. It would make a statement of convention-defying uniqueness for the wearer, maybe even suggesting a playfulness not otherwise apparent.

And if he was selling fun and variety, the customer needed five or even a dozen watches, better to ward off a creeping stodginess.

The end result of the entire process was a unique product with a unique message to the customer: "high quality, low cost, provocation, and joy of life."

MAKING TIME: AN INDUSTRY ON THE EDGE OF FOREVER

The global watch industry provides one of the classic, quintessential scenarios in the history of value migration. Value migration is sometimes about incumbents dueling; more frequently, it is a story of incumbents and newcomers. At times, the newcomers are economic neighbors; or, they are new companies taking advantage of an empty space that incumbents allowed to form inside the densely packed geometry of the current market structure.

The incumbent in the value migration story of timepiece manufacturing was the Swiss watchmaking industry. Ancient, steeped in tradition, and highly respected, this industry led the world market for decades, satisfying a spectrum of customer wants—from accuracy to style, and from luxury to tasteful excess (with price points to match, ranging from $100 to $500,000). The Swiss business design had not changed in more than a half-century. It still targeted conservative, well-to-do customers who paid premium prices for a product whose most important distinguishing feature was the small print that read "Made in Switzerland."

In the 1970s, a tsunami washed over the Swiss watchmaking industry and essentially destroyed it. The industry had represented about $10 billion in value in 1970. By the early 1980s, most of that value had migrated away from the traditional Swiss business model to new business designs owned by Timex, Citizen, Seiko, and Casio.

Employment tumbled in parallel with the drop in value. From the mid-1970s to the early 1980s, the number of workers in the Swiss watchmaking industry contracted from 90,000 to 30,000. The value seemed to have left the industry permanently. It had become a no-profit zone.

The common explanation offered for this disaster was the influence of technology, especially the development of the digital watch. No diagnosis could have been more misleading. The answer was not in the technology, but in the minds of Swiss managers. It was not the availability of digital technology that Japanese companies such as Citizen, Seiko, and Casio capitalized on. It was the inability of the Swiss, the traditional industry leaders, to modernize their antique business design—to create a different vision and structure, and to move to the next-generation business design in their industry.

Swiss watchmaking was a single unified system that drew into its orbit all the key players in the game—the suppliers, the distributors, the consumers, the gift receivers ("Oh, I received a beautiful Swiss watch for my birthday"), and the watch repair shops (mechanical gears made by craftsmen several thousand miles away require a local craftsman to repair them). Everyone's complicity was required for the system to work. Customers did not demand innovation on any level, and the suppliers did not provide it.

The Swiss industry's success had not been about technology. It was about craft, name, elite image, expectation, association, confidence in selecting the right gift, and certainty about its being perceived in the right way. Having prospered under these rules for many years, the Swiss held a very strong, deep-seated commitment to the old world of watchmaking.

As Casio, Seiko, and Citizen stared at the strategic landscape of the global watch industry, they saw this undersensitivity to innovation as their greatest asset. Behind every truly brilliant strategic victory, there stands a slow-moving competitor. That's what Casio, Seiko, and Citizen were searching for, and they liked what they saw.

Although this landscape looked inviting to Casio and Citizen, they knew they could make a fatal mistake in moving too timidly, in revolutionizing only one dimension of the business model, rather than fundamentally altering several levels in their new business design.

The Japanese firms focused simultaneously on manufacturing (creating extraordinarily low costs), distribution (creating ubiquity), and marketing (creating universal awareness). The profile of their new business model represented a powerful shift from the traditional Swiss business designs (Exhibit 6.1).

The sales explosion produced by their new business design was dramatic for Citizen and Casio. But it was not all new growth in the market; it was a major redistribution of market share, revenue, and market value.

When the Japanese knocked the Swiss watch industry on its back, the two Swiss watchmaking associations, ASUAG and SSIH, lost as much as $124 million on annual revenue of $1.1 billion.[4]

The Omega watch brand was the diamond in SSIH's strongbox; ASUAG was primarily a watch component manufacturer, although it owned the Rado and Longines brands. ASUAG was a patchwork of

---

EXHIBIT 6.1 *Business Designs: Swiss vs. Citizen*

	Swiss Business Design	Citizen Business Design
Customer Selection	• Upper-income buyers	• Low-to-moderate-income buyer
Value Capture	• Price/watch	• Price/watch
Differentiation/ Strategic Control	• Traditional "Swiss"	• Digital lowest cost position
Scope	• Full range	• Full line—short of high end
Manufacturing	• Craftsmanship	• Modern, lowest possible cost
Go-To-Market	• Specialty dealers	• Universal
Communication Investment	• Low • 1% sales	• Intense • 10% sales

100 companies—some big, some small, some efficient, some hopelessly backward.

ASUAG and SSIH were under pressure from their bankers to sell off or consolidate what few resources they had left. They turned to Hayek and asked, "What would your strategy be for this?" In the course of those discussions, he stepped into a leadership vacuum and took the initiative to rebuild the viability of the 300-year-old Swiss watchmaking industry.

"I got an assignment from the bank to make a report stating that the salaries in Switzerland were the highest in the world, five times what the Japanese were paid, and that we couldn't produce any more watches," he explains. "The bank advocated selling off brands such as Omega, for which it already had an offer from a Japanese buyer of 400 million Swiss francs."

A great debate swept Switzerland: Should its national treasures, the watchmakers, sell out to the Japanese? More than money was at stake; Swiss watchmaking is a matter of national pride.

Hayek changed the nature of the debate. He said, "We can once again become No. 1 in the world." The bankers laughed. They said, "If you study this, you will find out that it is absolutely impossible to fight against the low-salaried Japanese."

What Hayek actually discovered was that salary was not the main issue. To sell a watch for $107 in the United States, the Swiss must make it for $35. Only 20 percent of Swiss production costs were in labor. In fact, many of its fixed costs for shipping to the United States were the same costs incurred by the Japanese. And Japanese transportation costs were even higher because products had farther to travel.

To test his theory, Hayek designed an unusual marketing test.

"We made three watches that were exactly the same," he says. "One said, 'Made in Switzerland.' The second said, 'Made in Japan,' and the last said, 'Made in Hong Kong.' We priced them at $110, $100, and $90, respectively—the Swiss being the most expensive, the Hong Kong being the least. Then we put them in shops all over Europe, the United States, and Japan, and we followed consumer reaction. In Italy, 99 percent of consumers chose the watch 'Made in Switzerland,' even though the 'Made in Japan' watch was identical. Here in Switzerland, it was 97 percent. In the eastern United States, we were at about 65 percent for the 'Made in Switzerland' product.

And in Japan, the 'Made in Switzerland' product took 42 percent of the market compared with 51 percent for 'Made in Japan.'"

Even if the Japanese had zero labor cost, Hayek determined, there was still a market for Swiss watches. Japan was working hard to differentiate its products on price and distribution. Hayek's marketing test showed that the Swiss watch companies achieved significant differentiation without even trying. Hayek knew that the Swiss could recover, and even win the game, if other dimensions of their business designs were changed. Labor costs were only a minor obstacle. "It is not a question of salaries," he told his critics. "It is a question of management, innovation, marketing, and product."

The measures that Hayek recommended were implemented from 1983 to 1985. In 1985, Hayek and a group of investors acquired 51 percent of the combined assets of ASUAG and SSIH for 150 million Swiss francs (US$102 million).[5] The investment kept growing in value; he estimates his investment in the company is now worth 5 billion Swiss francs.

After taking control, Hayek's key move was to cross the threshold defining "economy timepiece" and move into an economic neighborhood defined as "accessory," "style," and "fashion statement." This was a world of broad-scale taste, not chronology; a world of design and fashion, not craftsmanship. It was also a world defined by marketing and communication, not by manufacturing method. Low cost was needed to play, but low cost was not enough to win.

Hayek took a creative gamble in customer selection. He was interpreting the 18- to 30-year-old consumer who was buying Nike athletic shoes, Benetton sweaters, Gap apparel, and Bruce Springsteen's music. Succeeding in this market required a finely developed sensitivity to shifting tastes, more so than knowledge of next-generation production technologies.

By the time Hayek took charge, Swiss watchmakers had about 90 percent of a shrinking upper-crust customer segment, but they had lost the growing middle market. (They were clinging to just 3 percent of it, according to Hayek.) As for the bottom of the marketplace, not a single Swiss watch could be bought for less than 100 Swiss Francs. Hayek's vision for SMH was held captive by that single fact. As long as Japanese watches were priced 50 to 70 percent below Swiss watches, any SMH attempts at differentiation through design or marketing would be futile.

Sensing a substantial opportunity in the face of enormous skepticism, Hayek issued an absurd challenge: "Find a way we can sell watches in Switzerland at a price of $30." And, he added, "I want to continue manufacturing Swiss watches in Switzerland, not in a low-labor-cost Third World country."

"I said, 'Let's make a plastic watch, same principle,'" Hayek recalls. His challenge inspired the team to create a series of breakthroughs. For example, they reduced the number of watch components from 155 to 51. With fewer moving parts, there were fewer opportunities for breakage, and the company needed far fewer expensive Swiss workers for the assembly process.

ETA, a unit of ASUAG, built an automated assembly line for Swatch watches that turns out 35,000 Swatches and millions of components daily.[6] Labor costs dropped from 30 percent to just 10 percent. "We got watches that were of the highest possible quality. Our watch never breaks. It is better than any other watch in the world—repairs are less than 1 percent. And the best watch in the world has repairs of less than 3 percent."

Armed with a high-quality product and a low price, the next issue for Hayek was head-to-head competition with similarly priced Hong Kong watches. Hayek differentiated his watches by giving them a soul. He created a message, an emotional sense that appeals to everyone, conveying a sense of fun, of style, and of lightheartedness. Then he wrapped it around indisputable high quality and low cost.

All Hayek's new product lacked now was a name. "We were working with an American advertising company," Hayek says. "We had the craziest names in the world and none pleased me. Finally, we went for lunch and this woman wrote on the blackboard 'Swiss watch' and 'second watch.' Then she wrote 'Swatch.' It helped that we were not very strong in English. We didn't know that 'swatch' in English meant a cleaning towel. If we had known, we wouldn't have started the company with such a name! Fortunately," he adds, "it sounds good in every European language, including English—and even in Chinese."

A watch with these characteristics—and that name!—challenged Swiss society. It also pumped new life into the older SMH brands, first by generating new dollars for marketing and promotion, and, more importantly, by restoring a belief that if SMH could build a better watch for $30, think what it could do for

$3,000! This multiple brand management concept was the cornerstone of Hayek's business design.

SECURING VICTORY

Hayek modeled the total SMH watchmaking business design on what he calls a "birthday cake" or product pyramid structure (Exhibit 6.2), analogous to the product pyramid created by Alfred Sloan at General Motors in the 1920s. In order to appeal to a broad income range, GM constructed a hierarchy of brands, from Chevrolet at the bottom to Cadillac at the top. Hayek built a product pyramid or "birthday cake" with three layers: the lower market segment with watches up to approximately Sfr. 100; the middle market segment with watches up to approximately Sfr. 1000; and the upper and luxury market segment with watches priced up to one million Swiss francs or more, or, as Hayek says, "the sky is the

---

EXHIBIT 6.2   *The SMH Product Pyramid*

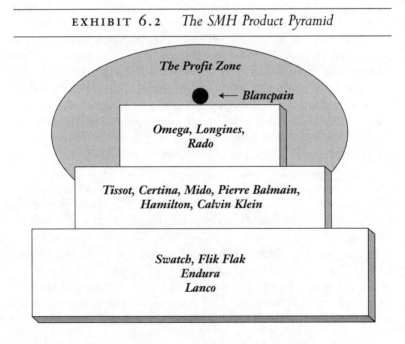

limit." But Hayek developed the product pyramid idea further. He believed that price point coverage had to be complete. Any gap on the spectrum would be an Achilles heel for a company trying to protect the profit zone that existed at the top of the pyramid. As an example, in the late 1960s, GM did not develop a profitable sub-Chevy model or a luxury model beyond Cadillac. Those openings allowed the Japanese and German automakers to make inroads in the U.S. market with low-end and luxury models.

Careful to avoid this pitfall, Hayek made Swatch his firewall brand at the bottom, which secured the low-end market and made it profitable. Then he protected and expanded his positions in the upper part of the pyramid including acquisitions (of Blancpain, in 1992) and licensing (the Calvin Klein license was acquired in 1997).

According to Hayek, there are four reasons why his new business design succeeded:

"The lower layer of the market is very important because each emotional product that you have—watches, cars, anything that is an emotional, mass-merchandised product—is seen on the wearer by as many as 5,000 people every year. That is to say, if you wear a watch, wherever you go, 5,000 people a year will see it, consciously or unconsciously. And from these 5,000 at least .1 percent will think it is a very nice watch and want to buy the same. So every customer who wears your watch creates publicity for you. This is why it is very important for you to be in mass production.

"Second, when young people start buying watches or cars, they do not have enough money for the most expensive ones so they buy the lower-cost items. But they won't be poor forever. If they get good quality, they will grow attached to the brand. Once they grow older and can pay more, they will stay with the brand, buying watches—or other similarly branded products—that cost more money.

"Third, if you manufacture in high volume, you can automate, you can increase quality, you can build experience, you can improve everything.

"The fourth reason is that, by getting the last portion of the lower market segment, you block your competitors and stop them from going up the layers where the highest profit is and taking the higher market segment."

SMH's range of brands is an effective tool against competitors, but Hayek does not see it only as a means to that end. Within SMH, each brand is an autonomous unit with its own marketing department and profit-and-loss account. Swatch is not the only line that has been infused with image and meaning. "Each brand is different, so each message is different. But each brand has a message. My job is to sit in the bunker with a machine gun, defending the distinct messages of all my brands. I am the custodian of our messages."

In a business where the brand is the basis for strategic control, protecting the brand can be the difference between success and failure. The brand impacts both the differentiation and value capture (through price premium) dimensions of a business design. Brand can be an extremely powerful way to make a product stand out against its competitors, but a powerful brand must be carefully cultivated and maintained. Hayek learned his first lesson in brand management when SMH was being formed.

Until the 1970s, Omega had been the prized brand of Swiss watchmaking. Its image was one of the highest quality and style. Demand far outstripped supply, and the Omega team began to wonder whether there was more money to be made. Production doubled, hundreds of new models were introduced, and management dropped prices to help move more volume.

By 1980, Omega's brand power had been badly diluted. The one-time luxury product had lost the scarcity that had set it apart from other watches. With both volume and price at low levels, the brand was losing money rapidly. When Hayek gained control of the company, he took a hard line, retracted all production licenses, cut the number of models almost 90 percent, and simplified the design. As he puts it, "Omega started making sense again. We gave Omega back its message."

This first lesson in brand protection was well learned. As Hayek prepared to launch Swatch, he knew that success depended on delivering the right message, and delivering it well.

SELLING THE SIZZLE

Hayek is not a typical businessperson, and the campaign he mounted for Swatch was not a typical new-product launch. Swatch (the company) didn't have much money for advertising in the beginning, so Hayek needed inexpensive ways of reaching the maximum number of consumers with each effort. More importantly, Hayek was launching a product whose differentiation was critically dependent on image and message. One failed advertising campaign could derail it forever. Hayek's team fired a shot that was heard 'round the world. They designed an enormous Swatch watch, 500 feet long, displaying the basic message:

SWATCH
Swiss
DM 60

It was hung from the headquarters of Commerzbank, the highest skyscraper in Frankfurt, and created an immediate sensation. The German press did the rest of SMH's advertising gratis.[7]

"We provoked the whole society by putting such a low-priced watch on the building of the most sophisticated bank in the country," Hayek recalls with glee. "In two weeks, everybody in Germany knew what a Swatch was."

A second giant Swatch was hung in Tokyo, in the Ginza. By the end of the year, the returns were in. Swatch was a go. Not only would the idea live, it would thrive. Customers fell in love with it and wanted more and more choices in color, composition, and styling.

Hayek added a completely different dimension to the watch industry. His brand had succeeded, and Swatch was building customer relationships and loyalty. Soon, Swatch was enjoying sales of multiple watches to individuals—increasing returns on SMH's advertising dollars. Clever promotions and limited-edition manufacturing had added another form of differentiation to Swatch products. Last year's Swatches were no substitute for this year's Swatches. Constant design innovation kept customers' interest at a peak.

Swatchmania is no mere coincidence. Hayek deftly fanned sparking consumer interest into wildfire. The company sells memberships in "Swatch—the Club," which offers special watches available only to members, a complete Swatch product catalog, and invitations to club events. Club members also receive the handsome *Swatch Watch Journal*, a quarterly, full-color tabloid magazine guide to all things Swatch.

Raman Handa, owner of the Lexington Jewelers Exchange Inc., in Boston, has seen the mania strike up close and personal. His New England operations include a fine jewelry store, two fine watch stores, and four Swatch stores, including the world's largest—in square footage (1,500) and sales volume ("quite a few million")—located in Harvard Square. Adjacent to the 1,500-square-foot Swatch store at 57 JFK Street is a 3,500-square-foot Swatch Museum.

"I sell watches for as much as $100,000 in the fine watch store," Handa says. "But the quality of Swatch is magnificent. And the styling keeps changing. Every time you think they'll run out of ideas, they come up with many more."

Handa, who spends a reported $500,000 annually on Boston-area advertising, has participated in a good many Swatch promotions and special-edition watches. "People go crazy collecting them, wearing them," he says. "We were unconvinced when we opened the store in December 1992. But the first time 400 people lined up overnight to buy a new release, the 'Chandelier,' we believed."[8]

"Now our expectations are much bigger," Handa says. "My chiropractor asked why I hadn't been around recently. I told her, 'I'm too busy!' Then I brought her to the store and she bought her first Swatch. Now she has 30. It's not just a watch."

The Boston watch merchant encourages visitors to his museum to design and submit their own ideas for new Swatches. He also sponsors activities for area Swatch collectors, including a cruise on *The Spirit of Boston* and a convention in the grand ballroom of the Charles Hotel. Swatch supports his efforts with limited-edition watches made especially for the events, such as two "Once Upon a Time" watches featuring Puss 'n Boots and Sleeping Beauty. Other watches commemorated the history of cinema, honoring directors such as Akira Kurosawa, Robert Altman, and Pedro Almodovar. The manufacturer and its distributors take great pains to make Swatch a real part of people's lives. On paper, SMH still sells watches, but Hayek has realized that the true scope of his business is much broader. For the customer, a Swatch watch is a souvenir, a piece of history, and a work of art.

To say that Handa believes in the magic of Swatch would be a serious understatement. "Hayek has done an amazing job. He's a genius!"

Hayek does possess an imaginative understanding of the customer that goes beyond pure economics. Like Michael Eisner, he has a "golden gut," a strong intuitive understanding of what customers like and will like. What stands between what Swatch accomplished and being just another fad is not taking the customer for granted—customer-centric thinking. Fads are fads because no one tried developing their ideas further. Swatch captured the customer; then it consistently refreshed the fashion watch concept, never becoming static.

One of the key aspects of value migration is understanding the patterns that have played themselves out in other industries. Swatch is only one of the companies that tapped into the value migration patterns of the 1980s. Swatch joined Nike, Benetton, and The Gap in opening new customer territories.

RUNNING LIKE CLOCKWORK

The Swatch business design introduced in 1983 created enormous value growth. By 1992, sales of SMH (the parent company) had risen to $2 billion, profits were at $280 million, and the market value of the company exceeded $3.8 billion (Exhibit 6.3). In 1984, Hayek was trying to sell his fanciful, colorful watches to anyone who was young, or young at heart. In the 1990s, he has learned to approach every demographic group through a tailored message for each new watch design.

The simple plastic Swatches of the early years were supplanted by designer timepieces and watchbands by everyone from Kiki Picasso to Yoko Ono, plus one inspired by M. C. Escher. Limited-edition box sets appeared for special events such as the Summer Olympic Games in Atlanta and Christmas. One watch celebrated the 50th anniversary of the United Nations. Film director Spike Lee starred in commercials for the "Black and White" Swatch set, one called "White Hours," the other, "Black Minutes." The most far-out was "Swatch Access to Space," a batch of 100 watches that actually circled the earth aboard the U.S. Space Shuttle "Columbia" on February 22, 1996, with Swiss astronaut Claude Nicollier. Swatch's boldest move was its "Irony" line, made of various metals but no less whimsical than its plastic versions. It also produced the water-resistant "Scuba" and the sun-powered "Solar" lines.

Hayek has raised not only watches, but brand development, to an art form. He has made people need any Swatch they see, so he makes sure that his customers see a lot of them. Swatch advertising

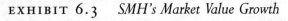

EXHIBIT 6.3   *SMH's Market Value Growth*

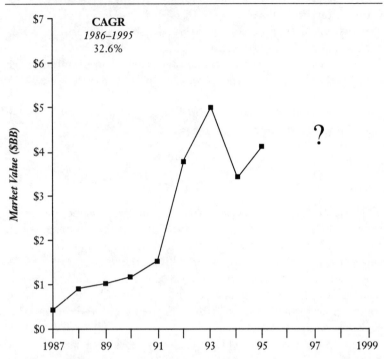

stands above other watches' promotions in both quantity and style. Making a product both unique and ubiquitous is a difficult feat, but Hayek's business design for SMH excels in its differentiation and value capture components.

In the 1990s, Swatch keeps building the strength of its business model through innovative partnerships. For example, Swatch was the official timekeeper and partner of the 1996 Olympic games.[9] Swatch Timing (a wholly-owned company of SMH) not only assumed technical responsibility for timekeeping and scoring, but also developed innovative measuring instruments and systems for this event.

Omega and Longines, other companies in the SMH family, were the watchmakers more typically associated with sporting events. In Atlanta, for the 25th time (out of 28), a company in the SMH family was the official Olympics timekeeper. For the 1996

Centennial Olympiad, however, Hayek sought the spotlight assignment for Swatch.

"I needed the 4 billion people watching the Olympics on television to see a product of ours that they could afford," reasoned Hayek, with his eternal customer focus. "Not everybody in Asia can afford an Omega or a Longines. The Olympics gave Swatch a very big boost, particularly in the U.S., because in every household in America they saw Swatch timing."

Literally. Every time the television networks showed the final times for an event, a logo indicated "Swatch Timing." And every scoreboard with a timed event bore the Swatch logo.

Hayek began the march on Atlanta a year earlier, commissioning and subsequently erecting 12 "Swatch O'Clocks"—artsy Olympics time towers—in a dozen world capitals. Even bolder, on July 18, 1996, Hayek himself was one of the last runners carrying the Olympic torch to Atlanta.

Determined to exploit every opportunity for image-building, Swatch developed and publicized its "Integrated Sport System" for the Atlanta Games, a time link that connected the automatic timing and scoring systems, the real-time display in its various forms, and, through IBM, deferred-time data processing and display.

Hayek's marketing gamble paid off. More than $350,000 worth of watches were sold daily in a 25-square-foot point-of-sale kiosk at the Swatch pavilion at Centennial Olympic Park. The "Swatch Irony Victory Ceremony Series"—a set of three gold, silver, and bronze watches made in the same quantities as the number of gold medals won—as well as the Olympic Legends series—featuring Mark Spitz, Nadia Comaneci, Katarina Witt, Sebastian Coe, and others—registered sellouts (Exhibit 6.4).

HAYEK'S NEXT OPPORTUNITY

Over the past 14 years, Hayek has built up an impressive array of assets. Besides an invaluable amount of management experience, SMH now holds two key weapons: one of the world's most recognized brands, and a mountain of highly sophisticated proprietary technology. Recognizing that these two assets work best in tandem,

EXHIBIT 6.4   *SMH Business Design Reinvention*

	1985	1990s	2002
Customer Selection	• Style buyers	• Style buyers • Collectors • Luxury buyers	
Value Capture	• Watch price • Movements	• Multiple purchases from repeat buyers • Movements • Luxury brands	
Differentiation/ Strategic Control	• Emotionalize the product • Style • Own the low end	• Proliferate the product • Style • Affinity/Olympics sponsorship • Own the customer relationship	**?**
Scope	• Full price range • Sell components	• Full price range • Sell components • Brand extensions	
Product Design	• Streamlined design/few components	• Continuous style innovation • Maximum variety	

Hayek has leveraged the Swatch name to promote pagers, cellular phones, and other telecommunications devices that use the same technology SMH has perfected through decades of watchmaking.

Now Hayek has his eye on something bigger. His customer-centric perspective has led him to a totally new product for the same customer set that buys Swatches. In partnership with Daimler-Benz, SMH has announced the development of the Swatchmobile. Hayek is working to change the traditional concept of what a car is. The traditional players in the auto industry make cars that can operate over long distances, that run on gasoline, and that are conservative in design. Hayek has seen an opening. He will target young, urban European drivers who need to travel only across town, who need to park in crowded cities, and who want their car to be a statement, not just a vehicle.

The auto giants—American, German, and Japanese—left an enormous opening in the market, at the imaginationless lower end of the ladder. Swatch made a fortune by entering such a space in the watch industry. It just might happen again with the Swatchmobile, which will be priced below $10,000.

The initiative could fail, of course. But there is no sustained value growth without the psychology of major moves, and there is no series of major moves through time without some magnificent failures. We study the major moves of others to keep improving our odds and to minimize our own mistakes, but we can never eliminate them completely.

LESSONS FROM HAYEK

SMH's success has hinged on customer-centric and profit-centric strategies that have brought prosperity to companies in many industries. CEOs across all industries face the same issues that confronted Hayek. Few leaders persistently ask themselves the right questions, and fewer change their business designs to match the answers. Learning to do so is the single most profitable lesson from the Hayek experience.

Hayek's customer-centric train of thought started with the question, "How does the industry view its product and its customers' priorities? Are industry players responding to customers, or are customers simply accepting what is offered by the industry? How can I be the company that offers something different to the customer?"

Based on the answers to these questions, Hayek differentiated Swatch from other low-cost competitors by redefining his offering. He understood that customers were simply accepting what the industry offered them and that there was an opportunity to provide more. Hayek ignored or reversed other watchmakers' most basic assumptions about the customer, and designed a watch that was far more than a timepiece, and far more than a fashion statement. It was a product that had behind it a philosophy and a revoluntary technology which enabled SMH to create a high-quality, high-tech, high-appeal consumer product. By crafting his product to fill the needs of an unserviced customer group, Hayek created mass demand for an item that had been a boring staple. Hayek then kept Swatch from becoming a boring staple with a constant stream of fresh ideas, fresh designs, and careful shepherding of customers into higher-level SMH brands.

Hayek didn't stop questioning. He asked himself, "How can I keep demand healthy and make this trend long-lived? Which aspect of customer priorities can be the basis of sustained growth for my company?"

From this line of questioning, Hayek realized that Swatch had to evolve as fast as popular culture did, in order to sustain demand. Swatches could have been a boom-and-bust fad, but Hayek carefully stimulated customer interest by creating new designs and funding creative advertising. The Swatch campaigns brought young people swarming to buy yet another fashion accessory. The quality of SMH's watches was not lost on its low-end customers. As they grew older, seeking elegance rather than flamboyance, these loyal buyers became higher-end customers for SMH's more expensive lines (Exhibit 6.5).

Hayek's questioning was focused on profits as well as customers. With a view to protecting his position, Hayek asked himself, "How might my competitors use customer relationships as a stepping stone into my key market? Should I be aggressively strengthening my product range to serve a wider spectrum of customers?"

Hayek knew that the role of the Swatch brand isn't just to earn profit at the low end. Rather, it is profit protection. Swatch prevents slow erosion of SMH customers by competitors who start at the bottom and move upward. That protection was overlooked by the Detroit automakers in the 1960s. They ceded the low-end, entry-model car market, first to Volkswagen, then to the Japanese, who later moved up the product pyramid, capturing even the luxury car buyers.

Hayek's second profit-centric question was, "How can I get more value out of the assets I already have?" With a strong brand, an international reputation for quality, strong manufacturing expertise, tremendous know-how and outstanding technologies in micro-mechanics and micro-electronics, and a very efficient international distribution network, Hayek wondered, "How can these

EXHIBIT 6.5   *Product Line Management at SMH*

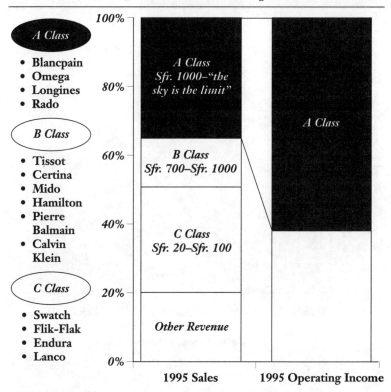

Source: Merrill Lynch.

assets leverage one another? What combination of innovation and reliance on current expertise will create the most value?"

The answers led Hayek to move beyond being a pure watchmaker. SMH became a leading supplier of watch components. More recently, Hayek has utilized his strong brand, international reputation for quality, and manufacturing expertise to extend the power of the SMH brands to new applications of its technology in telecommunications and transportation. He is also looking further afield for ways to respond to the needs of his chosen customers, wherever those needs may lie, and will use his brand as an entry method for new industries.

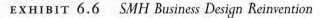

EXHIBIT 6.6   *SMH Business Design Reinvention*

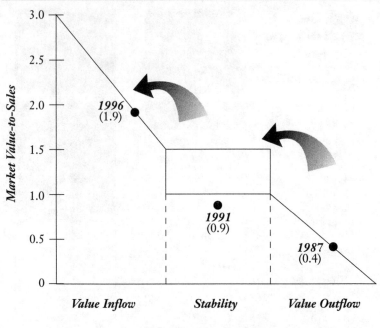

Value Creation Performance

Hayek will continue pursuing customer-centric and profit-centric questioning because he enjoys it so much. Business leaders can easily learn from that kind of thinking and from the highly valuable business design (the product pyramid) that it created (Exhibit 6.6).

BUILDING THE PRODUCT
PYRAMID BUSINESS DESIGN
Pilot's Checklist

☑ *Is there a product pyramid business design waiting to be built in my industry?*

☑ *If a product pyramid model already exists, how can I build a better one?*

☑ *Do I understand the attitudes, culture, and beliefs of the customer vis-à-vis my product? Do I understand how my product works in the mind of the customer?*

☑ *Have I built a low-price firewall brand at the base of the pyramid, to protect system profits?*

☑ *Have I designed my firewall brand to be profitable, despite its low price?*

☑ *Have I created every opportunity for my customers to buy multiple products?*

☑ *Have I built enough high-end, high-profit brands to maximize the profitability of the entire system?*

SEVEN

ROBERTO GOIZUETA

The Manage-the-Value-Chain Business Design

- *Is the profit zone in my industry in a part of the value chain that I do not control?*

- *Do I have to change the nature of my relationship with my distribution channels to get access to the profit zone?*

- *Do I have to fix my business design first, before pursuing global growth?*

IT WAS three-thirty in the afternoon. It had been a long, hard meeting, and there were many hours to go before it was over.

"Would anyone like a drink?" Kevin Burke asked, as he tried to break the tense atmosphere that was crowding the room.

"Sure, why not? That would be great," came the responses from the dozen or so people in the meeting. Kevin called his secretary, and within five minutes, a beverage tray and ice bucket materialized. People happily popped the cans and poured themselves an assortment of colas, bottled waters, and lemon-lime drinks.

"Do you have a Snapple?" someone asked.

"No, sorry," Kevin's secretary replied. "But our cafeteria does have Lipton Iced Tea."

"That would be great."

"Any others?" she asked.

"How about a Diet Pepsi?" someone asked.

"Sorry," she said. "We don't have it. But if you'd like, I can run downstairs and get some for you."

"No, that's OK. Diet Coke would be fine."

She left for the cafeteria to get a couple of iced teas. The rest of the people drank their Cokes, their diet Cokes, their Sprites, and their Poland Springs.

From cola, to iced tea, to bottled water, they drank what was available. What was available in carbonated beverages was Coke and Sprite (made by Coke).

What they drank was not determined by preference, but by availability. And availability was determined by the hard work of the local bottling company that had won the cafeteria contract and the vending concession for the building.

The local bottling company, a part of Coca-Cola Enterprises, the world's largest bottling organization, was the front line of the Coca-Cola system's determined effort to be the one choice available, to be *there* to provide refreshment to a thirsty world.

*　　*　　*

The modern-day story of Coca-Cola is much more complex than the way it is usually told. Coke's success is usually ascribed to its dominance of the international scene. What this narration misses is that such dominance would not have occurred if Roberto Goizueta had not fundamentally altered the relationship between Coke and its bottlers.

As the company's new CEO in the early 1980s, Goizueta inherited a Coke that was powerless to manage the profitability of its own system. In the beverage industry, the value chain consists of syrup manufacturing, bottling, logistics, distribution, marketing, and consumer relations. Moving from syrup maker and advertiser (Coke's business design in 1980) to value chain manager (Coke's business design in 1997) helped Coca-Cola capture the most profitable zones of the beverage industry.

Goizueta's analysis of this problem, and the action he took, are important lessons for managers at every level. Industries that lack rapid technological change and experience modest growth offer opportunities to move into the profit zone and to create extraordinary value growth.

*　　*　　*

As a product, Coca-Cola is more than a century old and has no flashy innovations or high-tech gadgetry to generate excitement. It competes in an industry where, since the early 1980s, per-capita soft drink consumption has grown at rates of 3 percent and 8 percent for domestic and international markets, respectively. Yet the company's market value, propelled by CEO Roberto Goizueta's innovations in Coke's business design, soared from $4 billion in 1980 to $130 billion in 1996 (Exhibit 7.1). Goizueta's most significant business design innovations were managing the value chain, and focusing investment on the high-profit zones. He regained control of profit opportunities by redefining who his customers were.

EXHIBIT 7.1   *Coca-Cola vs. Pepsi: Market Value Growth*

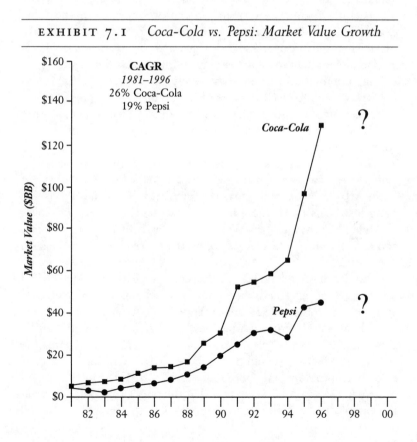

Goizueta built his business design on the foundation of some very innovative thinking about who Coke's primary customers were. An effective business design requires selecting who the customers are, deciding what you will do for them, and planning how you will make money doing it. In 1980, Coca-Cola's bottlers were the most potent force blocking Coke from moving into a more attractive profit zone. While the consumer and point of sale were essential downstream customers, the bottlers became Goizueta's primary customers and the object of his most significant strategic business design moves.

By 1996, Goizueta had built an extraordinarily powerful business design (Exhibit 7.2). Its elements are: a highly aligned manufacturer–bottler–distribution system, which has created the lowest-cost manufacturing, bottling, and logistics in the industry, and which purposefully focuses investment on the profit zones in the value chain; the world's strongest brand; the world's most cost-effective advertising, plus licensing and signage; and the most pervasive collection of dominant market positions in international markets.

This dominance did not come easily. In the late 1970s, Coca-Cola was an unfocused organization. Its diversified portfolio included shrimp farming, plastic straw manufacturing, and other unrelated businesses. These investments were slowly pulling the company under.

"Goizueta is extremely focused in terms of the core business, which is exactly what Coke needed," says Mark Rowland, president of the Atlanta-based money management firm of Rowland & Co. "He never lost focus on that. He lives and dies on the number of Cokes sold. He's like the anti-Jack Welch. Welch has a diverse conglomerate and he makes it all click. Roberto, on the other hand, is in the soda pop business."[1]

After he assumed power, Goizueta cleaned up the diversified portfolio and redefined the company's old business model as a syrup maker to include stronger strategic control in the distribution channels. He created a business design that captured significant value for Coca-Cola. "Goizueta," says Tom Pirko, managing partner of New York-based Bevmark Inc., LLC, a management consulting firm that includes both Coke and Pepsi among its clients, "is extremely good at understanding that the only thing that counts at the end of the day is the value of the stock to the shareholders."[2]

EXHIBIT 7.2   *Coca-Cola's Business Design:*
Manage the Value Chain

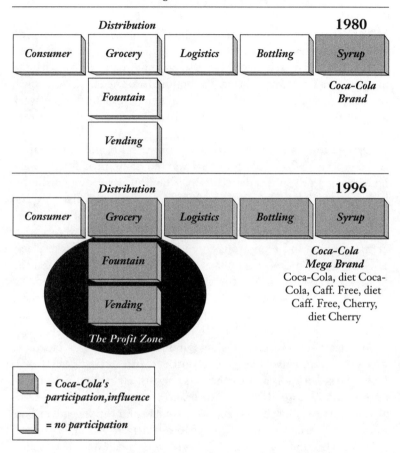

In the 20 years between 1977 and 1997, Coke changed its business model from a syrup maker and advertiser to a value chain manager. Besides expanding the scope of its operations in the value chain, Coke clarified its market strategy and persistently focused on the most profitable channels in both the domestic and international arenas.

CHANGING THE BOTTLER RELATIONSHIP

In the early part of this century, The Coca-Cola Company built a nationwide network of bottlers by granting territorial exclusivity of bottling and distribution rights to entrepreneurs, along with the promise of a fixed syrup price. By tapping into the energy of American entrepreneurs, Coke built an extensive distribution network that would have been prohibitively expensive to create by conventional means.[3]

Opportunities were ripe to build a powerful brand name across the country, and Coke's founders wanted their product in every household, store, and soda fountain. The bottlers provided the vehicle for getting there. By the 1920s, Coke had established 1,200 bottlers in its franchise system. Although hundreds of them covered counties with populations as small as 50,000, they were a powerful, hungry, and ubiquitous force loosed upon the marketplace. Each signed a "perpetual contract" with Coca-Cola that fixed the price Coke could charge for the syrup and granted the bottler exclusivity in its territory. The early franchise bottler model was a tremendous success. Consumers were delighted, entrepreneurs grew rich, and the Coca-Cola Company was No. 1.[4]

At that time, Coke's business model included two customer groups: Coke drinkers and Coke bottlers. In the first case, Coca-Cola marketed its brand to the end consumer through nationwide advertising. Those efforts led to brand awareness, but Coke actually sold its product, the syrup, to its network of independent bottlers. The bottlers' demand for syrup was driven by sale of the end product. Demand for Coca-Cola's syrup depended on the existence of ample growth opportunities for the bottlers.

Through the first half of the 20th century, Coca-Cola lived happily on the demand growth that its advertising created and its bottlers fulfilled. However, by the 1950s and '60s, many bottlers felt their territories were fully mature and foresaw only modest prospects for further growth.

With only limited apparent opportunities for growth, the entrepreneurial zeal of the first half-century gave way to a "mature market" mindset. Investing more energy and assets into modernizing the plants meant only increased costs. For many of the families who owned Coke franchises, the business focus turned from growth to cash flow. Investments were reduced, modernization slowed, and productivity suffered.

During the 1970s, Coke watched its market share leadership fade. The loss of share was particularly pronounced in the grocery store segment. Large regional supermarket chains, which opened up branches that cut across many Coke bottlers' territories, emerged as a powerful force. Coke's bottlers, accustomed to serving the traditional Mom-and-Pop stores that had dominated the grocery segment in earlier times, had difficulty meeting the needs of the new supermarket chains. The bottler network structure that had created such a dominant position for most of the century was now a liability as new, larger, more powerful customers emerged. Serving the chains required coordination, consistent pricing, and key account management. However, because the bottler franchises operated independently of one another, with different cost structures and profit margins, they often failed to agree on a single price. The supermarket chains would not accept different prices for the same product in neighboring markets, and the bottlers lost large contracts to Coke's arch-rival, Pepsi.

In the Pepsi model, the company owned many of its larger bottlers, allowing it to concentrate its efforts on the big supermarket accounts. Where Coke's bottlers cared only about their own cash flow, Pepsi's bottlers were a part of the larger company, giving Pepsi greater pricing flexibility in contracts with large grocery clients. Pepsi took advantage of this opportunity and priced its products below Coke's. Then, besides simply offering a lower price, Pepsi backed up its distribution strategy with effective advertising that targeted supermarket shoppers. Coke served all distribution channels equally, from Mom-and-Pop grocery stores to restaurants to vending machines. Pepsi focused on the rapidly growing supermarket chain segment—and won.

When Coke's national sales group approached the large supermarkets with the same services and low prices that Pepsi delivered, Coke could not persuade its local bottlers—an often strong-willed, ill-coordinated group—to drop their price. Coca-Cola couldn't compete because it couldn't unite its bottlers to address the priorities of this increasingly important customer group.

As it stormed grocery store shelves, Pepsi knew that its products would be stocked beside Coca-Cola's. In an effort to pulverize consumers' loyalty to Coke, Pepsi launched the "Pepsi Challenge." In this brilliant stroke of marketing, Pepsi "proved" that Coke drinkers actually preferred the taste of Pepsi. Pepsi eroded Coke's differentiation on taste, and consumers made more decisions based on price. Pepsi, because of its relationship with its bottlers, underpriced Coke and won.

Pepsi's business design masterfully exploited the biggest weakness of the Coke business model—a distribution system that prevented it from focusing its efforts on important customers or competing on price. While Coke catered to everyone, Pepsi grabbed the future by appealing to youth. Coke differentiated on brand; Pepsi, on price, the key variable for young beverage drinkers. The business design comparison in Exhibit 7.3 highlights the differences between the two models.

By 1977, Pepsi had achieved parity with Coke in the nation's supermarkets, bringing its overall market share to 24 percent, just 12 points behind Coke. By 1980, the overall gap had closed to 9 percent.[5] At that point, Pepsi seemed satisfied with its strategic position in grocery. It saw the Cola Wars battle as a virtual stalemate and turned its sights toward aggressive investment in its snack food and

EXHIBIT 7.3   *The Beverage Battle: Coke vs. Pepsi, 1977*

	Coca-Cola	Pepsi
Customer Selection	• All ages • All segments	• Youth • Grocery
Value Capture	• Syrup sales	• Syrup sales • Bottler profits
Differentiation/ Strategic Control	• Brand	• Price
Scope	• Syrup • No bottler control	• Syrup • Some bottler ownership

restaurant businesses. Pepsi acquired several restaurant chain businesses, including Pizza Hut, Taco Bell, and Kentucky Fried Chicken, which created new, guaranteed venues for Pepsi fountain sales.

The move to restaurant chains created new Pepsi outlets, but it brought some unanticipated disadvantages as well. Pepsi's focus on food increased the asset intensity of the company. More importantly, Pepsi's entrance into the restaurant market positioned the company as a competitor to many large fountain accounts. To restaurants such as Burger King and Wendy's, vendors of Pepsi products, the soft drink company was now a direct competitor. Selling Pepsi products was no longer an option. The No. 2 and No. 3 hamburger chains joined No. 1, McDonald's, in selling Coke products exclusively.[6]

FOCUSING INVESTMENT ON THE HIGH-PROFIT ZONES

Coca-Cola needed a modern, low-cost grocery system that presented a united front against Pepsi. But defense would not be enough. Competing in the grocery segment would bring revenue and market share, but it was increasingly becoming a no-profit zone. Goizueta wanted increased shareholder value, too, so he focused attention on dramatically increasing Coke's earnings.

As Goizueta tackled the question of where he could earn the highest profit, he thought about how consumers bought soft drinks. Coca-Cola drinks were sold in one of three venues: grocery stores, restaurants—which the industry still called "fountain"—or vending machines. As he put Pepsi's success in perspective, Goizueta took note that although grocery sales were necessary to promote the Coke brand with consumers, the real profit zone was in vending and fountain sales. Consumers pay about 2 cents per ounce for Coke in grocery stores, 5 cents to 8 cents per ounce in restaurants and vending machines.

Grocery store shelf space was plentiful for soft drinks—both Coke's and Pepsi's—so supermarkets would always be an arena of intense price competition and low profits. In a restaurant, consumer choices might include juice, alcoholic drinks, or soda, but few restaurants would offer both Coke and Pepsi products. Once consumers made the choice to have a soft drink, they would buy whichever brand the restaurant carried. Not only would being in the restaurant provide high consumption rates, but, with a semicaptive audience, soda prices and system profits could be higher.

With vending machines, this phenomenon was even more extreme. Most soda vending machines would be the only source of beverages in their location. The choice for the consumer would not be Coke or Pepsi; it would depend on who owned or controlled the vending machine. The choice would always be the owner's brand or nothing.

Gaining leadership in the high-profit zones meant establishing a totally different relationship between Coke and its bottlers. Supporting, modernizing, and focusing the bottlers was the only way of capturing the profits in the system. The bottler became Coke's primary customer. Without an effective strategic relationship with its bottlers, Coke could not make certain that the right level of investment was focused on fountain and vending. Goizueta knew that aligning the bottlers behind this strategy was crucial to Coke's long-term success.

MANAGING THE VALUE CHAIN

Entering the highest ranks of Coca-Cola officers in the 1970s, Goizueta looked for ways of altering Coke's relationship with its bottlers. He saw that, under the perpetual contracts, the bottlers held all the cards—fixed costs for syrup and weak incentives for participating in Coca-Cola's corporate strategy. When the company labs developed high-fructose corn syrup (HFCS), a low-cost substitute for the sugar in Coke, Goizueta championed it as a way to save costs and to reduce the company's dependence on fluctuating sugar prices. It was also a tool for fundamentally altering the power relationship between the company and its bottlers. The cost of the syrup was a large part of the bottlers' overall system economics, and Goizueta recognized that he could use the 20 percent price saving on HFCS as a bargaining chip in his negotiations with the bottlers. HFCS gave him the opportunity to help the bottlers reduce their own costs. But if they wanted access to this economic advantage, they would have to amend their agreement with Coca-Cola in a way that created more reasonable terms for the company. Most bottlers acquiesced.[7]

The new contracts were a vast improvement, but Goizueta was still not satisfied. Eliminating the fixed price allowed Coke greater margins from the sale of syrup, but it did not give the company the power to make its bottlers support an overall strategy for growth. Goizueta sought other ways to bring the bottlers into greater alignment with Coke.

Coke experimented with developing a stronger bottler relationship in 1981, when it purchased 30 percent of the Coke bottler in the Philippines, a laggard operation that had ceded 70 percent of its market to Pepsi.[8] Coke invested in the bottler, modernized its plant, advertised aggressively, and increased vending operations and marketing to key accounts. The improvements in market performance were swift and dramatic, convincing Goizueta that purchasing stakes in his bottlers was the right model for building a focused and united system.

Back in the United States, the Coca-Cola Company began to buy up franchises, purchase controlling positions, and encourage other sales to friendly and competent buyers. Coke brokered or financed many transactions that ensured the new ownership and management would drive the bottling business in a direction closely aligned with Coke's corporate strategy for growth and significantly higher profitability.[9]

For the acquired bottlers, it was a win–win situation. They discovered a new friend with deep pockets who helped them to modernize their operations and to market more effectively. Bottlers that were not included were now at a significant disadvantage. Without the financial and managerial resources of Coca-Cola Inc., they became less and less competitive in an increasingly competitive environment.

"The smartest thing Goizueta did was get rid of the archaic bottler network," Mark Rowland says. "The Coca-Cola bottlers, at times, took on a management vs. labor approach. They were like local politicians. There were a million alliances. And while some were pretty sharp, others were less so. Goizueta's effort to consolidate the bottlers was an extremely astute move. Coke was a captive of the bottlers. He was smart enough to say that while this was a 105-year tradition, it was time to go. That was pure Goizueta."[10]

There was one enormous disadvantage in Coca-Cola's acquisition strategy—it raised the company's asset intensity. High asset intensity leads to poor valuations from analysts, resulting in lower returns for stockholders. Owning the strategic control point in the value chain was critical, but Goizueta's focus on shareholder returns left him troubled by the growing asset base required to create that control.

As Goizueta continued consolidating the bottlers through the mid-1980s, he searched for a solution. In 1986, he found it. He created Coca-Cola Enterprises (CCE), a holding company for the large bottlers that Coke had acquired. Once CCE was created, Coke spun off 51 percent of it to the public. Because it owned 49 percent of CCE, Coke controlled it, but did not consolidate its financials. Consequently, Coke had control but had none of the bottling assets on its balance sheet and none of the enterprise's paper-thin margins on its income statement. Not only did the CCE spin-off leave Coke with control of the bottlers while reducing Coke's asset intensity, the Initial Public Offering (IPO) also raised $1.1 billion to fund the continued implementation of the "buy bottlers" strategy.

Coke's U.S. bottler-management business design was complete. Coke's primary customers in the United States were the major Coke bottlers, and their strategic direction was perfectly aligned with Coke's. The new model realized economies of scale, highly efficient fleet utilization, modern equipment, and a total focus on profit growth. Coca-Cola's business design was the cornerstone of an emerging low-cost system, which included control of concentrate, syrup, and bottling and was geared to constantly reducing costs, reducing asset intensity, and creating the strongest possible positions in vending and fountain.

Develop the Right Model, Then Expand

By the late 1980s, Goizueta had achieved control of the U.S. market with focused, low-cost distribution and an unshakable brand. Looking for new growth opportunities, Goizueta was attracted by a vast foreign market where Coca-Cola had a long history, but where broad distribution channels were underpenetrated by Coca-Cola and relatively underserved by Pepsi (whose corporate focus was American fast food and salty snacks). In markets free of constant price competition from Pepsi, Coca-Cola could sustain high margins on its products. As Coke executives increasingly understood how much profit growth was available abroad, the company's international efforts rapidly accelerated.

To avoid the focus problems it had encountered domestically in the 1970s, Goizueta knew Coke needed a strong international business design from the outset. His model had worked at Coca-Cola Enterprises, but the business design Goizueta foresaw was not a "global CCE." Instead of the American CCE model of controlling many smaller bottlers, in the international arena Coca-Cola would further create profit opportunities by working with several large, sophisticated "anchor" bottlers that would serve an entire region or country.

By 1990, Coke had established a network of powerful anchor bottlers in Western Europe, Eastern Europe, Australia, Mexico, Latin America, and Southeast Asia. And by 1995, the Coke market position in major markets was an investor's dream. In just one 202-day period in 1994, as chronicled by *Business Week* magazine, Coke opened—or reopened—plants in seven countries, including Poland, India, Russia, South Africa, and Vietnam.

"The only true worldwide beverage company is Coca-Cola," Tom Pirko says. "The money and profit that derive from that are Roberto's great idea."

Coca-Cola's well-planned and aggressively executed takeover of the global soft drink market resulted in a decisive leadership position. Coke owns 46 percent of the international soft drink market (compared to Pepsi's 21 percent), a business which, in 1995, accounted for more than 80 percent of Coca-Cola's $4 billion operating profit. Coca-Cola's market value is over $150 billion. But what would Coke be worth today if it had gone global with the franchise bottler business design that existed in 1980?

If Coca-Cola had not reinvented its business design, it would deserve and have a significantly lower valuation. Coca-Cola owes its current high market value to its steady transformation from syrup maker and marketer to value chain manager, running a

EXHIBIT 7.4 *Coca-Cola's Business Design Reinvention*

	1977	1987	1997	2002
Customer Selection	• All soda buyers • Domestic focus	• Focus on fountain & vending customers • Anchor bottlers	• International focus	
Value Capture	• Syrup sales • Equal emphasis on grocery, fountain & vending	• Syrup sales • Bottler earnings • Focus on more profitable channels	• Focus on strong leadership in fountain, vending, and international • Sales of equity in bottlers	**?**
Differentiation/ Strategic Control	• Brand • Secret formula	• Bottler relationship • Brand • Low-asset intensity	• Bottler relationship • Global megabrand • Low-cost global distribution	
Scope	• Syrup • Diversified conglomerate	• Beverage focus • Syrup • Domestic bottler relationship	• Global value chain manager	

well-integrated, effectively focused, international beverage company (Exhibit 7.4).

UNCERTAINTY

Goizueta's transformation of the company by consolidating the bottlers became an enormous success, but it started out as an enormous risk. Goizueta believed that by purchasing controlling interests in the bottlers, he could coordinate Coca-Cola's market strategy, create a low-cost distribution network, and create value for both his shareholders and the bottlers. But what if the bottlers still couldn't be aligned? What if investments in modernizing plant equipment didn't pay off? What if Pepsi mirrored Coke's moves, following it into fountain and vending, and driving down profits as it did in grocery? Goizueta made a tremendous bet, and no good leader will risk an entire organization when it is possible to hedge.

Goizueta's first hedge, the 1982 purchase of Columbia Pictures, expanded Coca-Cola's scope from beverage maker to movie producer, an investment that he hoped would help develop Coke into a "consumer lifestyle" company and add significantly to its bottom line. Wall Street analysts pounded Coca-Cola's stock price at the announcement, but under Coke's ownership the studio produced several blockbuster successes. Goizueta eventually sold Columbia in 1989 for a considerable profit.

In Goizueta's other major hedges, he tried leveraging the Coca-Cola brand to broaden Coke's appeal. Most managers opposed using the Coca-Cola name on anything but its flagship product, but, to Goizueta, not optimizing the profits from the company's greatest asset—its brand name—seemed to be poor economic thinking. In 1982, he introduced diet Coke, which became an enormous success. Over the next few years, the company also launched Cherry Coke and Caffeine-free Coke.

Not every bet is a winner, however. In the early 1980s, Goizueta and other Coke executives were disconcerted by Pepsi's "blind taste tests," which showed that consumers preferred Pepsi's sweeter taste. Worried that the taste of the Coca-Cola product was at the heart of the company's problems, Goizueta launched New Coke.

"The seminal event in the company's culture was New Coke," Bevmark's Tom Pirko says. "It was the beginning of the 'New Age.' It turned out to be a blessing in disguise. It was an event that rocked the company; it made them question who they are and what their relationship is to the consuming public. They put their trademark up for grabs because they were trying to imitate Pepsi. But consumers said, 'This is not the right thing to do.' You can't have that massive response and not have it affect you. They learned to change."[11]

The public outcry of loyalty to the old formula taught Goizueta an important lesson: It was Pepsi's business design and its effective marketing efforts, not its taste, that propelled Pepsi-Cola into contention as America's top soft drink.

"Coca-Cola was an ultraconservative company before New Coke," Pirko recalls. "It now is superaggressive, even ferocious at times. If it needs to go after Mountain Dew by creating Surge, it tells the world it will spend $50 million and debut the product during the Super Bowl."

PEPSI AND THE FUTURE

The differences in Coke's and Pepsi's business designs are striking.

Coke is a focused beverage producer linked to a network of large anchor bottlers who are also its business partners and primary customers. It is a truly international business.

Pepsi is a food and beverage conglomerate that consists of soft drinks, snack foods, and fast food restaurants and is focused on the U.S. market.

Even within their beverage operations, the two companies' profits are generated from very different sources. Eighty percent of Coke's earnings come from international operations; 90 percent of Pepsi's beverage profit is generated domestically.

In the mid-1990s, Pepsi made some important moves that will reinitiate the Cola Wars. In early 1996, it appointed a dynamic new CEO, Roger Enrico. He was widely hailed as a creative manager who would do whatever it takes to turn around the company.

In order to catch up, Pepsi is likely to become more like Coke by doing three things.

1. Pepsi will focus its efforts. Enrico took steps toward this objective by announcing that Pepsi will spin off its restaurant businesses: Taco Bell, Pizza Hut, and KFC. The restaurants hurt Pepsi on two fronts. They represent a highly asset-intensive business that dilutes the profit margins of the beverage and snack food divisions. The restaurants also remove Pepsi from contention for contracts with the major fast food chains because they view Pepsi as a competitor. By severing Taco Bell, Pizza Hut, and KFC, Pepsi will be better positioned to compete for some of the prized fountain business that Coke currently wins almost by default.

2. Enrico may well follow Goizueta's lead and spin off Pepsi's bottling operations. (Pepsi still holds a large percentage of bottling assets on its books.) Removing the bottlers from its balance sheet would greatly increase Pepsi's return on assets and improve shareholder returns. "The bottling system is a drain on Pepsi," Bevmark's Tom Pirko agrees. "When you are in the business of owning and running trucks, it can be treacherous. It's better to be the keeper of the brand."

3. Pepsi will intensify the fight internationally. This will be difficult because of Coke's strong relationships in local markets and its brand recognition among consumers around the globe. Pepsi must establish the same strength wherever Coke is sold. Coke's international operations are supremely efficient. Unlike the grocery war of the 1970s, Pepsi can't undercut Coke on price. Pepsi's best chance is to compete intensely in emerging markets where Coke is not yet firmly established. Pepsi must then hope that Coke will concede some of these sales areas in order to avoid large-scale price wars throughout the entire international market. That's a lot to hope for, given how competitively oriented the entire Coke organization has become.

The strategic lessons and the key points of Coke's business design innovation were not lost on Enrico. Pepsi's moves subsequent to his arrival show that he understands the power of managing the value chain by controlling distribution and focusing on the areas of a business where the highest profits are available.

Spinning off CCE improved Coke's financial statements and return to shareholders, and international expansion provided Coke with the growth opportunities it needed. However, Coca-Cola's consolidated bottler system was the cornerstone of its global success. Managing the entire value chain has powered Coke's success for the past decade. Coke's issue now is not maximization but maintainability. It is a subtle challenge, one few have solved. With Pepsi making the kind of moves that could vault it back into contention, Goizueta must reinvent his business design again, to remain ahead. Every move Goizueta made—from switching to high-fructose corn syrup, to creating a new bottler relationship model, to focusing on vending and fountain—reflects an intensely profit-centric style of thought. The question is: What innovation will allow Goizueta to continue to occupy the leading position in the profit zone in the next decade?

The stage is set for an extraordinary contest. Led by aggressive, visionary thinkers, both companies have fortified their positions and are preparing for the next decade's battle over value growth.

BUILDING A "VALUE CHAIN MANAGER" BUSINESS DESIGN
Pilot's Checklist

☑ *Have I clearly pinpointed where all the profit zones in the value chain are today? Tomorrow?*

☑ *Do I need to manage the value chain to get to the profit zone?*

☑ *Have I designed an opportunity to test my new business design in a low-risk environment?*

☑ *Have I changed my relationship with all the other value chain players to create alignment behind a profit-centric strategy?*

☑ *Have I developed the* least *asset-intensive way to create a value chain management system?*

EIGHT

CHARLES SCHWAB

The Switchboard Business Design

- *Does my industry treat customers as customers or as sales targets?*
- *Does my industry make life difficult for customers?*
- *Do buyers and sellers both incur unnecessary costs?*

JOHN DAVIS did not become a Charles Schwab & Company customer until October 1993. In the several preceding years, John had begun to move his money out of low-yield bank accounts into the stock market.

His broker, who represented a traditional wirehouse, made many buy and sell recommendations, but John felt that the broker was making more money on trade commissions than John was making on asset growth. John gradually began to shift his money to mutual funds. He felt that fund managers' expertise could provide him with better financial performance than his broker was providing. Besides, he saw himself as a "sales target" for the broker, rather than a customer with real needs to be met and real concerns to be addressed.

By 1993, John had placed his modest, but growing, investment portfolio with five different mutual funds. He was reasonably happy with their performance, but record keeping was an enormous hassle. He received statements from all five of them (as well as from his broker and his bank), and the time and inconvenience involved were getting to be a burden.

John heard about Schwab's OneSource from a friend who had been a Schwab customer for 5 years. The friend's enthusiasm for Schwab was infectious. John moved his money into OneSource and was delighted with his new experience. Instead of struggling with statements from several different providers, he got one consolidated statement every month. He also got a checking account, and easy access to a discount brokerage service. Although he bought fewer stocks directly (most of his money was in mutual funds), he did trade occasionally, and he shifted his business from his traditional broker to Schwab. He was pleased to learn that he could execute orders by Touch-Tone phone and receive even further discounted commissions, besides saving time and money. And when Schwab introduced e.Schwab in 1996, he was one of the earliest users.

"All this financial work had been such a hassle for me, with one broker, five mutual funds, and a bank checking account. I got seven different statements every month. I now get *one* statement, the service is better and my costs are lower—on everything: on brokerage, on mutual funds, and, most recently, on insurance. And it all takes a lot less time than it did 3 years ago, in my pre-Schwab days."

John has been recommending Schwab to his friends. He feels confident that they will be pleased as well.

It took 20 years for Charles Schwab to create this level of service for his customers. A consistently customer-centric approach to building his business served as a compass. The needle kept pointing toward the *next* set of customer needs to be served in the world of financial services, and the next opportunity to create a highly lucrative profit zone for his company.

Schwab's customer-centric mindset sharply contrasted with an industry dominated by a product-centric point of view. Historically, the financial services industry's many sectors, from brokerage to banking to insurance, focused on product-out rather than customer-in. The customer was a "sales target," not a person with needs, concerns, and aspirations. The point was to sell as much "product" as possible (a brokerage account, a checking account, or term life insurance), rather than figure out how to invent the next good deal for the customer.

This product-centric, customer-as-sales-target approach in financial services created an arena full of opportunity for innovation.

But only for a radical thinker who could see beyond traditional industry lines and thought processes.

THE MAVERICK

Charles Schwab—friends and associates call him "Chuck"—has always had an angle, whether it was using Cliff Notes and Classics Illustrated comic books to help overcome dyslexia in school, or raising chickens for extra money and selling them door-to-door for all they were worth—eggs, manure, or poultry.

A graduate of Stanford with a bachelor's degree and an MBA, Schwab actually started his career running a $20 million mutual fund that was shut down in 1969 by the state of Texas because it wasn't registered in that state. He lost $100,000, and his first marriage, to a futile court battle.

Starting over again with two rooms, a telephone, and $100,000 of his uncle's money, 32-year-old Charles Schwab started First Commander, a brokerage firm, in 1971.

The new firm grew slowly in the early 1970s, wooing customers with free cameras and other inducements, and doing whatever it took to build the clientele of his no-name organization. Schwab's starting business model had the same customer selection, products, services, and pricing as a conventional brokerage, but it had no brand, no technology, and almost no client base. Schwab struggled to find a way to differentiate himself from the pack.

On May 1, 1975, the Securities and Exchange Commission (SEC) outlawed fixed commissions, and Schwab seized the opportunity to completely change his business design from conventional broker to discount broker.[1]

The investment game of the early 1970s contained only one kind of player—the full-service broker. A traditional brokerage house commanded high fees because it provided investors with advice and counsel as well as trading capabilities. The premium charged for the advice was unavoidable because brokers sold the advice and trading functions as a "bundled" package. There was no option for investors who only wanted access to low-cost trades. A discount brokerage, like the one Schwab formed in 1975, was a new way of doing business: A savvy investor could pay only for the trades themselves, and escape the high fees of traditional brokers.

At a discount broker, if a customer has his or her own ideas and doesn't want any advice, the customer can call the broker and say, "I don't want any advice. I just want execution and I want it cheap."

Shifting to discounting was only a first step. The discount broker business model attracted customers and generated revenues (the full-service firms resisted dropping rates, and, in many cases, raised them, especially for smaller customers), but dozens of other discount brokers were flooding into the market, and none had any particularly strong differentiation other than the promise of a lower price.

As with First Commander, Schwab quickly faced the problem of differentiation. He had to develop a compelling answer to the question: "Why does the customer want to buy from *me*?" To answer that question, Schwab constructed a different model, that of a value-added discounter. To differentiate his company and add value to his customers, he reinvested every cent of profit into a blossoming branch network, spent $2 million on computers and technology, provided basic information to investors, and established his brand name through substantial advertising. Although his fees were slightly higher than those of other discounters, he delivered greater value to his customers, while keeping his fees 50 percent below those of the full-service firms.

By paying salaries rather than commissions, Schwab further aligned the operations of the firm with the interests of its customers. The overall effect of Schwab's efforts was to make investors feel comfortable with the company.

Schwab's business design demonstrated an understanding of what was important to customers, beyond just the execution of trades. Schwab's investments in building his brand name and branch network were made to provide to customers the trust, convenience, and reliable information they were looking for.

The Schwab value-added discounter model went beyond simple unbundling of trading and advice. It served moderately sophisticated investors who sought inexpensive access to the market. By executing trades at low cost to the investor, Schwab differentiated itself from full-service brokers; by advertising, providing basic information, and establishing a local presence, it stood above other discount brokers.

It wasn't long before much of the public knew exactly who Charles Schwab was. He began appearing in most of the company's TV, radio, billboard, and print ads—"just about everywhere but the side of milk cartons," wrote *Fortune* magazine's Terence P. Pare.[2]

Advertising for such old-line firms as Smith Barney deliberately painted it as a faceless institution. Merrill Lynch was literally a bull in a china shop. But anyone who walked into a Schwab office knew that Chuck himself stood behind the company's trades. For a generation of Baby Boomers raised on TV, he was their natural choice. As *Business Week* once put it, "[Schwab's] genial face is a marketing tool."[3]

Schwab crafted a business design that was unique in the industry, and its economic power was reflected in its rising revenue, profit, and market share. From 1977 to 1983, revenues grew from $4.6 million to $126.5 million. By 1984, Schwab commanded 20 percent of the entire discount brokerage business.

By 1988, revenues at Schwab had grown to $392 million and market share of discount brokerage to almost 40 percent. More importantly, it was highly profitable market share because Schwab's model provided customers with what they wanted and didn't incur cost by adding things customers didn't want. Thanks to his up-to-date technology, his trades were more easily executed than his competitors'. Schwab had built a strongly differentiated discount brokerage model that created powerful revenue and value growth.

Despite the success and durability of the value-added discounter model, Schwab knew that competition for sophisticated individual investors would grow more intense over time. Most companies, when faced with competition, will try to hard-sell new products to their existing customers. Schwab, with his customer-centric perspective, took a different approach. He surveyed the financial services landscape, looking for ways to share his superior capabilities with new contacts. Shifting market forces then brought Schwab a new set of customers.

SCHWAB'S SECOND BUSINESS DESIGN: SERVING THE FINANCIAL PLANNERS

In the mid to late 1980s, a small but growing new force emerged in the financial services world—independent investment advisory services. A revitalized stock market awoke investors to the possibility of equity investments, and customer priorities shifted from savings to investment, which brought greater return on their money without significantly increased risk. But the world of investing was more complex, and advice and guidance emerged as increasingly important priorities for investors. The industry's traditional players were slow to recognize and respond to this shift. Independent investment advisors, frequently referred to as "financial planners," flowed into the vacuum.

These new participants in the financial services world were largely ignored and often disdained by the traditional players, who thought little of the small and medium-size investors the planners attracted.

Financial planners emerged for a reason, and Schwab saw clearly what the reason was. The traditional model in the industry no longer met investors' needs for advice, information, and guidance. Investors needed and wanted independent financial advice unvarnished by the broker commission structure that was inconsistent with that need. Planners provided an important, legitimate new service to customers. Schwab reversed the industry's point of view with regard to the planners. "Industrythink" viewed them collectively as a competitor, but mostly as an annoyance. Schwab viewed them as a potential customer, an ally, and a new channel to the ultimate customer—the investor. Where traditional industry players saw low-rent poachers, Schwab saw resource-rich partners with unmet needs, such as backroom operations to generate invoices, orders, and monthly statements (services he could certainly fulfill) and a growing source of investor assets that he could tap into.

"We are partners with those investment managers," Dan Leemon, Executive Vice President of Business Strategy for Schwab, says. "There are some things they do extraordinarily well that we can't, like prospecting for customers and building relationships with customers."[4]

Schwab's customer-centric view of the market enabled him to understand the utility that financial planners provided his customers. Recognizing them as a potential ally and a potential bridge to new customers, he expanded his business design accordingly, treated financial planners as his customers, and developed new services for them.

Most planners operate as sole proprietors or in small partnerships. For small-scale operators, account processing and trade execution are tedious, burdensome, and expensive tasks. Schwab recognized that these independent and scattered professionals would need an inexpensive, efficient, and equally independent clearinghouse for their transactions. The resources Schwab provided enabled them to do a better job for their customers, the investors, and made the planners' independent operations more profitable. In return, they represented a vast resource for referring new customers to Schwab.

The Schwab Institutional Enterprise, the program linking Charles Schwab & Company with small- to medium-size independent financial advisers, was not an instant success, however, as one early participant recalls. "They knew they had something but they didn't know what to do with it," according to Mike Kabarec, president of Kabarec Financial Advisors, Ltd. of Palatine, Illinois. "You name it, they screwed it up, everything from trading to paper flow. They had made promises they couldn't keep. But they got their act together and have been on a roll ever since."[5]

In the early days, the independent financial advisers were served via their local Schwab branch office. But the relationship didn't really mature until the financial advisers had their own regional Schwab service centers.

"What Schwab has done is create 6,000 branch offices without the overhead," Kabarec marvels. "I manage $110 million in assets. If I had this kind of volume without Schwab, I'd need at least two more people on staff." In his 10-year relationship with Schwab, Kabarec has seen his staff shrink from 12 to 6, but his assets under management have multiplied 20-fold.

What really amazes Kabarec is that he and his industry counterparts have become Schwab's "virtual sales force"—they sell Schwab product but get no payment from Schwab. In fact, they pay Schwab for the privilege.

Over time, Schwab became the de facto back-office operation for several thousand financial planners. A new revenue stream was generated as financial planners increasingly referred their clients to Schwab.

"Our business would exist without Schwab," says financial planner Mike Davis, founder of the Orlando-based Resource Consulting Group, "but it wouldn't look like it does today. Without them as our backroom paperwork processor, we'd have twice the staff. They've made our lives extremely easy. I don't think our clients have any idea what Schwab does for us in terms of making our lives easier. If we had to do all this manually, our fees would be much higher. We've done well, Schwab has done well, and our clients get a tremendous deal in the process."[6]

The financial planners' referral process was made smoother with SchwabLink (software for financial advisers), which allowed financial advisers and their clients to interact seamlessly with Schwab from anywhere.

Greg Lathrop, president of Lathrop Investment Management of Little Rock, Arkansas, spent the first half of his career working in bank trust departments. When he went out on his own as a financial adviser, Lathrop tried relationships with brokers other than Schwab. He was a skeptical latecomer to Schwab's institutional program. But as he grew more wary of the traditional brokers, he made a leap of faith and switched to Schwab.

"I went to them expecting to not get much, other than saving on trades. But for a firm our size—$170 million under management—they can handle anything we need to do," Lathrop says. "Schwab's culture is that of order-takers, with its people on salary. They're perfectly happy to take a small fee because they know the money is coming to them. And in the long term, they know the game is all about gathering assets because eventually, the asset is going to turn over."[7]

Schwab's initiative with the planners produced no response among the industry's traditional players. They just didn't see what he saw—at least not until it was too late to catch up.

Actually, such a nonresponse happens quite frequently across many industries. It happened when the established steel mills failed to respond to the Nucor minimill model. Exactly the same nonresponse occurred when the national hub-and-spoke airlines failed to craft an effective answer to the Southwest Airlines point-to-point model, or when traditional discounters failed to respond to the next-generation Wal-Mart discounting model.

Nonresponse happens all the time, and Schwab took full advantage of it.

Schwab's financial-planners move affected every strategic dimension of his business design. Customer selection was increased, and it included financial planners as well as investors. Value capture was expanded to include fees and referrals from financial planners. Strategic control was enhanced as Schwab's cooperative approach to the financial planners created a new and unique channel to market that was unavailable to most other financial service firms. Scope was expanded to include operational support for financial planners.

Schwab had invented a new way of doing business in the investment world. By allying himself with the planners, he had made potential competitors into partners and reached customers that his original business model could not have reached. Preserving the Schwab culture of friendly service with no sales pressure, Schwab's business design progressed to its next level, and produced tremendous revenue, profit, and value growth. By 1990, revenues at Schwab had grown to $387 million, profits to $16.8 million, and market share of discount brokerage to 39.8 percent. The company's market value rose from $152 million in 1987 to over $1.2 billion by the end of 1991 (see Exhibit 8.1).

As Schwab worked more closely with this new customer group, and Schwab's knowledge of evolving investor priorities deepened, his conceptualization of the company's next major move began taking shape. The move was announced in early 1992, catching the industry by surprise and representing the single most radical change in Schwab's business design to that point in time.

ONESOURCE: THE SWITCHBOARD BUSINESS DESIGN

Since the early 1980s, Schwab's close proximity to, and understanding of customers' needs and priorities had clued him into how radically those priorities were changing. This was especially apparent in the customers' embrace of mutual funds.

EXHIBIT 8.1 *Charles Schwab's Market Value Growth*

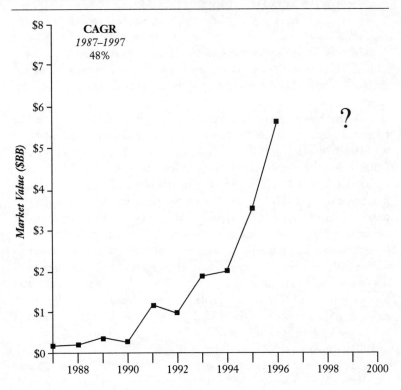

CAGR
1987–1997
48%

?

Market Value ($BB)

By constantly focusing on customers and not on just his own operations or his own competitors, Schwab more easily saw what the customers' next predicament would be. Where others saw a threat in planners, Schwab asked, "Why were financial planners emerging with such force?" He appreciated that they were a response to investors' important but unmet need for independent advice and guidance. As the mutual fund industry exploded in the late 1980s, Schwab again asked, "Why?" Customers were looking for investment convenience. Rather than making dozens of trades themselves, they wanted someone to help them make decisions. Mutual funds provided the solution, but another problem then emerged: Customers faced so many options, they needed a more convenient way of dealing with the complexity of too many choices. That problem was the genesis of the OneSource opportunity.

In 1980, investors held $135 billion of assets in mutual funds. By 1986, that amount had grown to $716 billion. By 1991, it reached $1,396 billion. The explosion in the number of fund companies and individual funds was equally breathtaking. In 1986, there were already 1,840 mutual funds offered by 261 fund companies. That probably seemed sufficient to most people. But just 5 years later, another 100 companies created an additional 1,600 mutual funds.

This evolution created two problems for investors: (1) a dizzying array of mostly unbranded fund options, and (2) extremely high costs, with many customers paying a 6 percent load *plus* a brokerage fee. In other words, fund placement could cost the customer as much as 8.5 percent of assets. No-load funds were growing rapidly, but they represented only a small portion of the industry's assets in the early 1990s.

The priorities of financial advisers were changing as rapidly as the habits of mutual fund customers. Increasingly, planners needed a convenient, low-cost mechanism to help their clients transfer assets from low-yield savings accounts to a well-designed mix of mutual funds.

Schwab began to see another opportunity to rationalize the system in the customers' favor. He examined the investment process from an investor's standpoint and was amazed by what he saw. It was not unusual for an individual investor to spread an investment across one company's "best of breed" fund, another's index fund, and so on, through equity and bond funds. But the strategy backfired when the customer reallocated assets among funds. Four separate telephone calls were required to make a sale. The customer then waited for four checks to arrive in the mail, resent deposits to the new target funds, and then made four calls to buy. Sixteen transactions in all: four sales, four checks sent; four buys, four more checks written. With a 7- to 10-day delay until funds arrived, there was an extended time during which the investor made no money.

To help the customer, Schwab sought to invent a different way to sell and buy mutual funds. He needed an easy-to-understand, accessible platform. He knew that nothing less than a revolutionary, comprehensive approach would move the market and stimulate consumers. Following his consistent philosophy of "low cost and high value for the customer," Schwab kept searching for a way to sell no-load funds at zero cost to the investor.

Schwab's experience following the 1987 market crash (when his revenue fell 20 percent) caused him to think harder about the economic advantage of shifting his own company's revenue mix away from an entirely transaction-based commission stream and toward one that had a much larger component of recurring fees. He focused not just on the customer but on profitability, searching for a business model that had a floor of recurring revenue, creating a much more powerful design.

OneSource was the outcome of this dual search for a better deal for the customer, and better value capture for the company. Launched in July 1992, it made mutual funds available to consumers with no load and no transaction fee. All funds in OneSource were accessible with a single phone call to Schwab and were tracked on one account statement. Traditionally, to acquire mutual funds from a broker, consumers paid fees that could total more than 8.5 percent of assets for each purchase. The introduction of OneSource dramatically changed these customer economics by dropping the customer's costs to zero.

It also marked a fundamental shift in the Schwab business design. The move was toward meeting the priorities of core customer groups, both investors and financial advisers, and it significantly improved the company's own economics by creating a high-profit, high-growth, recurring revenue stream.

The power of Schwab's model was that it not only made the investing process easier for the customers, it also made finding customers easier for mutual fund companies. It is expensive for the mutual fund companies to market broadly, and it is time-consuming for any customer to simultaneously deal with several mutual funds. What Schwab did was put a "switchboard" between them, making it less costly for the mutual funds to reach customers, and less complicated for the customers, who could now deal with several mutual funds through one point of contact and receive one comprehensive financial statement. By reducing the mutual funds' marketing costs and the drag on customers' time and nerves (Exhibit 8.2), the new switchboard business design added value for both sides.

EXHIBIT 8.2   *The Charles Schwab "Switchboard"*

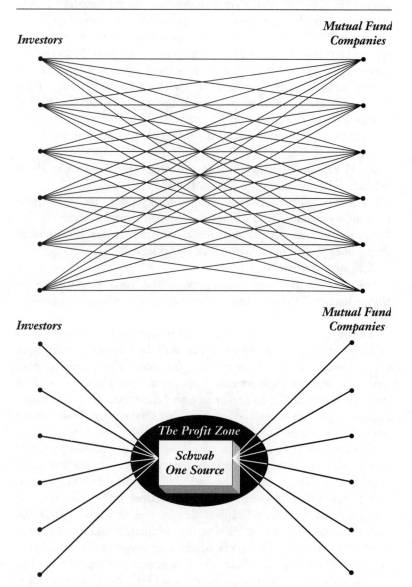

Schwab approached several mutual fund companies and persuaded them to pay him a commission on mutual fund assets distributed through Schwab—without Schwab's customers paying the traditional $39 minimum transaction fee. Eight fund companies agreed to do so, in hopes of gaining greater access to Schwab customers. With the close of the deal, Schwab effectively shifted the cost of acquiring mutual funds from the consumer to the fund companies. He charged a small fee to the mutual funds; he did not charge a fee to the customer. He made both of their costs lower.

Schwab, a pioneer in discount brokerage, had just invented discount mutual funds, radically reducing the customer's transaction costs. What the SEC had done to brokerage commissions in 1975, Schwab did to mutual fund fees in 1992.

"The OneSource program made a lot of sense to us," says Craig Litman, a principal in San Francisco-based Litman/Gregory & Co. "Schwab was in a unique position to do it, being an independent discount broker. The question was, could he deliver?"

The answer was yes.

"His people were young, very motivated, interested in making things happen," Litman says. "If we wanted something, it was done. That was very important to us."[8]

That's the resounding theme heard from most financial planners and advisers who hooked up with Schwab: by signing on with him, they no longer needed the personnel, automation, or office space required to support their mutual fund trades. "It was a tremendous time-saver not having to deal with every individual fund company," Litman says. "When we started in this business in 1986, before Schwab, it was a nightmare."

Key to Schwab's success was picturing the role technology would play in delivering services such as combined statements and quick trades—and making the investments needed to create that capability.

The OneSource move created a revolution in the industry, and the effect on Schwab's business design was enormous. In 1993, 2,000 workers were added, raising the company's total employment from 4,500 to 6,500. First-year advertising costs for OneSource exceeded $20 million. But Schwab's last-generation business model, having grown to $750 million in revenue in 1992—and $81 million in profit—had generated the scale of resources required to support such a major undertaking.

The industry scrambled to compete. There were three types of responses:

1. *Denial: Most financial services firms did nothing, hoping that Schwab's OneSource would be a passing fad.*
2. *Fee Structure: Forward-looking full-service brokerage firms introduced new share classes for their funds with low or no fees.*
3. *Imitation: Fidelity, realizing the growing importance of distribution in the investment management business, introduced its own Funds Network. Fidelity's offering, an imitator of OneSource, included 370 funds—their own and others'—with no loads and no transaction fee.*

Schwab also changed the direction of the industry. Smith Barney and others are now selling mutual funds that are not proprietary. Ten years ago, that would have been heresy.

"Virtually all the brokerages raced to offer marketplaces where they looked and smelled like Schwab," Greg Lathrop says. "But can a culture such as the old brokerages really change? I would argue that it can't."

None of these responses slowed Schwab's momentum. By 1994, 15 percent of Schwab's $1.07 billion in revenue was derived from mutual fund service fees. Schwab's mutual fund assets grew from $12.2 billion in 1992 to $19.7 billion in 1994. That momentum carried over into 1995, and by the end of 1996, Schwab was No. 4 behind Fidelity, Vanguard, and Merrill Lynch in total mutual fund assets under management.

As Schwab continued gathering assets, traditional players began seeing the competitive threat that Schwab's momentum posed. Mutual fund companies had a love/hate relationship with OneSource, which provided them with a new source of assets at a very low cost to serve. Schwab handled all account tracking and servicing, and simply mailed each participating fund company a single check. However, because Schwab maintained the customer relationship, investors who had previously considered themselves customers of a given mutual fund company started to see themselves as customers of Schwab. And Schwab, not the mutual fund companies, had direct marketing access to these people for future opportunities when it is time for their assets to move again.

Schwab's customer relationships grew stronger through both OneSource and the financial-planner program. The third party in every relationship between financial advisers and their clients in the Schwab network is Schwab.

Schwab's competitors were all at least a step behind. Fidelity and others belatedly recognized the value of the financial adviser relationships Schwab had developed, and they started courting them as well. Fidelity launched the Fidelity Investor Advisor Resource Group in 1992 to improve back-office service for financial advisers and to increase its line of Fidelity Advisor Funds (load funds).

While the industry players were preoccupied with thinking through and implementing their responses to OneSource, Schwab stayed one step ahead of the curve by bringing automation beyond Schwab's internal operations and into direct interaction with the customer.

"I wouldn't consider myself a techie," Schwab says. "I can envision, I can conceptualize solutions. I knew what I wanted and I had great computer people working with me who could understand that."[9]

The first major step in this direction had been taken in 1989, with the introduction of TeleBroker. Through the TeleBroker system, Schwab's customers executed trades with a Touch-Tone phone, reducing Schwab's costs and saving the customer time. Schwab's next innovation in this area was VoiceBroker, which uses speech recognition software to provide stock quote and account information to shareholders over the phone. Instead of keying-in relevant account and ticker symbol information, a single spoken word gave customers access to the information they needed. In 1993, Schwab introduced "StreetSmart" software for home computers, providing Schwab customers with 24-hour access to trading information and their individual accounts.

A much larger-scale change was the introduction of "e.Schwab" in 1995. Although Schwab had provided online trading capabilities since introducing The Equalizer in 1984, e.Schwab was a complete account offering designed specifically for active traders who can access the system via personal computers or laptops in their offices or homes, or anywhere in the world. Trades, which can be placed at any time of the day or night, are completed online with funds from an independent e.Schwab account and without the assistance of an account representative. With such a low-cost vehicle for completing brokerage transactions, Schwab offers active traders a fee of $29.95 per trade because there are no costs for unwanted services. Because of its consistent focus on the customer, and its persistent technology investment to serve customers better, the Internet was less a surprise than an opportunity for Schwab, particularly given the low age and high computer literacy of its customer base.

Schwab rapidly emerged as the easiest company to do business with in the financial services world, and the one that delivered the most value—from discount brokerage to discount mutual funds, investment information, and referral of financial advisers.

In 1985, Schwab's narrow business model was that of a highly differentiated, high value-added discount broker. In 1997, Schwab's business design was that of a highly differentiated, high value-added financial services firm operating a unique switchboard business model that created benefits for multiple customer groups: investors, financial planners, and mutual funds (see Exhibit 8.3). Schwab's business design reinvention led to dramatic improvements in the company's valuation (see Exhibit 8.4).

How did the industry allow Schwab to build such a powerful position? In industry after industry, we encounter this pattern of a business model innovation and nonresponse or a delayed response from the incumbents. Companies seem to pledge allegiance to their traditional way of doing business rather than asking, "How are customers changing and how can I add more real value to them?"— even if the answer means developing a business design that looks very different from the industry's traditional model.

Many companies now offer "fundmalls" of their own. Jack White, AccuTrade, and Fidelity offer sets of mutual funds and related services that mirror OneSource and its lack of transaction fees. Traditional brokerage firms such as Smith Barney, Merrill Lynch, American Express, and Paine Webber are also experimenting with fundmalls.

The collective force of these responses defines the next challenge to Schwab's business design. The corrosive power of the imitation effect is always at work, turning today's profitability into tomorrow's no-profit zone. This is the same issue faced by Nucor in 1988

EXHIBIT 8.3 *Schwab's Business Design Reinvention*

	1980s	1988	1992	1997	2002
Customer Selection	• Do-it-yourself investor	• Financial planners	• Mutual funds • Investors	• Regional banks • Regional brokers	
Value Capture	• Commissions	• Fees • Referrals	• Mutual fund fees	• Fees	
Differentiation/ Strategic Control	• Branches • Brand	• Business partner program with financial planners • Technology	• No cost to investors • Owning the switchboard	• Technology • Business partner program • Brand	?
Scope	• Discount brokerage	• Back-office services	• "Discount" mutual funds	• Discount insurance • Adviser referral	

⬇   ⬇   ⬇   ⬇

"Value-Added Discount Broker"   *"Financial Planners Service Provider"*   *"Switchboard Business Design"*   *"2nd Generation Switchboard"*

Schwab's business design progression is cumulative.
The elements of the prior business design carry over to the next generation business model.

as imitators rushed in to mimic its steel mini-mill business model, add capacity, and undermine its economics. The same issue was also faced by Wal-Mart in the 1990s, when it depleted its available reserves of "easy competition" markets, and began to compete with more sophisticated, operationally excellent rivals. Intel faced the same issue when it needed to introduce a major generational innovation every 36 months to keep its competitors at a distance and to keep itself operating within the profit zone.

EXHIBIT 8.4   *Charles Schwab Business Design Reinvention*

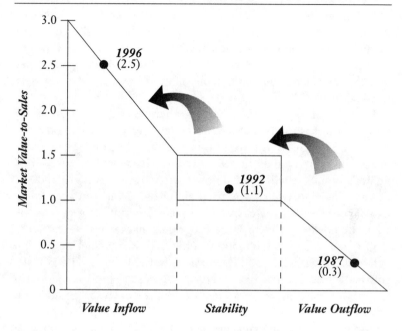

Value Creation Performance

STAYING AHEAD

Schwab continues to meet the financial needs of its customers, all the while drawing in new accounts. In April 1996, Schwab introduced SchwabLife Insurance Services—discount life insurance. After an initial trial period in 15 states, Schwab expanded the line to include 5-, 15-, and 20-year term plans. Schwab leveraged its name and reputation as a discount brokerage and mutual fund company, and began building a franchise in life insurance.

What's next? Schwab believes he can spread the influence of OneSource. In October 1996, he accessed a new pool of investors by offering OneSource through banks—a move that has not been without controversy, even among his own devotees.

"Some people think Schwab is trying to usurp our market by going into the banks," says financial planner Mike Kabarec. "But I think it's the opposite—that's business we're not going to get, anyway. The customers served by banks either don't want to pay our fees, or they're uncomfortable turning their investments over to someone else."

First, financial planner customers, then mutual fund customers; now Schwab has used OneSource as a gateway to bank customers.

Another Schwab innovation is the AdvisorSource program, begun in pilot studies in 1996. Under the new AdvisorSource, Schwab branches will refer its own clients who have $100,000 or more in their portfolios, and need more advice and guidance, to financial advisers in the Schwab network. It's not all gravy to the advisers, however: they pay the program's marketing expenses.

One way that Schwab maintains his lead in financial innovation is by listening harder to his customers, both at the retail and institutional levels. His customer advisory boards are probably more influential, regarding the practices of Charles Schwab & Company, than some boards of directors in multinational corporations. And not only does Schwab management solicit and listen, it acts on what it learns.

Another factor is cited by insiders: cross-training. Schwab executives don't learn one element of the business and stay with it for decades. They move across lines, learning multiple disciplines and business practices. They are far more well-rounded than their counterparts at the wire houses and traditional brokerages.

"Schwab also has an endless stream of young, talented people who they turn the keys over to and let them go to work," according to Lathrop. "And they don't care if you make a mistake. It's a culture where it's OK to make a mistake."

Charles Schwab & Company is also taking steps toward establishing a multilingual, international brokerage, by opening a Spanish-language facility in Miami and an Asia Pacific service center in San Francisco, staffed by employees who speak Mandarin, Cantonese, Japanese, and Vietnamese. It also bought a United Kingdom firm, ShareLink Investment Services PLC, as a way of entering potential new markets overseas.

THE LOGIC OF SUCCESS

Charles Schwab revolutionized the financial services industry by asking himself the right questions. When Schwab surveyed the brokerage landscape of the 1970s, he saw that the market basically offered one product—bundled trading and advice. He posed some basic customer-centric questions, "Can this single offering really be meeting all customers' needs? Which needs does it meet? Which are left out? How can I get those people who are not well served to buy from me?"

Schwab's early customer-centric business design took off, so much so that he knew imitators would soon follow. As competition for sophisticated individual investors grew, Schwab found a way to protect his profits. He asked himself, "What other customer sets have been neglected by the market? What tools do I have to serve their needs?"

Schwab realized that serving the needs of the planners, was a more efficient and profitable way to capture the assets of many less sophisticated investors. Schwab became the back office of thousands of planners, in a relationship that brought value to customers, planners, and Charles Schwab alike.

The late 1980s brought an explosion of investor interest in mutual funds. Investors appreciated easy diversification and were happy to pass off the job of stock picking. Schwab saw that mutual funds' popularity came from removing the need for investing expertise. He asked himself, "Has this industry shift created new customer priorities? If mutual funds have met the customer need for expertise, how can I work in conjunction with the funds to serve further customer priorities?"

Schwab had a profit-centric concern as well. He wondered, "How can I lower the risk associated with my revenues? Is there a way to convert transactional revenue to recurring revenue?"

Schwab found an answer to his customer-centric and profit-centric questions. He changed Schwab's business design to meet mutual fund investors' needs for less record-keeping hassle and lower transactions costs. At the same time, he made the mutual fund companies into Schwab customers by lowering their cost to bring in investors. Schwab's revenue mix also improved because he charged the mutual funds a small percentage of investors' assets each year. Rather than let himself be bypassed by changing industry trends, Schwab's customer-centric logic identified a way to create value as a switchboard for the two groups.

As he prepares to invent his next-generation business design, Charles Schwab will continue to ask himself: "How are customers' priorities shifting? What does the evolving logic of customer needs tell me about where the next best opportunities are located?"

By always looking forward, two moves ahead of the industry, Schwab owns the initiative—an invaluable commodity.

BUILDING A "SWITCHBOARD" BUSINESS DESIGN
Pilot's Checklist

☑ *Have I done everything feasible to help my organization change its mindset in order to treat customers as* customers, *not sales targets?*

☑ *Do I have a clear and complete picture of how much it costs my customers in time, money, and hassle to do business with me and with my competitors?*

☑ *What is the single best way to improve that picture?*

☑ *Is there an opportunity to create a high-value intermediary (a "switchboard") between sellers and buyers that improves the economics of both?*

☑ *Have I designed a program that builds on the switchboard position to work with others as business partners and to continue reducing customers' costs* and *sellers' costs?*

N I N E

ANDREW GROVE

The Two Steps Ahead Business Design

- *Have I struggled to keep my business in the profit zone in an industry that has seen enormous growth and innovation?*

- *What is the power equation in my industry? How can I manage it?*

- *Can I manage more of the value chain in my industry?*

- *Can I take my company into the profit zone by owning the relationship with the end user?*

THE MOVIE *Indiana Jones: Raiders of the Lost Ark* opens with the young archeologist, Indiana Jones, cleverly navigating his way through an ancient tomb in order to obtain a relic of great worth. He overcomes the obstacles that lie in his path: deadly traps, a den of spiders, an assistant who double-crosses him, and much more. After a series of harrowing escapes, he finally gets the artifact. But as soon as he picks it up, he triggers the mother of all traps, and the ancient tomb begins to fall apart. Frantically, he races back through the passages. Right behind him is a giant boulder that threatens to obliterate him should he fail to stay two steps ahead of it.

Moviegoers watch this scene and their hearts race. Can Indiana Jones stay ahead of the giant boulder? If he doesn't, he will surely perish. Somehow, Jones manages to stay two steps ahead of it as he races out to safety.

Andrew Grove at Intel might as well be Indiana Jones in the ancient temple. Like Jones, Grove has managed to overcome all of the obstacles that lay in Intel's path. Like Jones, Grove has grabbed the valuable relic—he is in the profit zone, in a very big way. And, like Jones, Grove has a great boulder racing behind him. If the competition catches up, Intel will be flattened. But, like Jones, Grove manages to stay two steps ahead, thereby keeping Intel in the profit zone. But it is a precarious lead. As soon as Intel is no longer two steps ahead, Intel will be out of the profit zone.

Who benefits from understanding Intel's two steps ahead business design? Anyone who is in a neck-and-neck race with a great competitor and can't break away. Anyone whose traditional sources of growth, profit, and power are losing value. Anyone whose innovative efforts will become ten times more valuable if accomplished in half the time. And anyone who can leverage a franchise in a remote region of the value chain in a way that strengthens its economic position throughout the chain and ends up as core—vs. remote—in the eyes of consumers.

Everyone in business talks about compressed cycle times, the increased rate of technological innovation, and similar issues. Yet who has found a way to manage these factors in a way that creates and protects extraordinary levels of profit?

Grove has done this at Intel. In its 28-year history, the company has produced more strategic history and more strategic business design innovations than other companies have done in a century. It has faced more life-or-death junctures, made more do-or-die decisions, and created more value than almost any other company its age.

Grove has found a way to manage these crises over two decades of change. How? By constantly causing the organization to keep a laserlike focus on customer priorities and on the profit zone. From his first days at Intel, Grove has used customer-centric thinking and has provided customers with what they want, be it functionality, solutions, higher processing power, or a brand. Grove has managed to control the value chain in the PC industry, and, unlike his early competitors, has made the distinction between the apparent customer and the economic customer. Other chip manufacturers have always considered their customer to be the PC manufacturers. In contrast, after establishing the x86 standard with the PC OEMs (original equipment manufacturers), Grove shifted his customer focus to the end user. And his understanding of this customer has allowed Intel to remain two steps ahead of every other contender in the computing industry.

Furthermore, Grove has employed profit-centric thinking during his tenure as CEO of Intel. He recognized that it is better to be two steps ahead on one product than at parity on a dozen others. Grove saw where the profit zone could be and did what was necessary to take Intel there.

THE EARLY DAYS

Intel was founded on profit-centric thinking. In the late 1960s, the memory component of computers consisted of magnetic cores that accounted for 60 percent of the computer's total cost. This older technology provided a great target for new breakthroughs in silicon technology. Bob Noyce, Gordon Moore, and Andy Grove decided to build a company that would participate in this emerging market. They were determined to make the company a leader in the industry.

Based on their expertise in the emerging "chip" technologies, Intel introduced its first general-purpose microprocessor, the 4004, in 1971. Whereas other companies in the computing industry at the time presumed that the value of technology would speak for itself, Intel took a dramatic departure and went to great lengths to prove the value of microprocessors to the customer. Its "Intel Delivers" campaign targeted a wide range of users, such as industrial equipment manufacturers, automotive firms, instrumentation companies, and manufacturers of cash registers, calculators, and coin changers. This included literally thousands of firms engaged in thousands of projects that could use microprocessors.

What distinguished the Intel Delivers campaign from other marketing campaigns of its time was the effort Intel expended for each customer. Rather than rely on the customer's ability to find uses for a great technology, Intel took it upon itself to develop a business design that identified the customer's needs and clearly explained how an Intel microprocessor would address those needs. Intel was not selling merely products—it was selling solutions to customers' problems. It was enabling its customers to run their own business better, through improved product development and faster time to market.

Intel's early focus on the customer gained in intensity throughout the 1970s. For example, Grove rallied the company behind one of the shortest corporate objectives in modern business history: "Book Ford." Ford was an attractive customer because it represented so many units of output. Most industrial equipment makers produced several thousand units per year. Ford produced millions. Grove knew that if Intel and its products were to be a success, he would have to land highly profitable accounts such as Ford. In pursuit of this objective, a tremendous sense of organizational alignment swept the company; across all functions, employees focused on a common aim. The objective took years to realize. In 1981, one of Intel's early microcontroller designs for Ford, the EEC-III, was used on a limited number of cars. By 1983, Ford was producing 150,000 cars a month with Intel microcontrollers.

OPERATION CRUSH

Book Ford was merely a precursor to the type of profit-centric and customer-centric thinking that would come to characterize Intel's business model in coming years. For the industry, it should have been the harbinger of a dangerous rival that was playing for keeps. Most competitors would not realize this until it was too late.

In the semiconductor industry in the late 1970s, Intel and Motorola were neck and neck. Intel realized that, should this continue, the chances of achieving attractive profitability were slim to none. Somehow, Intel had to create a business design that would put it two steps ahead of Motorola—and squarely in the profit zone. The profit zone was in the customer, not in the product. Intel would take no prisoners in creating this business design. Such was the genesis of "Operation Crush."

On its face, Operation Crush was one of those "impossible objectives" that the management literature so highly recommends to the ambitious manager—impossible because of the overwhelming scope of its results. Formulating impossible objectives is not difficult; achieving them is. The crucial moment that determines whether an impossible objective can be realized is when colleagues and employees look a manager in the eye and feel, unambiguously, that the manager is serious about the impossible objective. "Uh-oh," they think, "this is for real. We are not going to get away from this one. He really means it."

The articulation of Operation Crush was enough to inspire the full spectrum of emotion—from inspiration to fear—within the organization. The goal of Operation Crush was to capture 500 new design wins in 2 years, not 50—not 200, but *500*. (It is important to note the focus on the customer account rather than on Intel's market share. Although many industries, such as advertising, accounting, and consulting, use customer accounts as the measure of success, most are service industries. Operation Crush was unique in a computing industry populated by product-centric business designs that are focused on market share of units sold as the primary measure of success.)

Operation Crush was run from a war room; a world map jabbed with pins identified design wins. SWAT teams of engineering, applications, and marketing people were combat-ready for countering any threat to a prospective design win.

The first step in Operation Crush was to generate sales leads. Company-wide, Intel generated tens of thousands of sales leads, in order to achieve its targeted number of design wins. Design wins would not, however, just trickle down from sales leads. The blueprint for Operation Crush reflected the fact that Intel would have to sell—and sell hard. Drawing on the lessons from Intel Delivers, the Operation Crush program focused on creating positive results for the customer rather than focusing only on the sale of specific Intel products.

The first area of focus was time. Time-to-market was important from the customers' perspective because it provided differentiation for their products. Time-to-market was important from the supplier's perspective because the first entrant could charge a price premium. Operation Crush focused product development efforts on time-to-market as a key performance variable for the entire organization.

This focus on time-to-market was not enough to yield the design wins that Operation Crush mandated. The irony was that customers were still wary of the new technology, so the first entrant had the additional burden of proving its worth to customers. As a result, customer solutions became the second key element of the

Operation Crush campaign. In the Intel Delivers campaign, Intel's marketing division had sold programming and other development tools to help create the customer's need for the microprocessor. Now, in the Operation Crush battle, Intel went beyond that and offered field support. It created an education program about the microprocessor, with more than 50 presentations and seminars a year. It compiled a handbook that mapped the future evolution of Intel's products and systems, to give comfort to customers who were concerned about future compatibility. It broadened its product line of chips and ancillary products, to make the customer's design and development tasks easier. Operation Crush was structured to remove customers' concerns regarding the incorporation of Intel's products into their designs.

Grove's efforts worked. Operation Crush was a total success. Intel's customer-centric approach was well received by customers, and the company received 2,500 design wins in 1980. Intel's products became ubiquitous; they were incorporated into hundreds of new applications every quarter. With this ubiquity came power. This track record of success was a key factor in one of Intel's biggest (history would say, the single biggest) design wins: IBM's selection of Intel's 8088 chip over Motorola's competing design for a forthcoming personal computer—the IBM PC. The IBM design win was the most significant win of Operation Crush. Winning Ford had been big; winning IBM was bigger.

Intel's rise to preeminence in the microprocessor market was not a foregone conclusion. In 1978, two years prior to the success of Operation Crush, Motorola had introduced its 68000 chip. It received rave reviews from industry experts. And Motorola had nearly twice the semiconductor sales of Intel. In the early days, Motorola was in at least as strong a position (if not stronger) as Intel for dominating the microprocessor market in the decade ahead. Yet, by 1984, all of that had changed. Intel's 8086 microprocessor was outselling Motorola's 68000 microprocessor by 9 to 1. Why the shift?

It is often said that Intel's value growth in the 1980s was the result of serendipity—being chosen as the chip for the IBM PC was pure luck. But strategists familiar with the industry know luck had nothing to do with it.

In 1978, both Intel and Motorola had the resources to execute Operation Crush—Motorola's income was $83 million, Intel's was

$87 million. Yet Intel took a dramatic and unconventional departure with its business design. Intel sold more than just the product. It sold solutions: the product plus the applications plus the support. Moreover, Intel's differentiation efforts were exceptional in their organizational alignment and tenacity.

Motorola began the race with a better product; Intel won it with a better business design.

FOLLOW THE VALUE, NOT THE VOLUME

While Operation Crush was creating a two-step lead for Intel's microprocessor business, a different drama was unfolding in Intel's other major business: DRAMs, or Dynamic Random Access Memory chips. In the late 1970s and early 1980s, the market for DRAMs was growing frenetically. DRAM memory dramatically changed the economics of building computers (remember, core magnetic storage was 60 percent of the cost of a computer in the late 1960s) and adoption was extremely rapid. Revenue and unit volumes were high. The market held lots of value, but as Japanese competitors—Fujitsu, Hitachi, Mitsubishi, Matsushita, Toshiba, and NEC—entered the market, they viciously sought cost leadership. As their manufacturing techniques improved and the dollar gained strength, the Japanese product poured into the U.S. market. In 1978, U.S. DRAMs had outnumbered Japanese DRAMs by 3 to 1. Intel had succeeded in becoming a market leader. By 1985, the situation was totally reversed and Intel was losing money. The DRAM business was very asset-intensive—getting down the cost curve demanded continued investment in capacity—and offered a limited return on capital. Moore (then CEO) and Grove (then President) saw that staying in memory chips would require investing all of the corporation's assets in what appeared to be a war of attrition. Intel's overall performance was suffering as it maintained its commitment to producing DRAMs.[1]

They realized that DRAMs had become a no-profit zone. Intel had to quit the field and deploy its resources where the probability of success was much higher. This was a hard-nosed decision not easily made from either a business or an emotional standpoint. Intel was founded to make memory chips! Leaving the business would be like a book publisher deciding not to publish books or a carmaker deciding not to make cars. But Japanese memory chips, based on improved manufacturing techniques, were flowing into the U.S. market. Intel's survival required turning its back on everything that had made it great. There were deep layoffs—nearly 30 percent of Intel's workforce was let go. But Intel's leaders decided that Intel had to shift to a profit zone in which future value would be created, not just follow the volume and compete for market share in a capital-intensive business that was profitless.[2]

CREATE UNIQUENESS

After the painful retreat from the DRAM market, any fuzziness around Intel's future identity was gone. The company's future was now pinned to the microprocessor; there was no safety net. Faced by this sobering truth, Grove focused attention and resources on optimizing the business design around the microprocessor. In creating this focus, he fundamentally altered key elements of the business design, changing the company's value capture, primary source of differentiation, and scope.

Throughout the early 1980s, Intel had licensed its microprocessor design to AMD and other manufacturers of the microprocessor. For the 8086 microprocessor, Intel had 12 licensees who captured 70 percent of the market. Intel licensed its microprocessor design for four reasons. First, IBM required its suppliers to second-source the product and the technology. In this way, if a mishap befell Intel, IBM would be assured a constant flow of chips. Second, encouraging other producers of the same microprocessor pushed the Intel architecture as the de facto standard. Third, Intel was uncertain about investing the capital required for manufacturing microprocessors until the demand was certain. And fourth, by licensing its technology, Intel discouraged its competitors from building up their own capability for designing future generations of chips.[3]

As it moved out of DRAMs and focused on the microprocessor, Intel shifted its value capture approach away from licensing.

Intel's decision to steer the value capture and scope elements of its business design away from licensing had important implications for the company's basis of differentiation. When Intel had pursued a licensing strategy, its basis of differentiation was superior chip design and architecture. However, competitors quickly began reverse-engineering the nonlicensed designs, effectively cloning Intel's chips as little as 12 months after launch. In this environment, Intel realized that its long-term viability depended on developing and marketing successive generations of chips faster than the cloning companies could reproduce them. Not only did rapid development create new high-margin, low-competition product lines for Intel, but it hobbled the clone makers by reducing the customer appeal and pricing levels of their older, reverse-engineered chips. Speed became the essence of Intel's new business design and its primary source of differentiation.

Intel's focus on creating a speed-based business design was only reinforced by an understanding of the power equation in the industry. Intel was one of the earliest companies to experience the force of unlimited customer power. Intel sold to giants. Its customers were IBM, Compaq, Toshiba, and NEC, all megabuyers. What power did Intel have before these Goliaths—especially if the Goliaths had good alternatives? Absolutely none, unless Intel could be unique, even if only for a year or two. If it could be unique, it could at least partially rebalance the power equation toward a more level and more profitable relationship.

Intel did not achieve its speed advantage without a tremendous struggle. Thousands of hours of management time and attention poured into making the improvements required at every level of the development process.

Technology investment played a critical role as well. From 1984 to 1988, Intel invested $250 million in computer-aided design—more than any other semiconductor maker. This investment in process improvement represented about 20 percent of Intel's total R&D spending.[4]

Eventually, this accumulated effort and investment paid off in significantly shortened product development cycles. From 1985 to 1989, Intel reduced development time on many of its chips by more than 50 percent, from 90 weeks to 44 weeks. The cycle compression effect worked in very large-scale projects as well. Even though the

486 was vastly more complicated than the 386 (with 4x the transistors and 2.5x the cost), its lead time was shorter. How long would it take the competition to copy this feat? Certainly more than a year. The competitive lead was increasing.[5]

Diligence in technology leadership and cycle reduction led to an additional benefit for Intel. It restarted a powerful upward spiral in attracting and retaining engineering talent in the company. Its rebuilt reputation was a powerful magnet for many of the best engineers in Silicon Valley. In an industry known for high turnover, upper-level churn at Intel was lower than that of the industry.

Compressing the cycle increased Intel's lead over the competition, but Grove was not satisfied. He recognized yet another business design choice that was available.

Grove believed that by parallel-processing the development of three different generations of chips, Intel could gain significant differentiation from its competitors. So, instead of beginning a development effort every four years, Intel would initiate a development effort almost every year. The P6 generation development effort was announced in 1990, a year after the beginning of the P5 design. The P7 came even sooner after that. To implement this staggered development plan, Intel expanded the scope of design activity to three locations: California, Oregon, and Israel.

This combination of rapid and staggered development created profound economic consequences for Intel and its competitors. For Intel, six-quarter exclusivity on the latest generation of microprocessors created pricing flexibility and high margins. Grove recognized that the overwhelmingly predominant need for customers was processing power. The more power a processor had, the greater its functionality for the consumer. PC OEMs competed to bring the latest Intel generation to market as quickly as possible. Consumers were willing to pay more for greater functionality. Competitors tried in vain to make up the lead by intensifying their reverse engineering. Yet, as competitors launched a cloned chip, Intel reduced prices rapidly, severely limiting the window of profit opportunity and investment cash flow available to imitators of its technology. Competitors such as AMD saw operating margins rise as the volume of processors increased, and then fall as Intel shortened its product development cycle to put it two steps ahead (Exhibit 9.1).

EXHIBIT 9.1   *Operating Margin Comparisons*

	1986	1987	1988	1989	1990
AMD	–13%	–3%	3%	6%	–3%
Intel	–11%	19%	25%	22%	28%

The business model that Grove created—a combination of focused investment, speed, and timing—had become a powerful profit engine. It was squarely in the profit zone.

COMPETE FOR VALUE IN THE CHAIN

Most companies would have been content at this point. Grove's profit-centric and customer-centric moves had leveled early competitors. In the late 1970s, the Operation Crush initiative had destroyed Motorola's hope of capturing the industry's strategic control point, the 2-year lead. Exiting the DRAM business in the mid-1980s moved Intel away from a space that was becoming a no-profit zone because of Japanese competition. And Grove had successfully created uniqueness through an accelerated development program that left competitors behind. But Grove was still wary. At the height of its success, it was time for Intel to begin looking for its next problem and its next business design move.

Since the early 1970s, Intel had been more than a chip company; it had also been in the systems and peripherals business. Its involvement in that business had allowed Intel to deliver solutions to its customers during the Operation Crush days, and that capability had given Intel significant control over the demand for its products. It was able to influence design and product development. As Grove looked at Intel's customers, the PC OEMs in the late 1980s, he realized that any lapses in functionality improvement by those customers would slow the growth of consumer demand and would threaten Intel's basis of differentiation. Intel's Two-Steps-Ahead business design (Exhibit 9.2) was predicated on significant demand growth for processing power. Grove couldn't leave that to chance—or to the OEMs.

Grove decided to push his business further and move Intel down the value chain. Intel started making chipsets, and then motherboards, the guts of a computer, for machines that used Intel chips. Grove's move increased Intel's influence over the entire value chain. When PC makers were not improving as rapidly as they should, Intel could intervene by selling more motherboards to new

EXHIBIT 9.2 *Intel's Business Design: "Two Steps Ahead"*

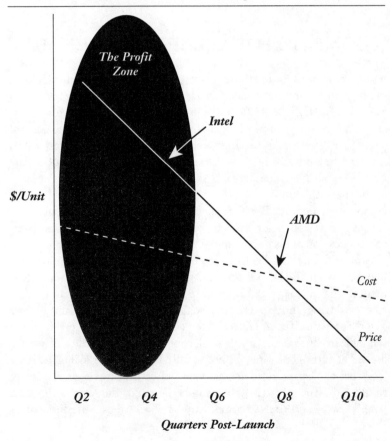

Quarters Post-Launch

entrant PC manufacturers. By making motherboards—the most technically challenging part of the PC—Intel reduced entry barriers to the PC assembly business. Intel effectively commoditized the PC market and seized the strategic control point of the personal computer value chain.

This strategic control enables Intel to have an impact on the "rate and pace" of the game for the entire industry. This means that other players must adapt to Intel's product development, capability, and product launch schedules. Hardware vendors have a choice of either running an engineering and development schedule to the launch schedule of Intel's processors, or losing significant market share and profitability for a 3-month cycle.

OWN THE CONSUMER RELATIONSHIP

Grove had established strategic control of the PC value chain, an important vantage point from which to manage the hardware vendors. Grove's customer-centric thinking, however, pushed the company still further out in the value chain. He asked: What gave him a strong position with hardware vendors? The answer that came back could be summed up in one word: end users. The end users could not be satisfied; they had a need for greater and greater processor speed. They wanted bigger and better applications, and those required more powerful processors. So long as the end users clung to that need, Intel could maintain its Two-Steps-Ahead business design.

Grove had to find a way to develop a relationship with these customers. He knew Intel had to begin consumer advertising. One can imagine the debates that swirled around consumer advertising issues at Intel. The powerful voice of strategy traditionalists said, "Our customer is the PC OEM. Our focus should be on that customer, on building a stronger position with that customer, on maximizing our share with that customer." But by moving Intel further into the value chain, Grove had transformed the traditional supplier–customer relationship into a contest for power in the value chain. In this contest, the party that owned the relationship with the end users could gain the upper hand. The company initiated the "Intel Inside" marketing campaign.

The Intel Inside campaign was another in a series of moves to rebalance the power equation in the industry. It was also a move that was not possible in the late 1980s because consumers were not a factor in the power politics of the computing world. Consumers were hardly a factor even in 1991. In fact, they were a tiny blip on the marketing radar screen. In 1991, while consumers spent $6 billion on TVs, set-top boxes, and VCRs, they spent less than $1 billion on PCs and peripherals. But that relationship was changing. Consumer PC spending grew at rates in excess of 50 percent. This growth momentum meant that consumer spending on PC hardware could exceed consumer spending on TV-related hardware by the mid 1990s. The shift in consumer buying behavior created a brand-building opportunity for Intel.

The Intel Inside campaign was an unorthodox move, especially when it was initiated—in 1991. Many observers were puzzled. Some believed that because Intel's business model generated too much profit, consumer advertising was a good way of using up excess earnings in a way that might prove beneficial in the future. But for those who understood Grove, these observations reflected a fundamental misunderstanding of how he thinks. Grove abhors waste and bad moves. This move was not capricious; it was essential. It was a down payment on a powerful franchise with PC consumers. Intel Inside provided Intel with a tool that added value and helped manage the decisions of many PC manufacturers that used Intel chips. By 1995, when the brand was in full bloom, it successfully narrowed the degrees of freedom available to PC manufacturers in their chip selection decisions. The sheer magnitude of Intel's brand investment—more than $300 million—created yet another formidable obstacle for Intel's imitators.

Intel's advertising campaign transferred the consumer's attention and loyalty away from the PC OEM and toward the chip maker as the source of primary value to the customer. This switch changed the balance of brand equity in the value chain, taking it away from leading assemblers such as IBM, Compaq, and Dell, and toward Intel. Compaq was furious. Intel's motherboards technically enabled new low-cost competitors, and The Intel Inside campaign limited Compaq's central processing unit (CPU) choices. A public falling-out between Compaq and Grove made headlines for months. But what could Compaq do? Intel held the strategic high ground, the end-customer's relationship and confidence.

The other factor motivating franchise-building with consumers was the gradual convergence of the computing, communications, and entertainment (content) industries. Intel knew that, as these sectors began overlapping, the hottest PC market would be the home, where computers would compete with televisions for leisure time. Intel wanted to be the brand of choice in this rapidly expanding arena.

EXHIBIT 9.3   *Intel's Business Design Reinvention*

	1980	1985	1997	2002
Customer Selection	• Industrial equipment manufacturers	• PC OEMs	• PC OEMs • Consumers	
Value Capture	• Chip manufacturing and licensing	• Chip manufacturing	• Chip manufacturing • Limited value capture in motherboards • Brand premium	**?**
Differentiation/ Strategic Control	• Technology	• Speed	• Speed • Motherboards • Consumer brand • Compatibility	
Scope	• Memory chips and solutions	• Processor chips	• Processor chips • Chip sets • Motherboards • Value chain management	

The story of Andy Grove and Intel is not the story of a single move, a single reinvention, a single innovation. Grove, probably more than any other reinventor, created enormous value through a series of moves that created a mutually reinforcing system of strategic control (Exhibit 9.3). Each of the moves—Intel Delivers, Operation Crush, quitting DRAMs, Two Steps Ahead, value chain control, and building a consumer brand—was brilliant in its own right, but the mindset that allowed for continuous reinvention in the face of success is the most unique element.

Competing against Intel is a tall order. By the time a competitor begins to make headway in responding to the first business design innovation, Intel has made two new moves that put it further ahead (Exhibit 9.4).

EXHIBIT 9.4   *Intel vs. AMD: Market Value Growth*

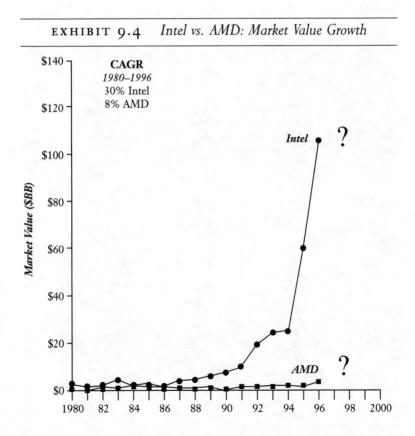

By 1995, Intel had so outdistanced its rivals that its primary economic pressure came not from competitors, but from direct customers and the software makers' failure at developing exciting new and power-hungry applications. Intel's problem wasn't AMD—which struggled to clone the Pentium chip—but the OEMs to whom it sold chips. The OEMs were still too powerful and too slow. Intel contained their power through consumer brand-building and forward-integration into motherboards. Now it focused on provoking more rapid performance improvement on their part. Intel was caught in a classic value-chain squeeze, when weakness in a neighboring part of the value chain can seriously impair a leader's performance. Intel used its strategic position and gained control of the industry's pace of improvement. Laggards, beware! If the OEMs don't innovate, Intel will . . . two steps ahead of anyone else.

BUILDING A "TWO STEPS AHEAD" BUSINESS DESIGN
Pilot's Checklist

☑ *Have I selected a subset of projects to create a 2-year lead, rather than parity for all?*

☑ *Have I done* everything *possible to compress the cycle?*
  Resourcing
  Brilliant project management
  Technology
  Parallel processing

☑ *Having gained the lead once, what am I doing to*
  Maintain it?
  Increase it?

TEN

MICHAEL EISNER

The Profit Multiplier Business Design

- *Is more and more of my business becoming an intellectual property business?*

- *What are the rules for creating maximum value growth in that kind of business?*

- *How many companies in my industry have fully exploited those rules?*

IN 1984, the Andersens, a family of five, living in St. Louis, were planning a summer vacation. They were trying to decide where they could go with their three young children. As they discussed possibilities, Bob Andersen remembered that a friend from work had talked about his family vacation at Walt Disney World. They'd all had a good time and it sounded like fun. Bob mentioned Walt Disney World to his wife, Jane. She was interested. Neither she nor Bob had been to Epcot Center, which had opened several years ago. "Why not?" they decided.

The trip went well. The kids enjoyed the rides and the games. And Bob and Jane enjoyed the meals and the weather. In fact, the vacation couldn't have been much better. Bob also thought that the trip was fairly economical. The plane tickets for the whole family had cost about $800; the hotel, $700 for the week; meals and snacks, about $500; tickets for the park, $200 for the four days that the

Andersens visited; and the miscellaneous items, like a rental car and merchandise for the kids, $500. Not a bad deal for under $3,000.

Six years later, in 1990, the Andersens were planning a winter vacation. The kids, now older, were even more difficult to travel with. They didn't like long car rides, and their trip that summer, to some National Parks, had been less than successful. Although it had been fairly inexpensive, it was difficult to organize, there wasn't enough for the kids to do, and the weather was lousy. Bob and Jane struggled for a few weeks to come up with an idea. In the end, it was the kids who decided for them. They had been watching the Disney Channel and asked when they could go back to Walt Disney World. A good question. Bob had just bought his daughter a set of Little Mermaid toys for Christmas. And his son was still watching the video of *Dick Tracy* that Bob had bought. In fact, now that Bob thought about it, his kids had been watching high-quality Disney videos for the past 5 years. Walt Disney World might be just right.

The trip turned out to be remarkably hassle-free. Walt Disney World had changed significantly since their visit in the summer of 1984. There were some new rides and a lot more strolling cartoon and movie characters, and Bob even got in a few rounds of golf while Jane took the kids swimming. Although the trip had cost almost $4,000, a lot more than the trip to the National Parks, it was worth it. Bob had spent $1,000 on plane tickets, $1,100 at a Disney resort, and about $750 on food. He didn't need a rental car because the shuttles at the Disney resort picked them up at the airport, and the internal transportation ferried them to all parts of the park every day. The park fees—about $600 for 6 days—seemed a bit higher than the last trip, but there were more areas to visit and more rides at each area. Bob spent almost $300 on various merchandise for the kids and a bit more on miscellaneous stuff. But, he figured, the extra cost was easily worth the convenience.

*   *   *

Comparing the two trips, Disney captured a much larger share of the Andersens' spending in the second trip. Of the $2,700 the Andersens spent in the first trip, Disney captured $200 for the tickets to the park, $200 for the meals and snacks they ate in the park, and about $100 for the merchandise they bought their kids. All told, Disney captured less than 20 percent of the Andersens' spending.

However, on their second trip, of the almost $4,000 that the Andersens spent in 1990, Disney captured all of it but the plane tickets—that's 75 percent. Disney owned the hotel, the park, the merchandise, and the restaurants that served the Andersens. Disney provided just about everything for a high-convenience, low-hassle vacation. And the Andersens had no complaints. Disney had found a way to provide a better experience for its customers and to increase its profits by capturing a significantly larger share of its customers' spending.

* * *

Today, nobody works harder for Michael Eisner than the animated characters that have been the staple of the Disney organization for the past 60 years. The basis of Eisner's—and Disney's—success has been a business design that maximizes the value capture of this intellectual content. One piece of intellectual property—be it Mickey Mouse, Aladdin, or The Lion King—works not once or twice but seven, eight, or ten times to provide both a better experience for customers and greater profit growth for shareholders.

With Disney, it seems self-evident that Mickey and his colleagues are the basis for knitting the entire Disney empire together: films, theme parks, theme park hotels, video sales, retail sales and licensing. But what may be self-evident is not necessarily easy to accomplish, otherwise all of Disney's competitors would have mastered it. Compare Disney's business design to that of one of its major competitors, Time-Warner (formerly Warner Brothers, Time, Inc., and Turner Broadcasting). Although not a perfect comparison, it does offer insight into the successful sequence of business design choices that Disney has made. Like Disney, Time-Warner has movie studios, theme parks, and a powerful franchise in animated entertainment. Yet, unlike Disney, Time-Warner has not moved as quickly and aggressively to pursue innovative value capture opportunities, or to build distribution capabilities that maximize the worth of its creative assets (Exhibit 10.1).

For example, despite having a rich cast of animated characters led by Bugs Bunny, Superman, Batman, and even Alfred E. Neuman of *Mad Magazine* fame, Time-Warner has not moved as aggressively as

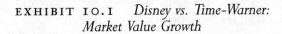

EXHIBIT 10.1   *Disney vs. Time-Warner: Market Value Growth*

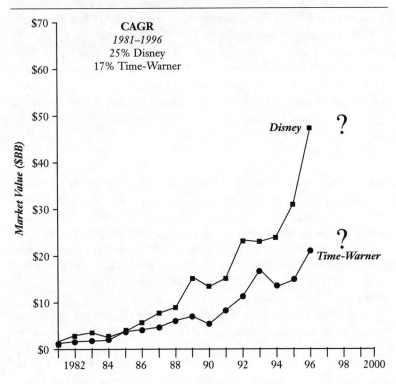

Disney into merchandise licensing. Only in the past 3 years has the company built distribution capabilities emulating Eisner's moves into retailing.

Time-Warner's use of its animated characters at the Six Flags theme parks represents another comparison of different rates of value capture from intellectual property. Although fully 85 percent of the U.S. population lives within a day's drive of a Six Flags park, the company only recently used the park network as a significant distribution mechanism. The appearance of "Batman" adventure rides finally linked the parks with Time-Warner's filmed entertainment business through common characters and experiences for the consumer population.

The business design that Michael Eisner and his team have built at Disney offers a significant model for managers in almost any industry with buried assets that await creative use. Eisner's business design innovation and creativity have been equal to or perhaps even greater than the artistic innovation and creativity for which Disney has historically been known. For instance, Eisner increased Disney's customer selection. He extended the audience from children to the entire family. And Disney has created a spectrum of offerings that can entertain these customers—children, families, or adults—for an hour, an evening, a day, or a week.

Eisner has also expanded Disney's scope. When he arrived at Disney in 1984, Disney produced box office movies, operated theme parks, and licensed consumer products. Today, in addition to these core activities, Disney's scope includes television production, TV and radio network broadcast, cable networks, videocassettes, retail stores, theme park hotels, vacation packages, sports teams, Broadway musicals, cruises, and much more.

From its inception, Disney differentiated itself as the family entertainment company. Now, thanks to Eisner's business design reinventions, such as his expansion of Disney's scope and customer selection, Disney has become the entertainment solutions company. Eisner has created a much larger profit zone for the company. Disney thinks harder about value capture than any other company. It invents or enters new businesses that interact with each other in a way that enhances their profitability. Disney's profit multiplier business model has created more value growth than any other media conglomerate in the entertainment industry.

Intellectual property created in the Disney system is much more profitable than property created in any other entertainment system, achieving the kind of significant resource generation that is the basis for sustained value growth.

Eisner did not have an easy time creating his profit multiplier business design. Before this design could be put into full effect, he had to reinvent the business design of Disney twice, starting with the epitome of "cost overrun" businesses: films. His first challenge was to build a business model that was capable of producing films profitably.

THE PROFITABLE
FILMMAKER MODEL

When Michael Eisner joined the Walt Disney Company in 1984, it housed three separate business designs under its corporate roof: filmed entertainment, consumer products, and theme park operation. After years of neglect, all three had slipped into value outflow.

Disney's movie studios, which had been considered a major power in the 1950s and '60s, were positioned in the industry's third tier. Excessive overhead costs (35 percent of revenue versus the industry average of 20 percent) had driven down profits every year since the late 1970s. The studios lost over $30 million in 1983 alone. And Disney's theme parks, once the world's favorite vacation destinations, had a decline in attendance during 3 of the 4 years prior to Eisner's arrival.

Eisner's first set of strategic moves at Disney was designed to restore Disney's basic operations to profitability. In a product-centered world, Eisner had to be concerned about Disney's basic product: films. If Eisner was unable to make Disney's films profitable, he would be unable to catalyze the profitable evolution of Disney's business model. His approach: resist and defeat the cost-overrun ethos of the film business.

His first step was to assemble the best executive team in the entertainment industry and charge it with instilling an intense work ethic in all of Disney's employees. The previous management had allowed the staff to become accustomed to short days. The new management expected early arrivals and late departures during the week, as well as time spent in the office on Saturday and Sunday. On the subject of weekends, a favorite saying around Disney was, "If you don't come in on Saturday, then don't bother coming in on Sunday."[1]

The intensity of Eisner's work ethic brought a new corporate ethos to Disney, and his techniques for generating ideas were revolutionary. Eisner created, evaluated, and then implemented ideas with an alacrity unrivaled since the days of Walt Disney himself, almost two decades earlier. Eisner personally led executive brainstorming sessions. Ideas that were bad or didn't fit in with Disney's business design were quickly killed; ideas that held promise were implemented immediately.[2]

In short order, Eisner succeeded in transforming Disney's culture from one of institutional memory and lack of energy into one that would actively and energetically support him as he reinvented Disney's business design a first, a second, and a third time.

Having created the appropriate success environment within Disney, Eisner was ready to challenge the power position held by the Creative Artists Agency (CAA) and other talent agencies. CAA was by far the most significant strategic factor in the industry. Founded in 1975, CAA had quickly grown into the most powerful talent agency in Hollywood. Its success was based not only on the extraordinary framing and negotiating skills of its founder and president, Michael Ovitz, but on an outstanding business model based on the inherent weaknesses of the traditional Hollywood production studio business design.

Ovitz's first and sharpest insight into the business of Hollywood was that studios depended on stars, but stars depended on stories. Whether Paul Newman or Robert Redford scored a major cinematic success was heavily dependent on the quality and power of the scripts that became available. Most of the Hollywood studios believed that the star made or broke the film. Ovitz believed that the story was the linchpin, and he allied himself with a New York literary agent who helped him locate great stories.

With the story as the seed of his new system, Ovitz put into effect his second major move: packaging. Armed with a great story, he would recruit writers to convert the story into a script, then combine the script with a director, lead actors, and supporting actors, creating one integrated unit. When Ovitz approached a studio, he held all the cards—story, script, and talent. This approach was very convenient for the studio: all of the key elements of a potential blockbuster were preassembled. But the studios paid dearly for this convenient package. Most of their profits went to CAA and to the talent that CAA represented.

CAA realized phenomenal profits from this business model because Ovitz was generating a fee from representing four to six key talents on each film, not just one. And, he was negotiating from a position of strength. He owned the strategic control point: the story AND the talent package. Ovitz's unique business model created an upward spiral for CAA. Over time, more and more talent flocked to CAA because the odds of success were higher as part of a CAA package than in a stand-alone negotiation. Ovitz had built a brilliant switchboard business model, interposing CAA between the studios and the talent. (See Chapter 8 for further discussion of switchboard business models.)

Eisner saw the power Ovitz and similar talent agency executives held in the entertainment industry and was determined not to allow them to gain control over Disney's business model. He made certain that Disney built the capabilities to assemble its own movies in-house. Disney wrote the script, found the stars, and provided the production capabilities. No other studio executives had done this so successfully since Louis B. Mayer and Samuel Goldwyn in the Golden Age of Hollywood.

Eisner, like Ovitz, knew that the success of a movie depended on its story. Disney had to have high-quality scripts, so Eisner hired a team of top-notch staff writers. Although Disney was far from being a top-level studio, aspiring writers were so abundant that the company could hire two dozen outstanding creative talents for less than a top star's financial guarantee for a single film.

In selecting stars, Disney always used brand name talent if it could find it on sale. Actors *du jour* were expensive, but down-on-their-luck actors were not. For example, when Disney was casting *Down and Out in Beverly Hills*, it capitalized on a low point in Bette Midler's and Richard Dreyfuss's careers and signed them for a fraction of what it would have had to pay the hottest stars. Opportunistic purchasing became a key part of Disney's business model. "There was no way to overestimate their stinginess," complained Dreyfuss's agent after the *Down and Out* contract negotiations. That sentiment would be shared by hundreds of Disney's suppliers, collaborators, and advisers during the years to come.[3]

Although it significantly distinguished itself with its own script writing and the hiring of off-peak actors, Disney was like all the other studios in that it produced its own films. However, unlike the other studios, Eisner saw that he could keep costs down. In moviemaking, angst and haggling over casting decisions can drain the energy out of the project team even before the cameras roll. Actual shooting stretches out month after month. Every day delivers another opportunity to spend over budget and destroy the profitability of a film. Many a Hollywood project has been nudged toward unprofitability in the name of artistic decisions that are ultimately lost on the audience. Then editing becomes a tug-of-war between the quality of the overall product and dozens of powerful egos reluctant to see their work end up on the cutting room floor. Eisner exercised draconian control over the budget to ensure that costs were kept at a minimum.

Eisner also worked to help spread Disney's financial risk. He saw, early in his tenure, that building stability in Disney's profit model required low-risk, moderately profitable films, not the high-risk, expensive films most studios were after. Disney needed to build a track record of turning out profitable films before it could move to making blockbusters.

Eisner worked with the Wall Street brokerage firm of E.F. Hutton to create Silver Screen Partners, a vehicle that allowed investors to finance Disney films. The investors received a share of the profits, but only after all expenses had been paid. If a given film was not profitable, Disney would have 5 years to return the investors' original contribution. As a result, investors' principal was safe, and they had upside potential. In exchange, Disney received an interest-free pool of funds with which to turn itself into a major studio. From 1985 to 1989, three successive Silver Screen Partners investments generated nearly $1 billion of financing for Disney films.

Within 2 years, Eisner had put in place the business design he needed to build a successful studio operation. *Down and Out in Beverly Hills* was released in January 1986. It performed respectably at the box office, and, thanks to Eisner's draconian cost control, it was profitable. In fact, fourteen of the first fifteen films produced by the new Disney were profitable.

With so many profitable films, Disney's studios were starting to build scale; by 1987, the Disney activity had grown to thirteen films, up from three in 1985. Eisner had restored profitability and productivity to Disney's moviemaking operations. The foundation had been laid for a business design that moved into a more lucrative profit zone (Exhibit 10.2).

THE BLOCKBUSTER MODEL

Although Disney's film production unit had become a viable business, it had not yet delivered the blockbuster needed to establish

EXHIBIT 10.2   *Disney's Business Design vs.*
The Industry Standard

	1986	
	The "Cost Overrun" Industry Standard	*The Disney "Profitable Filmmaker" Model*
Customer Selection	• Adults • Some children	• Children • Families
Value Capture	• Own the risk • Breakeven films	• Profitable films • Diversify the risk • Theme park receipts
Differentiation/ Strategic Control	• Star-driven	• Story-driven
Scope	• Many films • CAA/Agent packaged	• Few films • Disney assembled • Theme parks
Operating Approach	• Cost overrun	• Strict budget control; low-cost stars; low-cost locations

reputation and momentum, and to produce a significant effect on the market value of the company. As time ticked on, the pressure to deliver a blockbuster kept rising. Blockbusters were eminently more profitable than average films. Why? Consider the arithmetic. The costs for films vary from $20 million to well over $100 million (depending primarily on the stars, special effects, marketing budgets, and shooting location). The revenues for films range from $10 million to $300 million. A profitable film that has $50 million in revenues and $30 million in costs brings only $20 million to the bottom line. A blockbuster that has $300 million in revenues (to the studio) and $150 million in costs brings $150 million to the bottom line. Ever profit-centric in his thinking, Eisner sought to move Disney's business design from the profitable filmmaker model to the blockbuster model.

One of the key elements of Eisner's blockbuster business model was a move beyond product focus to a total system focus. Eisner recognized in his early years that a profitable film was based on a good story; he also recognized that a blockbuster needed much, much more than a good story and good execution. It needed: (1) a great marketing and launch campaign, and (2) great distribution.

A movie cannot become a blockbuster without a successful launch. The first ten days after release determine whether a film will succeed at the box office. That, in turn, determines how well it will do in the lucrative videocassette market. In this high-stakes environment, movie executives watch box-office receipts for the first ten days as vigilantly as the faithful watch for puffs of smoke from the chimney of the Vatican.

In 1987, Disney introduced sophisticated and extensive marketing and launch campaigns for two new movies: *Three Men and a Baby* and *Good Morning, Vietnam.*

Disney had originally prepared *Three Men and a Baby* for release around Christmas, one of the best release times for a movie. But, to let the movie build audience and momentum before the Christmas season, the launch was moved to late November.

Around Thanksgiving Day, scenarios of triumph alternated with visions of deepest despair in the fevered minds of Disney executives. Jeffrey Katzenberg promised to dance a jig on the conference table if the film took in more than $4 million on the Saturday after Thanksgiving. As the weekend approached, the entire company seemed to hold its breath.

On Monday morning, Katzenberg started dancing. In the weeks that spanned the holiday season, *Three Men and a Baby* went on past the magic number of $100 million. Disney had its first real blockbuster.

Eisner worked to continue Disney's success with a second blockbuster in *Good Morning, Vietnam.* The strategy for this marketing and launch campaign reflected the creativity and tenacity that would ultimately become key ingredients of Disney's blockbuster system. The star of the film, Robin Williams, best known as the quirky extraterrestrial on the 1970s sitcom *Mork & Mindy,* had a narrow franchise with the public. To broaden Williams's appeal, Disney lined up appearances on *Good Morning, America, Today,* and *Oprah.* It also ran two sets of commercials—a racy set intended to draw in 12- to 25-year-old viewers, and a "sensitive" set, for older audiences, featuring the hero's work with illiterate Vietnamese peasants. To gradually build the public's awareness of the film, Disney experimented with an unprecedented slow rollout, initially releasing *Good Morning, Vietnam* in only three cities.[4] By covering every base and using innovative methods to shore up potential liabilities, Disney significantly improved the odds of major box office success. Within two months, *Good Morning, Vietnam* had also generated over $100 million. Disney had turned the corner.[5]

Little by little, Eisner had been refining the basic profitable filmmaker business design into a blockbuster business design, supplementing strict cost control with marketing and launch techniques to maximize revenue.

The next component of Disney's blockbuster business design involved creating a more potent distribution capability that would improve both box office and videocassette sales.

When Eisner arrived, Disney's distribution unit, Buena Vista, was active only within the United States. To bring its films to market overseas, Disney contracted with the distribution unit of Warner Brothers. Eisner moved decisively to increase Buena Vista's domestic clout and to build global capabilities. Within 2 years, Buena Vista was challenging Warner Brothers for leadership in the film distribution industry. Better distribution helped sell more tickets. By investing in Buena Vista, Eisner raised the odds of creating future blockbusters in Disney's favor.

In 1985, Eisner saw that the penetration of VCRs into American homes was increasing rapidly. More homes were still viewing films via cable TV, but Eisner realized that the lines would soon cross, opening a lucrative videocassette market. Eisner was determined to release Disney's filmed entertainment on videocassette and release it effectively. When the company rereleased a big-screen version of *Pinocchio* in theaters at the end of 1984, he saw an ideal opportunity to pilot a videocassette launch.

The results were less than impressive: Disney garnered a paltry $9 million. Undeterred, Eisner followed the theater rerelease of *Sleeping Beauty* with a specially priced collectors' set of animated videocassettes, including *Sleeping Beauty*, *Dumbo*, and other titles. Eisner's tenacity was rewarded: 5 million copies were sold.[6] From his first success with videocassette sales, Eisner never looked back. Within 5 years, Disney owned 6 of the 10 biggest sell-through titles on videocassette.

The success of these animated films in videocassettes reinforced Eisner's focus on rebuilding Disney's animation unit. When Eisner had arrived at Disney, animation was out of fashion in American moviemaking. Studios that had invested heavily in animation technology and human resources in 1980–1981 had realized poor financial returns. A strike by the Screen Cartoonists Guild in 1982 further raised studio owners' anxiety about committing wholeheartedly to animation.

Eisner saw things differently. Consistent with his early assumptions, which were the basis for the profitable filmmaker business design, Eisner knew that an animation film would be successful if it had a good story, and that animated films had more long-term profit potential. Although relatively few animated films are released, they were often extremely successful. Of the 50 full-length animated films ever produced, 22 were on *Variety*'s list of the top 100 grosses of all time—and not one used the hottest stars.

Animated films had been financially successful because they had much more staying power than live-action films. Although *Pinocchio* lost money when it was originally released in 1940, subsequent rereleases grossed $64 million, much of which fell directly to Disney's bottom line. Furthermore, Eisner knew from the public's response in Disney's existing theme parks and in consumer product sales that the animated characters in a movie can be repackaged in many different ways. The multiple packaging opportunities represented by animated characters would later serve as the foundation for Eisner's profit multiplier business model.

Eisner had helped Disney further its value capture through rereleases of Disney classics. In rereleasing a film, Disney had to pay for only the marketing and launch and some minor distribution costs. It then captured all of the revenue from work previously completed. From 1987 through 1990, Disney rereleased *Snow White, Cinderella, Bambi, The Fox and the Hound, Peter Pan*, and *The Jungle Book*.

Motivated by animation's economic potential and the success of the rereleases, Eisner began to reconstruct the company's dilapidated animation division. The first major success of the revitalized unit was a collaborative effort that created *Who Framed Roger Rabbit?*,

EXHIBIT 10.3   *The Disney Blockbusters*[7]

Release Date	Title	Box Office Receipts in Millions of Dollars	
		United States	Overseas
1987	Three Men and a Baby	$168	$65
	Good Morning, Vietnam	124	35
1988	Who Framed Roger Rabbit?	154	160
1989	Honey, I Shrunk the Kids	130	80
1990	Pretty Woman	178	200
	Dick Tracy	104	50
1991	Beauty and the Beast	146	180
1992	Aladdin	217	250
	Sister Act	140	20
1994	The Lion King	313	400
	The Santa Clause	145	60

which surpassed all expectations, grossing over $300 million worldwide in 1988. By the 1990s, Disney's animation division had become a well-oiled blockbuster machine, capable of conceiving, producing, and marketing a major animated film every 12 months (Exhibit 10.3). *The Little Mermaid, Beauty and the Beast, Aladdin, The Lion King, Pocahontas, The Hunchback of Notre Dame,* and *Hercules* have all generated significant profit.

THE PROFIT MULTIPLIER
BUSINESS DESIGN

In the late 1980s, as his blockbuster business model proved its success in increasing shareholder value, Eisner saw that the rising costs of producing films were threatening to move even the blockbuster business model away from the profit zone. He intensified a search for ways to more aggressively utilize the hidden assets within Disney and keep Disney securely in the profit zone. He also looked for ways to make the components of his business interact in a way that would multiply the profitability of the system. Two major strategies emerged: (1) a profit-centric focus on distribution, and (2) the creation of solutions packages for family entertainment.

One of Eisner's most successful ventures has been to transform Disney from primarily a creator of content to a creator *and distributor* of content. Much of the profit in filmmaking lies beyond the content itself. To move Disney further along the value chain and capture more value, Eisner took control of more of the channels through which Disney products flowed, and he introduced several new channels (Exhibit 10.4).

From its creation in the 1920s until the early 1980s, Disney had been primarily a content creator: it made animated or live-action films that told stories suitable for children and families. Disney also had produced a TV show in the 1950s, currently had four theme parks, and made no small amount of money from licensing its characters. But Disney's creative, financial, and strategic energies had always been focused on developing characters and stories. Eisner rechanneled much of these energies into finding new ways to increase Disney's value capture from its creative assets.

One route that beckoned was to move Disney into retail. For six decades, Disney had licensed its characters to manufacturers, who then sold their various products to retailers. When Eisner came to Disney, this was still the practice. Roughly 7 percent of the wholesale price of the merchandise inspired by its characters was captured by Disney. In 1984, that translated into $100 million in revenue. Eisner saw that Disney could capture much more value from its products.

At another part of the value chain, retailers were capturing a significant amount of revenue and profit from Disney products. Eisner questioned the economic and customer logic of this arrangement and began to formulate a radical move. By entering the retail business, Disney could both share the retailers' economic rewards and create a more direct and valuable link with its customers. Eisner's emerging plan to enter retailing represented more than recognition

EXHIBIT 10.4   *Disney's Business Design Reinvention*

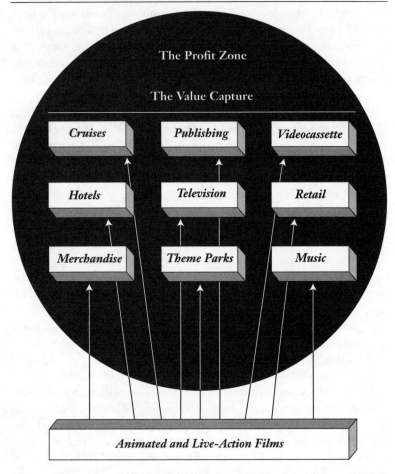

The Foundation

that business design moves are choices rather than "givens." Eisner was effectively reaching outside the existing spectrum of business design options to create a new one that held the promise of significant value growth.

Within the Disney organization, Eisner's intention was met with extreme skepticism. Running a chain of retail stores was remote from Disney's proven core competencies. How could Disney compete with the likes of Toys R Us, Macy's, and FAO Schwartz?

Eisner envisioned Disney Stores designed to provide customers with a better shopping experience. By leveraging the Disney brand name and the Disney service culture, he created a positive customer experience and a whole new vehicle for capturing value.

Despite doubts within the organization, Eisner carried the day. The first prototype Disney Store was opened in the Glendale Galleria, a suburban mall near Disney's home base in Burbank, California. It stocked a broad line of products at all price levels: Disney watches by Lorus, Disney collectors' coins by Rarities, and classic plush Mickeys and Donalds manufactured by Hasbro.

The Glendale Galleria store, in its first year, generated sales of $1,000 per square foot, double or triple the numbers posted by leading retailers. As soon as the Glendale store's financial performance became clear, the debate about whether to enter retailing was over. The debate now shifted to the issue of how to further develop the Disney retail concept. From 10 stores in 1988, the Disney retailing presence has expanded to some 630 stores around the world today.

In the video realm, the capacity of Buena Vista, Disney's distribution channel, has been gradually increased since 1984, first to additional national outlets, and then to international locales. Prior to Buena Vista, Disney distributed its movies through a competitor's distribution mechanisms. Now, Disney distributes its competitors' films. One of Buena Vista's greatest successes has been the distribution of Disney's videos. Audiences across the country have repeatedly elected to rent and buy Disney films more than films produced by any other movie studio. Eisner's decision to invest in Buena Vista has allowed Disney to capture even more value from the success of its films.

A third facet of Disney's move from content into distribution has been Disney's purchase of ABC/Capital Cities. As owner of a major TV network and several key cable channels, Disney now has more access than ever to the homes of America. Disney's studios can produce television shows—animated and live-action—for programming on ABC, thereby gaining enormous distribution of its content to consumers. ABC has access to 100 million American households, and typically, in prime time, reaches 20 million of them. ABC's ESPN network has promised Disney an important head start into the potentially lucrative markets of Asia.

In addition, the repeal of long-standing regulations now allows TV networks' fledgling studio operations to grow into full-fledged studios. The last thing Eisner needed was for ABC, CBS, and NBC, all with the cushion of guaranteed distribution, to start putting tens of millions of dollars into the studio business. With control of ABC, Disney preempts a major potential competitor.

The Disney profit multiplier business model also provides a safety net for Disney movies. Should films such as *The Hunchback of Notre Dame* or *Hercules* merely turn a profit rather than become blockbusters, Disney has numerous ways to still make money from them. Or, should a successor to *The Mighty Ducks* or *Angels in the Outfield* be an unexpected success, Disney's distribution network significantly raises the value of current Disney characters *and all future characters Disney creates*. Whenever a new character is conceived, it can be disseminated through hundreds of stores. With a film studio, a videocassette business, an aggressive licensing policy, proprietary retail operations, theme parks, and a major TV network, Disney can usher its characters from concept to first medium, to second medium, and to nationally distributed retail products in one smooth and rapid process. The emerging system ensured that a Disney character would work harder for shareholders than any characters owned by other companies. The profit earned by any single character multiplies itself across Disney's entire business system.

Disney is also able to multiply profit through its entertainment solutions, particularly the business design moves in the theme park division, which represented both an optimization of the existing system and a creative expansion of the boundaries of the business. Today, besides earning an attractive return on theme park assets, Disney owns the preeminent brand name in family vacations.

Eisner's first innovation to the theme park business design was a go-to-market mechanism intended to increase the number of visitors. Because press coverage of major events amounts to free advertising (witness the New York media attention to the new Disney presence in Times Square, and the attendance at the after-dark parade in June 1997), few managers in the theme park division thought that investing in advertising would yield attractive returns. Several managers disagreed with this thinking and tested an advertising blitz on local TV stations and in newspapers in

Chicago, Houston, and Kansas City. The results were extraordinary. Every $1 million in advertising brought 154,000 additional guests to Disney's parks. On the heels of the successful Midwestern advertising test, Eisner was quick to approve a massive advertising campaign for Disneyland's thirtieth anniversary in 1985.[8]

Increasing the number of visitors to the theme parks was only the first step. Eisner saw a greater potential for profit. In the mid- to late 1980s, customers were extremely pleased with Disney's theme parks: the quality was high, the facilities were spotless, the service level was extraordinary, and the customers' overall experience was first-rate. After personally reviewing several glowing customer satisfaction surveys, Eisner decided that the most immediately pressing concern was value capture. Prices had not been raised in several years, and the company had made no efforts (until its recent advertising experiments) to increase the number of visitors. The utility created for the customer was superb; the value captured by the company was not.

With roughly 30 million guests attending Disney theme parks each year, Eisner knew that a one-dollar increase for admission represented another $30 million in annual operating profit. Many individuals within Disney debated the wisdom of raising the admission prices at the theme parks. For Eisner, however, the question was not *whether* to raise prices, but *how*. The answer to the conundrum was gradualism. Ticket prices at Walt Disney World, which had been $18.00, went up to $19.50 in the summer of 1985 and then to $21.00 during the winter. In another 6 to 8 months, there was another increase. Overall, the ticket price rose to $28 per day by 1988, but the increase was introduced in increments under 10 percent over a period of 4 years. As a result, Disney generated an additional $310 million in operating profit without suffering negative publicity.

Noting the increased number of visitors to the theme parks despite the higher admission price, Eisner sought to have the company "own" a much larger portion of the customers' vacation. Vacation expenses can be broken down into several major categories: travel, hotel, food, entertainment, souvenirs, and sundries. Disney was making money primarily in three of these areas: food, entertainment, and souvenirs. In the areas where the theme parks were located, Disney was creating vast economic benefits for local hospitality and attraction owners—benefits not unlike those that Disney merchandise created for retailers. Eisner posed a question: What percentage of a family's vacation spending could be captured for Disney?

Unconstrained by any conventional definitions or concepts of what an entertainment company is supposed to do, he invested in different components of the retailing and vacation value chains, fundamentally reshaping Disney's business design. The common theme was a desire to simultaneously improve the quality of the customer's experience and control the largest possible percentage of the revenue and profit associated with the Disney experience.

First, Eisner dramatically increased the company's presence in hotels. Henceforth, Disney would play host to families not just for a day at the theme park but for their entire vacation. By 1992, the company had increased its hotel room ownership fourfold. And while industry occupancy rates in Orlando hovered around 68 percent, Disney averaged 90 percent.

Pursuing other initiatives designed to capture a greater share of the consumer's vacation money, Eisner increased Walt Disney World's entertainment options. During his tenure, the complex has added MGM Studios and other major attractions. The resort offers parents the opportunity to play golf, attend conferences, or even study at the Disney Institute. By moving from theme park operation to complete vacation solutions, Eisner was beginning to create a formidable brand name in away-from-home entertainment just as the stream of animated classics had created a brand name in at-home entertainment.

For those unable to take a vacation or those looking for a Disney experience closer to home, Disney offers another alternative: Club Disney, the newest component of the profit multiplier entertainment business model. Club Disney is a local facility that provides an opportunity for a 2–3 hour spontaneous visit, where families will find dozens of different play zones for children, a restaurant, and a retail store. The first Club Disney opened in Thousand Oaks, California. Before the doors opened, over 1,000 Disney fans were waiting to get in. Eisner plans to roll out Club Disney centers across urban and suburban locations around the world.

As in the case of all the reinventions, not every initiative was a success. Some were outright disasters. In building the profit multiplier business design, Eisner experienced several reverses. The launch of *Pinocchio* on videocassette, Disney's first videocassette venture, achieved only modest results, because of the low level of household VCR penetration at that time.

An even greater reversal came with the opening of Euro Disney, near Paris. Many assumptions and calculations about the European customer turned out to be fatally mistaken. The errors ranged from pricing to assumptions about travel behavior.

The financial results of Euro Disney in the first few years were very poor; nor did the company achieve high levels of customer satisfaction. It took many years of hard work to begin repairing the mis-steps surrounding the launch of Euro Disney.

Although there were numerous other strategic and tactical missteps in Disney's past decade, the company's continuing ability to develop new ways to multiply profitability seems remarkable. Realizing that sustained value growth depends on the business model that he has constructed rather than on Eisner himself, Eisner has incorporated a profit multiplier position into Disney's hierarchy. Termed the Vice President of Corporate Synergy and Special Projects, this position exists to guarantee that Disney captures maximum value from its intellectual content. By creating the position, and the mindset that goes with it, Eisner has raised the odds that Disney's business model will continue to multiply its profits into the future.

THE NEXT REINVENTION

Thirteen years ago, Disney's greatest challenge was overcoming near-terminal stagnation. Within a few years, Eisner had developed a profitable filmmaker business model that eventually outdistanced Paramount, the longtime market-share leader. As filmmaking costs rose, the profit zone shifted. Consistent blockbuster productions were needed to maintain consistent profits. Eisner developed a blockbuster business model that did just that. And then, in the late 1980s and early '90s, Eisner reinvented Disney yet again, this time building on the blockbuster model to create a profit multiplier business model. Eisner has managed to move Disney into the profit zone as required by the increasingly competitive intensity within the entertainment industry (Exhibits 10.5 and 10.6).

Today, the profit zone is poised to shift again. The company faces a serious set of competitors, including Viacom, Time-Warner, and

EXHIBIT 10.5   *Disney's Business Design Reinvention*

	1984	1990	1996	2002
Customer Selection	• Children	• Children • Adults	• Children • Adults • Families	
Value Capture	• Film sales • Licensing	• Blockbuster films • Theme park sales, hotels • Retailing	• Blockbuster films • Profit multiplier model	**?**
Differentiation/ Strategic Control	• Copyright	• Copyright	• Copyright • Distribution • Brand	
Scope	• Film making • Theme parks • Licensing consumer products	• Theme parks • Blockbuster movies • Retailing of consumer products • Videocassettes	• Blockbuster films • Disney assembled • Theme parks • Retailing • Television • Sports teams • Multiple other forms	

Rupert Murdoch's News Corp. (Fox), all of which have recently begun to imitate Disney's profit multiplier business model. For example, Viacom promoted the hit movies *Clueless* and, more recently, *Beavis and Butthead Do America* on MTV, a division of Viacom. Viacom is utilizing tactics very similar to Eisner's early marketing and launch strategies in Disney's blockbuster business model. Viacom has also begun using educational materials from Simon & Schuster and programming from Nickelodeon to create an education network. How Eisner will respond to these business model imitations remains to be seen.

Disney also faces a subtler internal threat—success itself. By becoming so broad and so complex, is the Walt Disney Company on the verge of the IBM or GM problem: being all things to all people?

EXHIBIT 10.6   *Disney Business Design Reinvention*

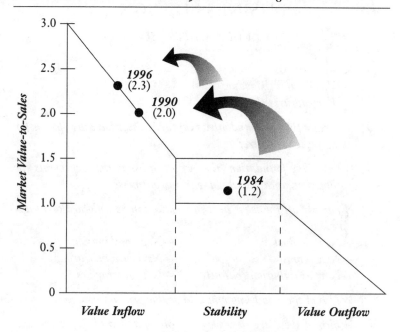

Value Creation Performance

Have Disney's customer selection and scope become too broad? Moreover, as Disney's business model increases in its complexity, it must struggle with new challenges. For example, although the acquisition of ABC/Capital Cities significantly increases Disney's distribution channels, will it cause even greater complexity? There are also new short-term pressures. ABC had solid No. 2 ranking when Disney acquired it, but it fell into the No. 3 position by the end of the season.

It remains to be seen whether this newly formed juggernaut—the largest, most profitable, and most intelligently constructed business design in the entertainment world—will maintain the flexibility necessary to stay ahead of its competitors and keep leading an industry that experiences a very high rate of value migration.

Eisner himself has stated, "A business needs to change itself every 7 years." If that is the case, Disney is ready for its next change.

BUILDING A "PROFIT MULTIPLIER"
BUSINESS DESIGN
Pilot's Checklist

☑ *In my business:*
  —*Who creates the value?*
  —*Who captures the value?*

☑ *If I create the value and others capture it, what are my options for changing that picture?*

☑ *What is the foundation, the key set of assets that represents the untapped or uncaptured value in my business?*

☑ *What are all the ways in which value can be unlocked or recaptured?*
  —*New product*　　　　　　—*New combinations*
  —*New forms*　　　　　　—*New customer groups*
  —*New distribution channels*　—*New geographies*

☑ *Which of these do I know how to do, but haven't done yet?*

☑ *Which of these are new ways to unlock and multiply value that my organization has to learn?*

☑ *Have I created a mutually reinforcing, profit-enhancing relationship among all of the components of my business?*

GEORGE HATSOPOULOS

The Spin-Out Business Design

- *Can I continually motivate and retain my most talented employees as my company grows?*

- *Is it necessary for my core businesses to be valued with one stock price?*

- *Is my company's stock price undervalued?*

- *Has the size of my company hindered its ability to stay one step ahead of my customers?*

IN 1990, Will Thompson was ready to make a career transition. He'd had a very successful career thus far. After college, he had worked at a big accounting firm for a few years, then took time off to get his MBA from a leading business school. Since then, he had been working at a major equipment manufacturer, and was learning a great deal as one of the company's most respected "fast track" managers. He was making a fair amount of money, had a great job, but just wasn't happy. He had strong entrepreneurial instincts and great business building skills. He had done a great job building two businesses in the past 6 years, but two things gnawed at him: (1) decision making was much slower than it needed to be and (2) his compensation growth was trapped in the structure of the company's pay scales.

He was looking for a new job. He had offers from several firms, but most of these companies were too large and too slow-moving for his taste. He thought about starting his own company in Silicon

Valley, but he just wasn't sure if he was willing to take that much risk or that much time. He knew a lot about building and running a business, but he knew that it would take a few years to build the resources to get something off the ground. He wanted to work with a company that was big enough so that he wasn't pressed to constantly find new resources, but still seemed small enough that it hadn't lost an entrepreneurial spirit.

The more he thought about it and the more he looked around, one company began to stand out in his mind as the only company that could meet his set of needs: Thermo Electron. He could work at Thermo Electron and enjoy the advantages of a small company as well as the advantages of a multinational. The fit seemed perfect. Will decided to explore Thermo Electron to see whether it was the best place for him to both develop his career and earn the types of equity rewards usually associated with entrepreneurs.

* * *

By 1982, Thermo Electron had been working with the same business design for almost 30 years. It had served the company and its founder, George Hatsopoulos, well. Sales were growing at a rate of nearly 30 percent as a continuous stream of new ideas for products came forth from the Waltham, Massachusetts-based company's R&D facilities. Yet Hatsopoulos was picking up signals of change in the world around him, persistent signals that suggested a need for a new business design.[1]

First, although government expenditures on environmental protection—a major Thermo Electron revenue source—had grown steadily throughout the 1970s, increasing at an average of 16 percent per year, spending had dropped by 4 percent in 1982. At the same time, the United States GDP fell in real dollars, indicating to many the onset of an economic recession and intensifying competition.

"The rug was pulled out from under our feet because of a recession that really hurt most of our customers," Hatsopoulos says. "Automotive companies, equipment manufacturers—customers with energy-intensive processes that relied on Thermo Electron to provide energy-saving technology—were no longer able to pay for our products. We lost a lot of our customer base."

The drop in spending, coupled with lessening public concern for environmental issues, indicated that Thermo Electron's future lay with different customers than those it had served in the past. Market changes necessitated a change in Thermo Electron's customer selection and product scope.

Hatsopoulos also believed that Thermo Electron's current business design was not being properly valued by the market.

"Thermo Electron's market value at the end of 1982 was $60 million," he says. "It had fallen from a peak of $180 million. But we calculated that if each of the parts went public, the value of Thermo Electron should be closer to $200 million."[2]

Hatsopoulos and the senior executives at Thermo Electron began thinking hard about new types of business design that would allow them to generate the most value for shareholders.

They were also concerned about Thermo Electron's employees.

During the start-up days of growth, everyone was excited and worked hard to see the company succeed. When Thermo Electron went public in 1967, Hatsopoulos motivated employees by rewarding them with stock options. But as Thermo Electron became involved in more and more technologies and the company grew in size, the force of these performance incentives became weaker. In a large company, the practice of rewarding divisional managers with stock options becomes independent of whether individual units or ventures succeed.

"Giving parent company stock options to each of our entrepreneurial groups meant that the reward would be the same regardless of whether any particular group was successful or not, because such options were not tied to specific achievements," Hatsopoulos says.

It was clear that Hatsopoulos needed a better way to motivate his most talented people.

At the same time, Thermo Electron's size was distancing him from his customers. In the 1950s, when Hatsopoulos started the company, he had hands-on involvement in both product development and client relationships; in 1982, as the head of a $240 million corporation, Hatsopoulos found it more difficult to manage day-to-day activities and still maintain relationships with his customers. Understanding customer needs was crucial. But his time also had to be spent running the Thermo Electron organization, instilling a "Know your customer" ethic in his employees.

Finally, Thermo Electron was hindered by a high domestic cost of capital. The public funding for Thermo Electron's projects was diminishing, and many of Thermo Electron's potential new technologies required several more years' funding before they could be brought to market. Hatsopoulos would have preferred debt financing for Thermo Electron; it would have allowed a tax deduction. However, he decided that given both the technical and business risk he was undertaking, it would be foolish to layer in the additional debt financing risk while his company had uncertain cash flow.

Seeing all these factors, Hatsopoulos knew that Thermo Electron's business design must change.

"We had a lot more on our plate than we had in the past," he says. "And with some of our businesses, like energy conservation, going downhill we tried to think of ways of accelerating the businesses on the drawing board. We needed a new way of managing start-ups. That's when the idea of taking our divisions public and letting them raise money for their own growth came along. This was the structure for our 'spin-out' strategy."

The spin-out design, Hatsopoulos believed, would address all the issues described above and, in addition, would create significant value for Thermo Electron.

And so, in 1982, Hatsopoulos began spinning out Thermo Electron's different businesses. Important to note is the distinction Hatsopoulos drew between Thermo Electron's *spin-out* strategy and the *spin-off* strategy that many large corporations use. Thermo Electron's spin-out strategy is just the opposite of the spin-off concept.

How so?

First, Hatsopoulos spun out Thermo Electron's core businesses; its most valuable businesses were the first to go. Most companies spin off only their peripheral businesses and keep their core businesses together. Hatsopoulos knew that in order to increase Thermo Electron's value, it was essential for Thermo Electron to spin out its primary businesses.

Second, Hatsopoulos decided that Thermo Electron would not sell its own shares of its subsidiaries.

"Very early in the process, we decided that we were never going to sell our shares," he explains. "Thermo Electron has never sold a single share of its subsidiaries. That's the opposite of what companies do with a spin-off. Most companies spin off subsidiaries to raise money for their core businesses. They say, 'We want to concentrate on our core business and we can raise capital for that by selling our peripheral businesses.' We wanted each subsidiary to have an independent valuation and raise capital for itself."

In this way, Thermo Electron would remain very connected to each one of its subsidiaries.

By spinning out Thermo Electron's businesses, Hatsopoulos allowed investors to view each individual company as a "pure play" in a particular market, offering specific products that they could understand. Hatsopoulos explains: "The only way to obtain capital at a reasonable price in this country is to focus on the entrepreneurial inclinations of certain investors, people who are not interested in a huge conglomerate because they cannot get a feel for anything it does. We repackaged our equities so that investors can buy a piece of any promising technology and business opportunity that excites them."

The change in Thermo Electron's business design made a significant difference in the way analysts looked at the company.

"Thermo Electron's culture does not seem like that of a company with 17,000 employees," according to NatWest securities analyst Paul R. Knight. "At many other large companies, it appears that several layers of management exist and that politics can be an element of individual success. Thermo Electron's decentralized structure and the fact that it allows employees to have the responsibility of running or being part of their own company creates a very open and non-politicized culture. Our experience is that several layers of parent company and subsidiary management are capable of handling institutional investor questions and that no employee has ever been told not to speak with stockholders."[3]

Setting up a structure of this type was especially important for a high-tech company. In the 1990s, technology stocks shot through the roof. Companies like Netscape created billions of dollars of value before posting even a single dollar in profit. Product cycle times became brutally short, but the huge potential upside of these stocks brought billions of investment dollars into this sector.

Hatsopoulos wanted a piece of this action back in 1982, and he knew that he had to set up a simpler way for investors to understand Thermo Electron's different technologies and markets. This new structure proved extremely successful as a value capture mechanism for Thermo Electron; it brought in the necessary capital for Thermo Electron's technological advancement.

EXHIBIT 11.1 *The Thermo-Electron "Spin-Out" Business Design*

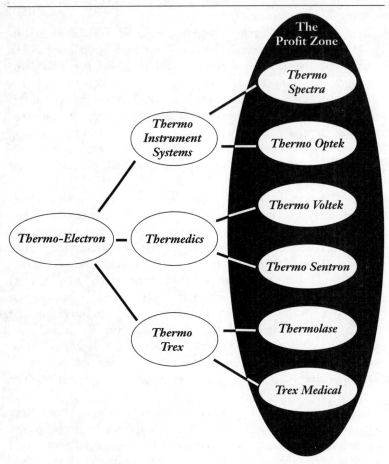

Moreover, Thermo Electron's new business design (Exhibit 11.1) created powerful motivation for employees. They gained a sense of ownership that caused them to become much more involved in their work. Their compensation was directly linked to the success of their division. They could see the direct benefits of good work, and there were no longer any excuses for poor performance.

"The public provides tremendous scrutiny, which helps in managing these units," Hatsopoulos says. "It helps because you can play a good cop/bad cop role with the manager. The manager says, 'The stock price dropped, but there is no good reason!' And you can respond, 'Oh, but there are good reasons. The public is concerned about the unit's earning power.' This system works beautifully."[4]

This business design effectively identifies and rewards good work.

The decentralized nature of Thermo Electron's business design also intensified the company's contact with customers. Most companies have a business design that decreases customer contact as the company grows; Thermo Electron's business design does just the opposite. Traditionally, as a company increases in size, the customer gets smaller in significance. The company is then both less able and less willing to listen to each individual customer's needs, let alone respond to them or adapt to them. Very large companies simply have too much internal mass relative to the customer. When Hatsopoulos first considered spinning out Thermo Electron's businesses, he saw massive organizations with pyramid structures that minimized management's contact with its customers. Hatsopoulos's business design for Thermo Electron made it impossible for Thermo Electron to become too removed or distanced in that way.

Hatsopoulos's spin-out business model maximizes the surface area of the company that is exposed to customer contact. Managers are sent out in the trenches to work elbow-to-elbow with customers, developing solutions to problems. In the course of doing so, they can soak up customer information like sponges.

For example, ThermoLase, a subsidiary of Thermo Electron, develops ways to use low-intensity lasers for cosmetic and industrial purposes. By maintaining a high level of customer interaction and providing an array of services tailored to individual needs, Thermo-Lase became one of the shining stars in the Thermo Electron constellation. As a manufacturer of skin-care and other personal-care products, ThermoLase spent much effort in marketing its new Soft-Light technology. Its method was to approach physicians directly through medical conferences. In addition, ThermoLase operates a string of Spa Thira clinics in which specialists use the laser technology to perform hair and tattoo removal and cosmetic skin resurfacing, and the company is moving to create a national network of physicians who will operate the laser equipment under lease—a very profitable arrangement for the company. This lucrative business design is a direct result of ThermoLase's independence; such innovative positioning would have been delayed or denied by the bureaucratic slow-motion of a larger conglomerate.

Today, Thermo Electron's products run the gamut. The company is a leader in environmental sensor instrumentation, such as air pollution and nuclear radiation monitors, and in recycling and biomedical equipment.

Industrial companies hire Thermo Electron to make their energy consumption more efficient and to monitor the emissions of various processes to keep pollution below specified levels.

The common denominator in Thermo Electron's vast array of products is that all were developed by employing the laws of thermodynamics to improve the efficiency or monitor the activity of some type of system.

With a market capitalization of over $8 billion on $2.9 billion in sales, Thermo Electron has a market value-to-sales ratio of over 2.5; this high ratio is the result of a business model like none other. Thermo Electron markets to customers who can benefit from its products either through more efficient energy consumption or improvement in processes. Value is captured through the sale, servicing, and support of these products.

From a technology company that developed and manufactured products, Thermo Electron transformed itself into a venture capital firm that spins out promising technologies into separate units and supports those units with financial backing, technical know-how, and other business resources.

FIND THE PROFIT ZONE
IN THE EARLY YEARS

George Hatsopoulos was born in Greece in 1927. As a child, he was fascinated by machines and science. Growing up in Greece during World War II, Hatsopoulos spent much of his time in the local library, reading about different people and places. He became fascinated by America's spirit of entrepreneurship and greatly admired American inventors such as Thomas Edison.

During the Nazi occupation of Greece, Hatsopoulos experienced many hardships. But instead of being oppressed by the war around him, Hatsopoulos looked for opportunities to help his people through technology. In the 1940s, for example, the Germans either controlled or manipulated radio transmission so that Europeans received only Nazi propaganda. Hatsopoulos built radio transmitters and receivers in his basement and sold them to the Greek underground. He risked being sent to a concentration camp. Hatsopoulos's radios were a success, eventually serving as the source of inspiration for Thermo Electron. Hatsopoulos realized that when the need is severe enough and arrives unexpectedly, there will be a great opportunity for someone to start a new enterprise.[5]

After the war, Hatsopoulos began his formal education at the Athens Polytechnic. Concentrating on thermodynamics, Hatsopoulos honed his skills in the sciences. But every fact he learned offered him two more questions. In 1948, Hatsopoulos came to the United States to continue his studies at the Massachusetts Institute of Technology (MIT). His lifelong relationship with the school began with his earning B.S., M.S., and Ph.D. degrees in mechanical engineering.[6]

Life in academia challenged his technical skill, but there was something missing. Hatsopoulos loved competition. He thrived on taking risks, and he knew that the business world was the one arena where he could combine his love of science and his love of risk.

In 1955, Hatsopoulos sat down with a friend (and recent Harvard Business School graduate), Peter Nomikos. Hatsopoulos had been working on a thermionic converter (a device that converts thermal energy directly into electrical energy without any mechanical parts) as the subject of his doctoral dissertation. The two friends discussed ways in which they could begin a business, and decided to go to Nomikos's father to ask for $50,000 in start-up capital. To their surprise, the money was granted without question and the two were off and running. They were unaware (until later) of the conversation that had occurred between Nomikos's father and Hatsopoulos's uncle, Costas Platsis. Nomikos's father had said, "Listen, Costas, I will give them the $50,000. They will lose it. Then George will go back to teaching at MIT and my son will concentrate on the family business. They will both benefit, and it will be a small price to pay for an important lesson."[7]

The lesson Hatsopoulos learned was different from the one Nomikos's father anticipated. After he successfully developed a working thermionic converter, he found that there were no commercial applications other than the space program. He had only focused on the development of the product for NASA. He realized that he had been stuck in the scientist mode for too long at MIT and had to become customer-centric if he wanted to succeed in business. He had to identify unmet customer needs before developing technologies for them.

Many companies of much larger scale invest vast amounts of capital into R&D efforts and create exciting new technologies. Because of their larger scale, these companies invest in intensive marketing, launch campaigns for the new technologies, and take them to market with little difficulty. Unfortunately, that same large scale often causes these companies to fail to develop technologies that respond to the needs of their individual customers. Instead, their focus has turned to the product. In the end, these technologies will fail and the company will have wasted significant resources. But the company, because of its large size, will still survive.

Small companies don't have that luxury. If they invest their limited resources in a technology, it must succeed. Otherwise, the company has no more resources and it folds. Hatsopoulos learned this early in his career, and he committed himself and Thermo Electron to remaining customer-centric.

"When I founded the company in 1956," Hatsopoulos says, "the central idea was to be on the lookout for emerging societal needs and try to address these needs through technology."

As Hatsopoulos turned the attention of Thermo Electron to addressing the needs of customers, he contracted out the company for research projects. Through work with these projects, Thermo Electron developed many of the technologies that are now full product lines. Additionally, with the success of early projects, Thermo Electron acquired companies with more manufacturing capabilities and marketing channels.

In the early to mid-1960s, Hatsopoulos directed many of Thermo Electron's efforts toward the space program.

"It was right after Sputnik went into orbit," he says, "and there was a lot of dismay in the United States that we were falling behind the Soviet Union. The space program was the rallying point that was picked up by then-candidate Jack Kennedy . . . [At Thermo Electron] we began concentrating our efforts to solve problems for the space program. Since our expertise at the time was energy conversion, we were able to offer a lot."

This momentum was short-lived, however. By the late 1960s, Hatsopoulos saw that America was becoming less involved in its space program. He was ready to change Thermo Electron's focus again.

"We already saw that America's space program would be petering out," he says. "We felt an urgency to go into a new enterprise using the same principles [as our earlier efforts]. We had many attempts. . . . Some didn't go very far, but some of them were very successful."

Hatsopoulos's intensely customer-centric approach served Thermo Electron well. As the technological needs of customers shifted, so did Thermo Electron.

The Clean Air Act of 1970 limited the nitrogen oxide emission levels of automobiles. The trouble was, there was no instrument that could measure such pollutants.[8] Ford Motor Company enlisted the leader in instrumentation, Beckman Corporation, to develop a product, but Beckman insisted it would take 2 years. Hatsopoulos went to Ford and promised, "Give us an order and we will produce the instruments in 3 months." The people at Ford didn't think it could be done, but they signed the contract.

"The biggest success over that period of time came in 1970 when we decided to pursue the instrumentation business," Hatsopoulos says. "The Clean Air Act imposed some requirements on the automobile companies to measure the emission of nitrogen with an accuracy that was not available in the instruments at that time. We saw an opportunity for us to solve the problem."

Less than 90 days later, Hatsopoulos delivered the first nitrogen oxide detectors. They were crude, but they worked. Soon afterward, the Environmental Protection Agency designated Thermo Electron's technology as the standard to be used on all automotive exhausts. Automotive manufacturers from all over the world began calling Thermo Electron to place orders.

* * *

Hatsopoulos built Thermo Electron by searching for and capitalizing on opportunities in the marketplace. Thermo Electron provided technology in the 1960s for the space program and medicine, and in the 1970s for the environment. But as the 1970s came to a close, Hatsopoulos saw that funding was drying up. The cost of capital was getting higher as interest rates were rising. The business world was changing, and Hatsopoulos knew that Thermo Electron had to change ahead of it.

THE MODERN SPIN-OUT BUSINESS DESIGN

Hatsopoulos's spin-out structure transformed almost every element of Thermo Electron's business design. Thermo Electron still serves its traditional customers with its technology product offerings, but it also serves two new sets of customers: investors and entrepreneurs.

Thermo Electron's business model serves investors by providing them with a range of investment options. Rather than being required to invest their capital in one stock—which, in many cases, represents dozens if not hundreds of independent initiatives within a company—investors can invest in the division of Thermo Electron they believe to be the most lucrative. Hatsopoulos works hard to serve this customer set and strives to ensure that their capital is well invested.

"We have a commitment to the stockholders that invested in Thermo Electron," he says. "We promise them that all the Thermo Electron companies will eventually be successful, although there may be periods in which they lose their market value. But we say we are going to do everything possible to get that company back on its feet, which may mean changing its strategic direction completely."

To best offer consistent value to these investors, Hatsopoulos selectively chooses, from Thermo Electron's many initiatives, only certain concepts as candidates for public offerings. He wants only stable and high-potential concepts to be offered to the public, thus creating a reputation for safe and profitable investment. To reinforce this policy, Hatsopoulos focuses on three main criteria: (1) a strong business plan, (2) a good management team, and (3) a receptive market. "Our track record has been very good," he says. "As a result, when we spin out something, there are buyers immediately."

Thermo Electron offers entrepreneurs the opportunity to take an idea or a technology to market by providing them with the resources to begin and then run a business through its own central R&D department. Rather than function as a standard R&D facility, developing new products, Thermo Electron's R&D capability literally develops new businesses.

"We call it an R&D center, but it doesn't do R&D for our divisions," Hatsopoulos says. "It is an incubator for new businesses."

The arrangement has worked so well that Thermo Electron has had to acquire more entrepreneurs as its customers. Those who were working in the R&D department were leaving Thermo Electron as each new business began.

"A lot of the people that worked in the R&D center would leave to work in the spin-outs," Hatsopoulos says. "When Thermo Instruments broke out, all the R&D people went with it . . . then Thermo Medics, then others . . . soon, we had no one left."

As a remedy, Hatsopoulos bought the Coleman Research Corporation (CRC), an R&D company, to replace the workers that had left its R&D department.

The fact that Thermo Electron's central R&D focuses on new business development does not prevent its spin-outs from becoming technology leaders with their own R&D departments. Profit growth from its numerous new ventures has afforded Thermo Electron the size and resources to further strengthen each new spin-out's R&D capabilities.

In 1995, for example, Thermo Electron spin-outs overall reinvested around 4.5 percent of their total sales, more than $100 million, back into R&D. In addition, Thermo Electron negotiated contracts in which its clients help fund the necessary R&D for a given product. These types of contracts can exist only because of the proximity to the customer that is afforded by Thermo Electron's customer-centric business design. In negotiations with utility companies, such agreements benefit both parties.

"Since their interest is to sell gas and ours is to make products," Hatsopoulos says, "we said that we would dedicate a good deal of our R&D to making products that burn gas if the utilities would pay for the research and development." Thermo Electron's deep well of technical knowledge, and the easy accessibility of its managers, made it a very attractive partner for the project.

Thermo Electron's spin-out business design also created a powerful mechanism for capturing value. Thermo Electron captures value through traditional means (product and service sales) as well as innovative means (investors). The ability to sell stock in its spin-outs gives Thermo Electron a significantly lower cost of capital compared to its competitors. The company uses the recorded profits from the sale of stock to invest in additional ventures. As long as new technological developments can support new IPOs, the company is virtually an endless value-creation machine that perpetuates itself through continued investment.

Although they are a significant portion of its business design innovation, the spin-outs are only half of the Thermo Electron story. Hatsopoulos loved the advantages of a small company, but recognized that large companies had an equal number of advantages. To benefit from these advantages, Hatsopoulos needed to centralize the activities that would keep the Thermo Electron family of companies a cohesive whole.

Hatsopoulos centralized human resources, public relations, banking functions, investor relations, strategic planning, legal services, and other administrative functions.

"Centralizing these activities makes the Thermo Electron business very lean," Hatsopoulos says. "Each spin-out can concentrate on doing the job it does best, which is to develop its products, customers, and manufacturing."

Like ABB's "global network of specialists" business design (Chapter 12), Thermo Electron's business model allows its spin-outs to specialize in a limited set of business activities. This increases their ability to create value for customers. The company's centralized activities help bring the divisions together to share a common vision for the future. The divisions can also count on the parent company for financial support, technical know-how, and legal advice.

Hatsopoulos also works hard to ensure that the spin-out companies are actively exchanging ideas:

"We have created an organization that we call the Thermo Institute, whose purpose is to keep everybody together. At our meetings, we spend three days comparing notes with members of every company and discussing their plans for the next year. We will also have a couple of meetings for the CEOs, a couple of meetings for the financial officers, and a couple of meetings for the divisional presidents of the spin-outs."

The meetings afford an opportunity for the spin-outs to exchange information and benefit from each other's experience. In return, Thermo Electron gets maximum value from its spin-outs' efforts, investments, and resources.

EXHIBIT 11.2 *Thermo Electron's Market Value Growth*

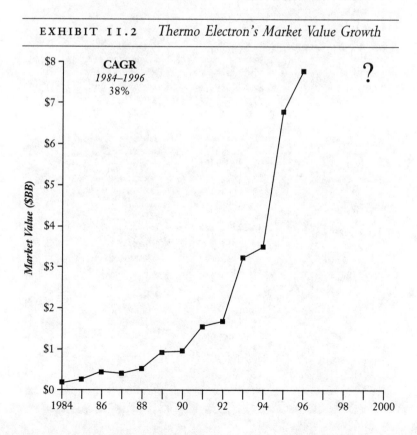

THE SUCCESS OF THE SPIN-OUT BUSINESS MODEL

Hatsopoulos's business design innovations at Thermo Electron have generated significant value growth. In 1982, Thermo Electron had a market value of $60 million. Today, Thermo Electron's market value is roughly $8 billion. From 1993 to 1996, Thermo Electron's market value tripled (Exhibit 11.2 on page 231).

EXHIBIT 11.3   *Thermo Electron's Business Design Reinvention*

	1956–1982	*1997*	*2002*
Customer Selection	• U.S. government • Utilities • Environmental organizations • Industrial firms	• Investors • Entrepreneurs • "Polluters" • Medical organizations	
Value Capture	• Broad array of manufactured products • Services	• Sale of products/services • Sale of stock • Financing and management of projects	**?**
Differentiation/ Strategic Control	• Proprietary technology • R & D capabilities	• IPO experience • Customer relationship • Track record	
Scope	• Environmental studies • Products to monitor pollution emissions/ make energy consumption more efficient	• Research contracts • Sale of products/services	

The company has created tremendous value for its customers, too. It has received an array of product endorsements that include the Seal of Approval from the Blue Cross and Blue Shield Association and Q1 (Quality 1) Certification from Ford Motor Company. Its Thermo Power division's TecoDrive 4300 natural gas engine became the first to receive the U.S. Environmental Protection Agency's certification as an Ultra-Low Emission Vehicle (ULEV). These EPA standards, the most stringent in the country, are scheduled to be put in place in California in 1998.[9]

Thermo Electron's sales increased 29 percent annually from 1991 to 1996, and many of its subsidiaries rose to the top of their fields. A core subsidiary, Thermo Instrument, is now the largest player in the $12 billion analytical instrument market, beating out competitors such as Hewlett-Packard and Perkin-Elmer. The company's

---

EXHIBIT 11.4   *Thermo Electron Business Design Reinvention*

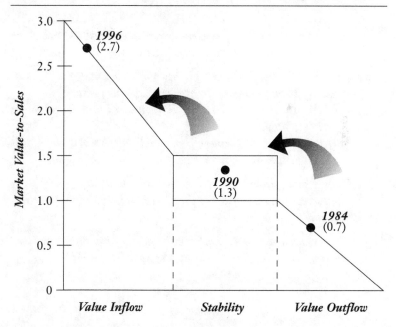

Value Creation Performance

newer subsidiaries are predicted to capture a significant share of fast-growing markets.

Hatsopoulos developed a business design at Thermo Electron that centers around the customer, motivates employees, and maintains an accurate and high stock price. Each division of Thermo Electron is small enough to stay open to change as the priorities of its customers change, yet large enough to be publicly traded. Thermo's business design has put it squarely in the profit zone (Exhibit 11.3 on page 232). More importantly, Thermo Electron's unique design positions it well to keep changing as customers and economic circumstances shifting, giving it the capability to identify and operate in the profit zone of tomorrow (Exhibit 11.4 on page 233).

BUILDING A "SPIN-OUT" BUSINESS DESIGN
Pilot's Checklist

☑ *Have I* searched *for every opportunity to establish subsets of my business as quasi-independent organizations?*

☑ *Have I structured the smaller units in a way that:*
— *Causes them to connect directly with the customer?*
— *Makes them accountable for their own resource consumption and profitability?*
— *Will make their managers and employees rich if their unit performs spectacularly well?*

☑ *Have I given them another unfair advantage by giving them access to central corporate resources, such as legal, administrative, tax, and technology?*

☑ *Have I encouraged the smaller units to start looking for further spin-off opportunities when they start getting too big?*

TWELVE

PERCY BARNEVIK

The Global-Network-of-Specialists Business Design

- *Is my industry characterized by underinnovation, poor performance for customers, and poor profit for suppliers?*

- *Is my industry overpopulated by small firms that all have the same business design?*

- *Does my industry provide major opportunities for profit growth through intense specialization?*

- *Does my company's global expansion limit its ability to stay in touch with customers?*

- *Does my industry contain opportunities for innovative value capture through solutions, financing, value-sharing, and long-term system maintenance agreements?*

FRANZ BOHMER watched as an ABB–GMI team installed new equipment in the local electric company's main plant building. German Manufacturing, Inc. (GMI) (a fictitious, but highly representative local engineering company) had certainly turned itself around in the past year, making radical changes compared to its pre-ABB days, Bohmer thought. He remembered the days when a GMI contract wouldn't get filled for two or three months; and even after such a long delay, the machines delivered would be of only adequate quality.

Bohmer, as head of purchasing, had actually considered switching to a foreign supplier—even though getting the machines serviced would have been a major hassle. When GMI had discussed reducing its offerings, Bohmer had spoken out, telling them in no uncertain terms that he couldn't be bothered with multiple suppliers. If he had to look elsewhere for *any* piece of equipment, he would be looking elsewhere for *all* of it. The threat had nipped any reductions in the bud, and Bohmer had even gotten a better price on his next contract. Still, his opinion of GMI sank to new lows.

All that changed when GMI joined the ABB network. The GMI facilities were modernized and converted to specialize in turbines, the company's area of expertise. When Bohmer asked how he was going to get other kinds of equipment, the sales representative of ABB-GMI assured him that other members of the ABB group specialized in each of the types of machines he needed, and that ABB-GMI would be responsible for providing what he needed.

ABB-GMI's sales rep proved true to his word. When Bohmer placed his next order, the rep volunteered a four-week turnaround time, rather than the three months Bohmer had expected. Furthermore, the model he bought was cheaper, and of much higher quality, compared to past GMI equipment. And now a team of ABB employees from the area were custom-fitting the new machine inside the utility company's plant.

The whole situation delighted Bohmer—he had gotten better equipment that was delivered faster, for a lower price. ABB service personnel were on call nearby and the utility company fulfilled its commitment to support the local economy.

*   *   *

In the early 1980s, the world power generation industry had stagnated. Bohmer's experience with GMI was the status quo. Equipment companies everywhere sagged with poor quality and poor financials. Customers were frustrated but accustomed to the mediocrity. Fortunately, Percy Barnevik, head of ASEA Brown Boveri (ABB), was about to provide the spark of innovation that improved both the equipment companies and the lives of customers like Franz Bohmer.

Barnevik took a closer look at the GMIs of the world and identified the source of their difficulties. He saw that the duplication of efforts—in research, administration, and manufacturing—was the source of enormous collective inefficiency in the power industry.

Each company within the industry tried to service *all* of its customers' product needs. This meant that few units within ABB, or the offices of its local competitors, were able to specialize in what they did best and to make a significant profit from the few products they made exceptionally well. Rather than focusing on a single activity, every office or company was a de facto generalist, a jack-of-all-trades. This translated to higher cost and lower quality for customers like Franz Bohmer.

Consider the complex problems faced by the CEO of a general equipment manufacturer in the power generation industry like GMI in the early 1980s.

German Manufacturing's CEO, a smart and ambitious veteran of the industry who had worked his way up through the ranks of GMI, couldn't seem to work his way out of the industry's low-growth, low-profit malaise. He hasn't seen profits so low for as long as he's been in the industry—over two decades. So, he continues to throw cash into GMI's R&D department. Meanwhile, he lowers overall costs. He is slowly gaining market share on his competitors, but only marginally. And, to do so, he keeps losing profits. Worst of all, he has to manufacture a whole host of products that his customers want, but on which he loses money. He can't stop making the products because, if he does, his customers may move to another manufacturer. As this profit-destroying cycle continues, the CEO watches GMI's margins continue to shrink.

In the past, he has sold to customers that were primarily in his region. Perhaps, he calculates, if he geographically increases his customer set, he'll be able to make a profit. Granted, he'll have to find new distribution channels to get his products to market, but won't the economies of scale more than make up for the difference? The CEO begins spending more money trying to sell GMI's products to customers outside of his core region. Because of the money he has invested in GMI's R&D departments, GMI's technology is slightly better than its competitors'. But, to attract the new customers, he has to lower his prices even more. After a few years, he finds that he has gained some new customers, but not as many as he had hoped. Most customers of manufactured equipment prefer to buy from local suppliers because, they say, buying from local manufacturing companies keeps the local economy strong. Many of these customers have had a relationship with their current supplier for two or three generations. And what if they have service problems? GMI wouldn't be able to respond immediately. Every moment of time lost, of facility downtime, represents a loss in revenues. Customers want a manufacturing company that can service and repair their equipment immediately. Why should GMI's marginally better and marginally less expensive products, which can't be serviced, cause them to switch suppliers? GMI's CEO lists the reasons, but none of them seems adequately compelling.

By 1985, GMI has outlasted many of its competitors from 5 years earlier. In a war of attrition, GMI is winning. But the cost of winning is high. The CEO finds that his own costs have increased because of the additional investment in R&D, the increased selling costs he has approved in order to attract more customers, and the high distribution costs that have resulted from the customers that are farther away. Moreover, he is stunned by how much he has dropped GMI's prices over time. Each drop seemed relatively minor at the time, but they have added up, and he is now charging significantly less for all of his products than he was when he began as CEO. GMI is making less money now than it did 5 years ago. For all his organization's efforts, he feels trapped in a no-profit zone.

In 1985, he has a choice. He can either close down his factory or he can try to ride out the lack of growth and continue to gain market share from his competitors, using the same tactics that he has been using for the past decade. Granted, this will erode profits even more, but if he can outlast his competitors, maybe—just maybe—he can move GMI back into a profitable business. Once GMI is the leading German company, the CEO knows, it will make money. He chooses to hang on for a few more years.

*　　*　　*

Once-strong companies like the fictitious GMI could be found across Europe. Barnevik saw this trend and began to think of effective customer-centric and profit-centric strategies to deal with it, strategies that would create value for both the customer and the manufacturing companies that were struggling in an ever-expanding no-profit zone. After the merger of ASEA with Brown Boveri to form ABB, Barnevik began to reinvent ABB's next business design, the global network of specialists.

THE GLOBAL NETWORK
OF SPECIALISTS

Barnevik's solution was simple. Instead of a world of subscale, un-connected generalists, ABB would create a global network of special-ists by acquiring smaller heavy-equipment manufacturing firms around Europe and around the world. He would help these firms to move out of their no-profit zone. He would restore their profitabil-ity and enable them once again to create value for their customers. He would do this by refocusing the scope of the affiliates, enabling them to specialize, to do what they do best, and to keep doing it bet-ter. Individual companies would no longer have to produce scores of items their customers required; other members of the ABB network could provide most of the products or services needed. Instead, each network member could specialize in the products it made best, elim-inating unprofitable activities and achieving the strongest possible economic position (lowest cost, highest quality, fastest response) in its specialty. When a customer asked for products that the local ABB affiliate did not make, the items could be acquired from an-other ABB member that specialized in the desired items.

The ABB model of specialization not only restored profitability through lower production costs, it also allowed ABB affiliates to dif-ferentiate themselves in new ways. They were able to purchase sup-plies and finished products at lower cost; deliver fast and reliable help; provide jobs locally; offer the best products; and benefit from a brand name. Consider again the highly representative story of GMI.

*   *   *

The year is now 1990. The CEO of GMI has won a long battle against his competitors. He has increased GMI's market share con-siderably and has improved the technology in GMI's products. He has sold to some major new accounts and has made GMI into a re-gional if not a national powerhouse in electrical equipment manu-facturing. And, perhaps most significantly, he has managed to keep GMI alive for over a decade in a no-profit zone. Granted, GMI's profitability is razor-thin, but GMI, unlike many of its competitors that have fallen by the wayside during the past two decades, is at least marginally profitable.

Yet the CEO is unhappy. He sees no possibility for additional growth. He knows that he could continue doing what he has done for the past 10 years—improve GMI's products, sell more products, cut the price, sell to more customers, and advance GMI's brand through heavy marketing efforts. But he knows that such a strategy will make GMI unprofitable. And, frankly, he is tired. It has not been an easy time for him as CEO. Each year of diminished margins has been another year of aggravation. What can he do?

ABB calls with a possible answer: Join ABB's global network of specialists. Barnevik is willing to pay what the CEO considers a fair price for GMI. And, Barnevik promises, within a few months, the CEO will begin to see higher profits again. The CEO is tempted. But what about GMI's customers, especially those whose working relationships predate the CEO's joining GMI? Barnevik promises that GMI can continue to work with them and will even be able to increase its quality of service and dramatically improve its technology offerings. More importantly, GMI will gain a whole set of new customers in other geographic markets, it won't have to pay massive distribution costs to get its equipment there, and it can use ABB's brand name for leverage with any new or existing customers. The CEO is intrigued—he agrees to sell his company and become part of the global network.

By the next year, GMI is making a profit. Barnevik's promises have started to come true. GMI's customers are more satisfied than they were before the acquisition; employees are taking home bonuses; and GMI is beginning to be well positioned for growth in the coming years. The CEO could not be more pleased.

Within a few months of joining ABB's global network, he has seen GMI's economic position and income statement improve dramatically (Exhibit 12.1). He has been able to get supplies and parts at dramatically lower costs because of the purchasing power of the network. In some categories, his cost of purchased materials has dropped by 15 to 20 percent. The CEO can also rely on ABB's global distribution network to transport GMI's manufactured equipment to its customers. Now that it includes the products of other network members, distribution is much less costly because large volumes are being handled by the network. No longer does the CEO have to worry about his distant customers. The global network has brought them much closer to GMI.

EXHIBIT 12.1   *GMI's Income Statement: The Power of Specialization*

	Pre-ABB	With ABB	Driver
Sales	100%	100%	
Purchased Materials	35	30	Purchasing economies
Manufacturing Cost	35	30	Specialization
R&D	3	8	Specialization
Sales, General & Administration	25	20	Distribution, Brand, Services
Profit	2	12	

THE PROFIT ZONE

Both of these cost reductions are minor compared to the ABB global network's other offering—the opportunity to specialize. GMI's biggest reduction in costs has come from the elimination (or transfer to other ABB units) of GMI's unprofitable products, together with increased production of its profitable products. The CEO has been able to eliminate almost 60 percent of GMI's previous product lines—all of those that GMI's engineers couldn't make efficiently or that GMI simply couldn't produce cheaply because of their small volume. GMI now specializes in the 40 percent of its former product line that carried GMI into the black for the past two decades. For those products that GMI no longer makes, it contacts another network member that specializes in them, and, via ABB's distribution system, the products arrive with more than enough time to get them to the customers.

GMI has also been able to make more of its profitable products than ever. GMI can sell its profitable products to any customer of any member of ABB's global network. GMI has exponentially increased its customer set through ABB's network. Where GMI was once a regional leader with a few customers scattered around western Europe, the company is now selling its products to customers in Asia, Africa, the United States, and South America.

The customers in these distant markets know that these are good products, not because they have heard of GMI, but because they know the ABB name. ABB has brand equity around the world, and GMI can take advantage of that brand equity.

GMI also is able to improve on the technology of its specialized products. Collectively, ABB's global network is able to do much more R&D than GMI can ever do on its own. ABB is delivering higher-quality, longer-lasting products to GMI and its customers than GMI had thought possible just several years earlier. GMI's customers are extremely pleased. They are able to get better technology quicker than before, at competitive prices. They reward GMI's CEO with more business.

And GMI responds to their increased business with faster and more reliable service. Where previously GMI has been limited by its geography, now it can request help from another network member, and GMI's customer receives service promptly.

ABB's brand name has also made it easier for the CEO of GMI to attract some of the best regional talent to the company. Previously, employees left to work for other companies with more opportunities; now, these same employees are coming to work at ABB. They perceive it as a viable option because, through the connections to ABB's global network, there is a possibility of working practically anywhere in the world. Additionally, ABB has staffed some outstanding engineers, division managers, and senior executives at GMI. They have brought to GMI expertise that GMI had been unable to attract as a freestanding company.

By 1995, GMI is more profitable than the CEO had ever believed possible. His customers are located all over the globe. He is making fewer different types of products than he made a decade ago, but he is selling more of them. Better still, all of GMI's products are the best technology in the industry, thanks to the combined power of specialization and ABB's R&D. Best of all, the products are highly profitable because GMI pays rock-bottom prices for distribution, marketing, R&D, and all of its supplies. Moreover, GMI now has the ABB brand name behind it. It can leverage this name to attract local talent and other international customers. The CEO of GMI has found a solution to his problems. He has become part of a business design that has put his company squarely in the profit zone.

*   *   *

ABB's global network business design provides the individual companies in the network with numerous economic advantages. These benefits have been instrumental in ABB's success, but they would have been irrelevant if the network had not added value for the customer. The real driver behind the success of ABB's business design has been its ability to recognize customer priorities and provide solutions to match.

Barnevik found a way to leverage the benefits of a local business design as well as the benefits of a global business design. He knew that ABB itself could not build its base of local customers, provide local jobs, or deliver fast and reliable help to all of its customers with a global business design. Yet he knew that (1) no local business design would be able to lower its costs as much as a global network could, and (2) a global business design could offer the best R&D and a brand name that no local business design could match. He crafted a business design that integrated the benefits of each (Exhibit 12.2).

However, customer needs are not static, and Barnevik knew that if his business design was to continue to add value for customers, it would have to be able to change along with them. As most corporations grow, adapting to meet customer needs becomes increasingly difficult. The executives responsible for directing the company generally have the least contact with customers. To ensure that ABB remains focused on the customer, Barnevik built ABB's business design so that the people responsible for making decisions are always in direct contact with customers. Barnevik has further divided each of ABB's network members into smaller profit centers. ABB's global network has some 1,000 companies and 5,000 profit centers across the world. By holding the middle managers who run the profit centers accountable for their own profit and loss, Barnevik has ensured that the company will always be able to feel the pulse of the customer and respond accordingly.

EXHIBIT 12.2   *The Benefits of ABB's Global Business Design*

Customer Need	Local Manufacturer Business Design	Global Manufacturer Business Design	ABB's Global Network of Specialists
• Convenient purchasing	✔		✔
• Fast, reliable help	✔		✔
• Companies that will provide jobs locally	✔		✔
• Low cost		✔	✔
• Best product (high quality, best technology)		✔	✔
• Brand name		✔	✔

CREATING A CUSTOMER-CENTRIC ORGANIZATION

ABB profit centers talk directly with their customers, identify their needs, and provide them with products and services from other ABB profit centers. Barnevik's business design has increased customer connectivity exponentially and marks a significant break from the conventional ways of doing business. Barnevik turned the company inside-out, removing the protective layers of a conventional corporate structure from its subdivisions. Furthermore, Barnevik himself makes sure to keep in touch with customers. He says, "ABB must have a customer-driven approach. We work very hard to be close to the customer. I personally talk to over 100 ABB customers per year."[1]

This customer-centric approach has helped Barnevik to recognize yet another customer need and respond accordingly. Barnevik saw that a growing number of ABB's clients needed more than expensive machines; they needed an easy way to purchase them. Smaller competing equipment manufacturers lacked the resources to be flexible with payment plans. Without a large reserve of capital, these smaller firms had to receive complete payment in order to cover their own costs, and their customers were forced to get financing from banks. ABB decided to differentiate itself by expanding its scope and offering its customers financing alternatives, either with credit or by organizing groups of investors.

The origins of ABB's financial services division date back to 1983, when Barnevik was the CEO of ASEA. Barnevik hired a senior executive from American Express to begin ASEA's financing division. Initially, it did not significantly contribute to ASEA's revenues. More recently, ABB has begun to use it as a value-capture mechanism. In 1994, ABB acted as a financial adviser on fifteen projects in which ABB was not itself an investor. Some analysts consider ABB's financial services division to be a key differentiator for ABB. For instance, in India, ABB's main competitor, BHEL, is the only company that offers a full range of power plant equipment and services—in fact, it offers more than ABB. In addition to having a larger scope, BHEL has cost leadership, which has allowed it to outbid ABB on a number of contracts, particularly those financed by multilateral agencies that award to the lowest bidder. However, BHEL does not have the ability to finance its own power projects. ABB does, and it is this ability that many customers need most. ABB's business design provides affordability for cash-strapped customers.[2]

ABB's value-sharing contracts offer customers a second way of making purchases more affordable. In a value-sharing structure, ABB agrees to a lower purchase price in return for a portion of the new value created by its equipment. Such contracts are extremely valuable to both ABB and its customers, for several reasons. First, value-sharing contracts allow ABB to engage in discussions with customers and market ABB's advantages during the negotiation phase. These talks can open doors to a host of projects that might otherwise have been unavailable to ABB. Second, value-sharing contracts create, for both the customer and ABB, value that is greater than either could achieve independently. By working with its customers toward solutions, ABB increases the positive impact of its products and services. Third, value-sharing contracts create a much stronger bond between the supplier and the customer. Not only are the two engaged in a business transaction, but in a long-term process as well. This weds them much closer than the traditional exchange of goods and services.

One example of a value-sharing contract is the ABB–Ford Oakville Paint-Finishing Project. In 1990, Ford needed an automotive paint-finishing line in its Oakville, Canada, assembly plant. It was to be one of the largest projects ever undertaken in the automotive industry: a 730,000-square-foot facility designed to paint 75 cars per hour. Ford planned on a cost of $300 million. Ford's key priorities were quality, timeliness, low price, and low risk.

ABB worked intensely with Ford in shaping its approach to the contract and, through a value-sharing contract proposal, won the bid. The two most important characteristics of the contract were: (1) a reduced appropriation price, which offered the promise of (2) an even lower final price, provided that ABB and Ford shared the value of any additional cost reductions and cooperative engineering. (Both Ford and ABB contributed to the design of the plant.) The value-sharing contract created the opportunity for additional profit to ABB and ensured a satisfied customer who would look to ABB in the future for its industrial systems needs.[3]

When necessary, ABB is also able to create total solutions outside of its global network. ABB's business model is to first develop a contract with a customer and then find the resources needed to fulfill it. ABB will bid for a contract even if it lacks the capacity to satisfy the deal by itself. If other capabilities are needed, ABB will find a business partner to carry out those portions of the work. The business partners are, in fact, specialists from outside the ABB network. ABB's approach dramatically expands the company's scope and increases the number of projects on which it can add value to the customer. For instance, in 1995, ABB led a consortium that built a 750-megawatt gas-fired, combined-cycle power plant in Barranquilla, Colombia. The contract paid $430 million; ABB contracted out roughly 40 percent of the work to business partners who were outside specialists.

As a participant in financing, value sharing, total solutions, and all parts of the global industrial equipment market, ABB has come a long way from its origins in ASEA. It integrates the benefits of a local business design with those of a global business design. And it creates enormous value for the customer.

ABOUT TIME, CUSTOMERS, AND PROFIT: A CONVERSATION WITH PERCY BARNEVIK[4]

Percy Barnevik took time out to talk about the inner logic that drove the creation and growth of ABB. In his commentary, there was an unmistakable passion for the topic—ABB's unique business design, which, though still a work in progress, has come so far in so short a time. ABB has expanded far beyond what anyone would have imagined in 1988.

"Time is the first factor," Barnevik emphasizes. "The industry areas where we compete were like a sluggish, slow-moving river. Everything took forever. That was the first thing that had to change. There's nothing that takes six months that couldn't be done in six weeks, and done much better."

If Barnevik had not applied this logic of timetable compression, what took 8 years would have taken more than 20. The business model would never have hit a critical rate of movement, and little value would have been created.

Moving fast is especially important in building a network business design. Hundreds of acquisitions are involved, and each could take months instead of weeks.

The second, less frequently discussed factor in the creation of the ABB business design is the fundamentally customer-centric mindset that drove the process forward.

"I speak to about 100 customers a year," says Barnevik. "You can't build a successful enterprise today without that kind of direct connection with the buyers and decision makers. Things change too quickly. Different things become important. Operating without that information flow is like driving at night—with your headlights off. Who needs that level of risk!

"Of course, the customers won't always articulate what they need or want. Sometimes they do, but not always. No matter. This kind of direct contact provides the clues you need to figure it out for yourself. That's the supplier's first challenge today.

"It's the customer that caused us to build such a network structure. The customer wants local presence. (Some of our member companies have served their customers for over 100 years.) The customers want local jobs, local service. At the same time, however, they also want the best technology, the best quality, the best cost—things you cannot create today without global scale. You have to exploit local positions, *and* the strengths of being global, to hit all these targets.

"The customer is, however, only half of the equation. The other half is profit growth. It keeps getting more difficult to get it.

"You always have to be inventing the next step. And it's a different step for Germany or Switzerland than it is for Poland, or Ukraine, or India.

"In Poland or Ukraine, you have extremely low labor costs, not just for workers, but for highly skilled engineers. We can capitalize on those low costs by selling throughout our system. Poland could never sell to Florida Power and Light. But ABB can, even if the equipment was manufactured in Poland. We make sure it was produced with quality, and we stand behind our product.

"In Western Europe, the game is different. Some of our Swiss factories have so little direct labor that we have to call together the maintenance crew just to be able to do a plant photo. They are world-class, low cost, but they take a different route to get there.

"The same is true about finding new ways to create profit growth. Our companies in Germany or the U.S., for instance, can't grow just through products, because the markets are mature, are stagnant. For them to do well, we have to develop systems and solutions selling. We go to a client account—a utility, for example—and say: 'We'll use our skills and capabilities to modernize your plant, to increase its efficiency, and be paid in part by sharing in the efficiencies that we create for you.'

"The path to profit growth in the future will not be the same as in the past. The network will grow by new means beyond the traditional acquisition route. In Eastern Europe, we have a logical economic progression that can work for a decade or longer. We started in Poland and made it work. The Poles speak Russian, and are our human resource bridge into Russia, Ukraine, and other members of the former Soviet Union.

"In India and other parts of Asia, there are fewer traditional acquisition opportunities. There, we'll take more of a greenfield approach. The network and its opportunities will grow, but in a way that matches the new market and talent situations that we face."

Behind the sparkling eyes are an active mind and an enormous spirit. An ability to use time to advantage, almost as a raw material in selecting and crafting the next business model. An ability to start with the customer in the strategic thought process, to make certain that the talent and resources of the network are always focused on doing what is needed to win in the tribunal of the customer's mind. And finally, an ability to invent new ways to create profit.

The network business design is not without its challenges: size, internal conflict, internal coordination, the need to constantly re-discover the internal balance point. But, for an industry with such unpromising prospects, the design is a remarkable creation. ABB is accustomed to speed and change. And that's important because the next 2 years are likely to require another reinvention of the business design. Market dynamics will inevitably change the answers to the questions that have driven the business design in the past: What's most important to the customer? Where will tomorrow's profit zone be?

FUTURE OPPORTUNITY SPACE

The competition for customers and strategic control across ABB's industries is fierce. Barnevik cites three levels on which ABB competes: (1) technological innovation, (2) process engineering, and (3) the global network. ABB's technological innovation does not give it an enormous competitive advantage, Barnevik readily concedes. Competitors can buy it, copy it, even steal it. In any case, in 12 to 18 months, the competition has caught up with ABB.

However, ABB stands well ahead of its competitors in understanding industrial, transportation, and power systems. Copying process engineering is not nearly as simple as imitating a limited set of product technologies. Rather, it involves an unusual and rare knowledge set, an understanding of the customer's whole system and its dynamics. It requires a unique relationship with the customer—as in the ABB–Ford value-sharing contract, where ABB intimately understands the customer's systems economics and decision-making processes. Thus, creating a strategic control point through superior process capability requires both a deep understanding of the economics as well as a very strong customer relationship. Barnevik understands that competitors cannot so easily wrest this strategic control point from ABB.

ABB's greatest competitive advantage, however, is its business model, the global network. No competitor—not Siemens, not MHI, not GEC-Alsthom, not even GE—can imitate it easily. "Our unique structure is the most difficult [for our competitors] to imitate," Barnevik proudly admits. In the business of creating systems, the

---

EXHIBIT 12.3 *ABB's Business Design Reinvention*

	1981	1996	2002
Customer Selection	• Local buyers	• Network members (acquired engineering firms) • Local buyers • Solutions seekers	
Value Capture	• Product sales	• Product sales • Value sharing • Long-term maintenance contracts • Financing • Solutions	**?**
Differentiation/ Strategic Control	• Price • Technology	• Specialization • Local presence • Global network • Customer relationship • Technology • Brand	
Scope	• Products	• International • Products • Services • Solutions • Financing • Collaboration with business partners	

ability to draw from the resources of over 1,000 companies around the world is a critical strategic control point for ABB.

ABB's ability to keep pace with changing customer needs has been the key to its success. Sustaining success will mean continuing to monitor and adapt as those needs change again. With its unique global network of specialists business design, ABB may be well positioned to do just that (Exhibit 12.3).

BUILDING A GLOBAL NETWORK OF SPECIALISTS BUSINESS DESIGN
Pilot's Checklist

☑ *Do I treat my acquired firms as my most important customers?*

☑ *Have I enabled them to specialize totally in what they do best?*

☑ *Have I provided every source of leverage to them, through purchasing economies, R&D, global distribution, and global brand?*

☑ *Have I enabled my network members to continue to be local to the customer?*

☑ *Have I developed new value recapture models (solutions, value-sharing, and financing) to further increase returns on their expertise?*

☑ *Have I developed a network of external business partners to enable me to offer my customers a complete product line/solution?*

THIRTEEN

BILL GATES

The Create-the-Standard Business Design

- *Is there any opportunity to create a standard in my industry?*

- *What exactly does it take to build a create the standard business design?*

- *How valuable would it be?*

MICROSOFT CREATES standards. That's what it is best at. That's what its business model has been designed to do.

It just so happens that a "de facto standard" business design is the most valuable type of business design. High margins, high profit protection, increasing returns to scale.

That's become generally well known—so much so, that many companies talk about adopting a "Microsoft" strategy or a "Microsoft" approach.

What's not well known is that, although a standards-based business design is the most valuable type of business model, it is also the single most difficult business design to create. That's what this chapter is all about.

Since 1976, Microsoft founder William H. Gates III has driven and presided over the most dramatic value creation in recent corporate history. Microsoft has grown from a pair of hackers working around the clock in a high school computer lab to a company with $170 billion market value. Microsoft is far from the largest company in the computer industry on a revenue basis, but it holds the largest market value. By building, developing, and owning the key components of computing, Microsoft leads the computer industry. Microsoft's success in capturing this position derives from its standards-based business design.

A standard is more than a physical product or technology. A standard is a fundamental building block around which an industry is built. Different moving parts of an industry work together and communicate. The development of the railroad required standard rail gauges. International telephone connections, faxes, and cellular telephones required standard communications signals. The existence of standards enables accelerated economic progress, and saves customers money. In many industries, the establishment of these standards has unlocked the market by giving customers confidence in compatibility and technology trajectory.

However, simply creating a standard does not guarantee capturing value from it. IBM created the dominant PC architecture in 1981, but by the mid-1990s its cumulative losses were in the billions. Matsushita's VHS format beat Sony's Betamax, but Matsushita didn't capture significant long-term value from the standard. Film studios and Blockbuster Video captured much, much more. Hayes built the standard protocols for modems, but ran into financial troubles in 1994 and had to scramble to avoid takeover attempts. Hayes saw value flow out of its modem business because of clones and other compatible modems that performed the same tasks for a lower price. Even though Hayes owned the standard—many modems are still referred to as "Hayes compatible"—its business design did not allow it to meet an important customer priority, *price*, and so it failed in the face of competition.

At the other extreme, a standard can open the door for tremendous value-growth opportunities—if the correct business design is built around it. By making the right choices on customer selection, value capture, additional differentiation, and scope, a company can create a degree of strategic control that allows extraordinary value growth. The technology inherent in a standard can be copied or replicated, but a standards-based business design will be very difficult for the competition to copy. The strategic control is embedded in the business design, not in the technological invention.

The economics of creating a standard can be quite attractive. In technology industries, developing new products often requires enormous sunk costs but low marginal costs. Profit is thus dependent on getting the highest return on the fixed investment. A company with a standards-based business design retains control of its product and market and has three value capture advantages: (1) high volume, (2) pricing flexibility, and (3) profit opportunities from upgrades. With the right business design, a technological standard can place a company squarely in the profit zone.

Microsoft has won several distinct battles for standards in its 20-year history. In each battle, Gates has used a common set of strategies to build a classic standards-based business design. First, he realized that to set any product as the basis for an industry, one must involve and deliver for all customer groups—from original equipment manufacturers (OEMs) to applications developers, end users, distributors, and those who will use the product as a starting point for their own business.

Second, Gates focused on the challenge of value capture. A classic standards-based business design brings enormous profit, but not immediately. The standard had to be secure, and volume high, before Microsoft could begin to offer upgrades and new and improved products. Third, to attain differentiation, he had to give the customer a compelling reason to adopt or switch. Gates knew that the most sophisticated technology in the world would never be adopted if it did not meet customers' needs and priorities, and most important among those priorities would be easy conversion from competitors' offerings to the new standard. Finally, he saw that his scope had to extend far beyond developing or finding new technologies. In the creation of a standard, great marketing is more important than great technology in persuading the key groups that drive the entire industry to adopt a product. The power of a standard is realized when the standard exists in the minds of the customers (Exhibit 13.1).

Constructing a standards-based business is no easy task, but Gates did it masterfully three times, using intensely customer-centric and profit-centric thinking in each case. For each of his standards, he focused on meeting customers' primary needs, whether they were quick delivery, low price, simplicity of use, or cross-platform capability. A second Gates strategy was eradication of the barriers—financial, technical, and logistical—to switching to Microsoft products. Third, he earned and secured the support of software developers who embraced the Microsoft standard and

EXHIBIT 13.1   *Microsoft's Standards-Based Business Design*

Customer Selection	• Immediate customers (OEMs) • Applications developers • End users
Value Capture	• Increasing returns to scale • Pricing flexibility • Upgrades/New offerings • Core applications

**Differentiation/
Strategic Control**
	• Create the standard
	• Meet most important customer priorities for each
	  major group of customers
	  —OEMs: Customization
	  —Developers: Support
	  —Users: Applications

Scope	• Development • Licensing • Developer marketing • User marketing

ensured the end users' satisfaction with the entire system. Finally, Gates was willing to trade current cash flow for future leadership and profit. He priced low each time, to draw his customers into the Microsoft system and to create near universality. The big profits would come later.

These strategies have served Microsoft well and have given it three successive standards. However, standards must be robust and constantly redefined for relevancy, or they will be replaced by new players who better understand and meet customers' priorities. In response to shifting customer priorities, Microsoft is now fighting to establish the company's next two major standards—on the Internet and in corporate networking. If history is any indicator, it will win on both fronts. In a value migration world, however, history is never an indicator. Each successive new business design must win on its own terms. Each time is like the first time. There are no guarantees of success.

WINNING LANGUAGES

In 1975, there was no personal computer industry, let alone any standards. Steve Jobs and Steve Wozniak were still tinkering with the pre-Apple in Woz's garage. IBM couldn't even get a prototype out of its well-resourced laboratories. MITS, an unknown, nearly bankrupt calculator manufacturer housed next to a massage parlor in Albuquerque, New Mexico, announced plans for a computer kit—the Altair—based on Intel's 8080 chip. However, the MITS "computer" lacked a language, keyboard, and disk drive, and came with no more than 4K of RAM (random access memory).

Without a language, the Altair was no more than a calculator with flashing lights. When Gates, a sophomore at Harvard, and his friend Paul Allen read about the Altair in the January 1975 issue of *Popular Electronics*, they never doubted that they could write the code that would make this machine usable. That wasn't an obstacle. The problem was that dozens of other people could write this code as well— and probably do a better job of it. To actually make money by writing the code, they had to win a contract with MITS. Pragmatic from the onset, the Microsoft founders' strategy was: Get the customer first; deliver the technology later.

This approach led Gates and Allen to make two key product development decisions that remain an integral part of the strategic code that defines Microsoft's business design today. First, they rushed to market pursuing a contract with MITS. That meant cutting corners and focusing on a pared-down product that wasn't perfect and wasn't elegant, but *worked*—period. Basic profit-centric thinking told them that to turn out a polished product one year later would be worse than useless. The window of opportunity was small. Second, Gates and Allen were bold about borrowing innovations. They embraced BASIC, cloning it for the Altair in the form of PC BASIC. For the sake of speed, Gates limited Microsoft's scope to adaptation rather than creation. They won the contract.[1]

Microsoft's first success was short-lived. Clones of the Altair began gaining market share, but Gates and Allen could not target them as customers because MITS owned the rights to license Microsoft's language. Gates saw that MITS cared about its own profits, not about making Microsoft's PC BASIC a standard. After a complicated legal battle, Microsoft walked away from MITS having regained control of its technology.

The Altair episode taught Gates about the double-edged sword of powerful OEM channel partners. Tie up the OEM as an exclusive customer and you benefit from the revenues derived from its business. But if you depend on those revenues and you lack the differentiation and negotiating leverage of a standard, that customer gains extraordinary power over your business. In the case of Altair, MITS controlled Microsoft. PC BASIC could not become a standard because it was captive to a powerful OEM customer.

Consider a world of software without standards; a proliferation of proprietary, incompatible products. This was the reigning model in the mainframe and minicomputer markets as Gates and Allen did battle with MITS. The software had value, but no power to protect it. Hardware was king. As Gates and Allen walked away from MITS in the fledgling PC industry, they sought to deliver software from the shackles of hardware.

CROSS-PLATFORM STRATEGY

Software began its career as a satellite, a complementary product to hardware. Microsoft's early challenge was loosening the hardware players' dominance of the microcomputer industry. Gates did this by creating software standards that ran on every hardware platform.

Gates was challenging the basic paradigm in the industry—customize the software to optimize the hardware platform. Convincing a critical mass of OEMs to adopt Microsoft languages was easier said than done. Microsoft's go-to-market strategy depended on an aggressive sales and marketing effort. As chief salesman, Gates himself delivered on his famous motto—"Get the business, get the business, get the business"—by pricing as low (and promising as much) as was necessary to close deals. Trying to minimize obstacles to adoption, he targeted a key customer priority—price. He sold on a flat-fee basis, encouraging OEMs to include the language with every machine sold.

Selling to multiple OEMs wasn't just a profit-making tactic. Gates knew that a language standard had to extend across all the hardware platforms in the market. He wanted ubiquity for Microsoft's language. To gain a wider share for his would-be standard, Gates designed his language so that only a few core blocks of Microsoft code implemented languages for myriad different platforms. Microsoft could easily translate—"port"—its language to any other hardware. Instead of just one revenue stream per product developed, Microsoft repurposed the product and built multiple revenue streams.

The result was a less-than-stellar product that was clunky, buggy, and not optimized for the hardware it ran on. However, it met the needs of its customers. OEMs simply wanted a language that worked, was available quickly, and was affordable.

Microsoft also met the needs of a second customer set—programmers. By implementing its languages on so many platforms, Microsoft created platform-independent standards that allowed programmers to write applications once and have them work across many types of hardware.

It improved the economics of the programmers, who could repurpose the code they wrote. Programmers returned the favor by creating an array of programs that created end user acceptance and pull for Microsoft's PC BASIC. An upward spiral was initiated.

Microsoft's campaign to create the language standard was a huge success. Microsoft's contracts with 48 OEMs, including Commodore, Texas Instruments, Apple, and Tandy, freed Microsoft of its dependence on a one-customer relationship. For 1978, Microsoft's revenues rose to $382,000, a one-year increase of more than 600 percent. Sales surpassed $1 million in 1979. The languages standard propelled Microsoft to unquestioned leadership that would last until the mid-1980s. This early success in languages defined the genetic code of Microsoft's methodology for creating and managing future de facto standards in its industry.[2]

WINNING DOS

While Microsoft was enjoying the fruits of its early success, the next act in the PC drama was already unfolding and a new profit zone was being defined.

IBM decided to enter the market, and its entrance had two implications for the PC industry. First, it legitimized the microcomputer. If IBM would build them, they were no longer "toys." Second, it likely meant flattening scores of tiny microcomputer players. This posed a threat to Microsoft's control of the language industry and its position as a software standards-bearer. However, for a customer-centric thinker like Gates, the entrance of IBM could enable Microsoft to take its standards-based business design to the next level.

End users' were growing increasingly frustrated with the rote typing of sequences of commands that performed basic tasks. Their priority became automation. Operating systems, an emerging technology that simplified file-management and printing operations, filled this need. Gates saw a new profit zone emerging.

In July 1980, Jack Sams was given a mission by IBM chairman Frank Cary: Develop the PC in less than a year! (This demand would have a profound effect on the future direction of the PC industry. Meeting this goal meant outsourcing software development and the microprocessor. The value creation template for the next 20 years was set as a result.) Sams developed a simple strategy: He contacted the No. 1 developers in the two major software segments: Bill Gates of Microsoft for languages, and Gary Kildall of Digital Research for operating systems.

With an installed base of 50,000 users, Digital Research's CP/M (Control Program for Microprocessor) was the leading operating system for personal computers, by a wide margin, in the late 1970s. Kildall was already developing the next-generation product that IBM wanted. But when Sams approached him, Kildall rejected the stringent time schedule that IBM demanded. Gates, on the other hand, was ready to respond to any important customer's priorities. He offered to provide both the language *and* the operating system for the new personal computer. Gates saw the dimensions of the opportunity IBM offered, if Microsoft could deliver the product in an impossible time frame. Winning the IBM contract virtually guaranteed massive distribution in the PC market that IBM would create. Microsoft would sell its languages and new operating system through IBM and become a de facto standard in the new PC market.[3]

The fact that Microsoft did not actually have an operating system was an obstacle that Microsoft had dealt with before. Get the customer, then make the product. Drawing on the experience of the languages battle, Microsoft swung into action, making good on every one of its completely unrealistic promises. Gates and Allen purchased a CP/M clone called Q-DOS (Quick and Dirty Operating System) which was based on CP/M. Gates knew that he had three customers to satisfy: (1) IBM, (2) programmers, and (3) end users. IBM wanted a system immediately, so Microsoft had to purchase and develop a system rather than take the time to write one from scratch. Microsoft's other customers (programmers and end users) would look for an operating system that supported many applications. Q-DOS met their priorities; the broad application base developed for CP/M could be easily adapted. Microsoft embraced and extended the existing Q-DOS program and called it MS-DOS.

Another part of Microsoft's standards-building methodology was to create end-user pull to complement the "push" effect that OEMs created. Microsoft made DOS an "open" system. IBM and Microsoft published programming specifications and encouraged developers to write DOS applications. Third-party applications developers catching the IBM PC wave created a burgeoning cottage industry of DOS applications. End users overwhelmingly chose the "IBM PC-compatible" format applications, which created "pull-through" for MS-DOS and built switching costs to protect against the incursion of other operating systems.

Cementing the standard, however, meant keeping the software independent from the hardware. While IBM was enjoying great success ($4 billion in PC sales by 1984), Gates was careful not to tie himself to a sole OEM partner. He convinced IBM to allow third-party licensing. Totally comfortable in its leadership of the computer industry, IBM never imagined the importance of this clause in the Microsoft contract.

By July 1982, Microsoft had locked in 20 American OEM contracts—including leading "clone" makers Compaq, Dell, and Packard Bell—and eight Japanese contracts. DOS became an enormous cash generator during the 1980s, and by 1991 had $200 million in revenues at 80 percent gross margins. Microsoft had created the first two major software standards, in languages and operating systems.

Once Microsoft's victory was ensured, Gates began tapping into the extraordinary profit power of his standards-based business design. During Microsoft's market penetration phase, Gates had pursued a low-price strategy to bring in customers. However, once Microsoft established a leadership position, Gates shifted gears to capture a virtual tax on every new hardware machine. First he moved from flat-fee pricing to per-machine pricing, and then he began raising prices. Gates had started to create an extraordinary profit zone in the computing industry.

WINDOWS

In markets that experience rapid introductions and adoption of new generations of technology, it is important to constantly reexamine the basis of profit power of a business design. Despite the strength of Microsoft's strategic control as MS-DOS became ubiquitous, Gates was constantly challenged to think about the next generation of customer priorities, and the next generation of standards.

When Gates visited the Comdex computer industry convention in 1982, he was horrified. VisiCorp, then the number one microcomputer application software company in the world (based on the first spreadsheet, VisiCalc), demonstrated a product called VisiOn, a mouse-driven graphical user interface shell for the IBM PC, as well as a suite of applications. This 1982 offering was a less powerful forerunner of the Windows and Office suite products that are ubiquitous today. Gates saw that VisiOn had the potential to sew up the applications and operating system markets in one move, under one standard. Not only did VisiCorp have a technically advanced product, but it brought the prestige and marketing capability that could attract a large market.

At Comdex, Bill Gates sat through three complete demonstration sessions of the VisiOn products. What VisiCorp showed off (to thunderous applause) was, in effect, an MS-DOS-killer. Microsoft's effort to establish the MS-DOS standard was in jeopardy.

Gates leaped into total attack mode. Microsoft's response to VisiOn set the pattern for many later reactive strategies against new challenges to its standards. First and foremost, Microsoft focused on winning mindshare away from VisiCorp. Even without a product, Microsoft had to establish its differentiation in order to stall VisiOn. In October 1983, when VisiCorp finally announced that it would ship VisiOn, Microsoft prepared its own announcement. It demonstrated an Interface Manager prototype—which it named "Windows"—that was no more than a graphics program that drew dummy windows representing files and applications. At Comdex 1983, Microsoft launched a no-holds-barred campaign to win the hearts and minds of customers. Banners at Las Vegas airport greeted conference delegates. Taxicabs were plastered with Windows ads. Cocktail napkins were printed with "Look Through the Microsoft Windows" and offered discounts at local restaurants.[4]

These mass-market tactics were aimed at disrupting the competition rather than driving sales, because Windows was not ready for the market. Gates's strategy worked. When VisiOn began shipping, soon after Comdex, it could not escape the specter of Windows. VisiOn products did not move off the shelves. Windows became the product the world waited for (few could guess how long the wait would be). *Fortune* magazine predicted that Windows would set the standard—without ever having seen a working copy of it.

VisiOn is an example of the failure of superior technology in the absence of the right business design. It illustrates how a standard is not adopted. VisiCorp's business design made end-user switching costs extraordinarily high. VisiOn was sold in shrink-wrap through VisiCorp's retail channel, so end users didn't receive it preinstalled on their systems. It was introduced at more than $1,000, a price point far too high for the retail channel. It could not run on most users' existing hardware setups without costly upgrades. It was a "closed, proprietary" system like the Macintosh, incompatible with the growing base of DOS software. VisiCorp actually discouraged third-party software development, planning instead to corner its own applications market. It charged developers a hefty fee for programming specifications, and coding required a DEC VAX, which few of them could access. This lack of applications software left an important end-user priority unmet, and the absence of end-user enthusiasm was the final nail in VisiCorp's coffin.

VisiOn's main failure was not with technology, but with business design. It met customers' need for an intuitive interface but didn't tailor itself to such critical priorities as low switching costs, price, convenience, and software selection. Gates understood these priorities and promised a solution. Even though he did not have the solution, the promise itself was more than VisiOn offered to customers. They would wait for Windows. This was the first step in creating significant end-user pull for Windows. VisiCorp did not survive the formidable attack constructed by Gates through preemptive marketing and strategic OEM relationships.

VisiCorp—battling a phantom product—lost $2.5 million in the third quarter of 1984. It was sold to Lotus by the end of the year for an undisclosed but certainly modest sum—still months before Windows' first launch. Windows never even competed with VisiOn on its own merits.[5]

CRAFTING THE CREATE-THE-STANDARD BUSINESS DESIGN

The success of the Windows program was built on two core elements of Gates's strategic business design: (1) maximum distribution and (2) perfect fit with customers' priorities. By the time the product finally delivered on its promise, with Version 3.0 in 1990, Microsoft had already established the standards-based business design that ensured its value creation performance.

First, Windows had a great channel. With BASIC and DOS, Microsoft secured valuable OEM relationships. With the launch of Windows, Gates drew on his OEM distribution channels to ensure that Windows would be preinstalled on every new machine. Second, Windows met the new customer priority of simplicity. Copying Apple's popular graphical user interface (GUI, pronounced "gooey"), Gates provided his customers with point-and-click convenience.

Gates knew that Windows also had to meet the customer priority of broad applications selection. Windows ran off the DOS shell and was compatible with DOS applications. But Gates went much further in his software efforts. He wanted a strong base of applications that would strongly motivate users to adopt the Windows interface. Microsoft encouraged adoption of Windows by, in effect, creating a new paradigm for how customers interacted with their computers. First, Gates prepared his own suite of productivity applications—Excel, Word, Powerpoint—ported from the Macintosh to Windows, that delivered on the promise of the GUI format's ease of use and matched the leading competitors in functionality. Lotus and Word-Perfect, two of the leaders in DOS applications, deliberately avoided developing for Windows, focusing instead on IBM's OS/2. They feared Microsoft's growing momentum and felt the growing power that was being wielded from Redmond, Washington. That suited Gates. Their boycott threw the applications software market wide open and made Microsoft Office (an integrated suite of Excel, Word, and Powerpoint) the "killer" application for Windows in 1991 (Exhibit 13.2).

Outside the arena of his three core productivity applications, Gates encouraged other firms to create new software that would excite users. He boosted Microsoft's applications developer marketing efforts. Gates became chief evangelist of a Microsoft team that actively wooed independent software vendors (ISVs) to develop for Windows. He spent hundreds of millions of dollars cultivating a cottage industry that delivers on the customer priority for more applications. In doing so, he tapped into an enormous reservoir of technical

---

EXHIBIT 13.2 *Microsoft's Business Design: Create-the-Standard*

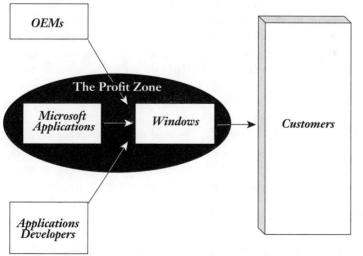

and entrepreneurial energy that unleashed hundreds of millions of dollars worth of R&D investment done by others on behalf of the Windows standard.

One area of focus was porting Macintosh applications to Windows. Microsoft hired a consultant who studied Apple's innovative developer marketing efforts. Microsoft cloned Apple's developer efforts—complete with annual developer conventions, beta-testing assistance, and product briefings—and then expanded and improved them. Developer marketing was aimed at widening selection, especially in entertainment titles, statistical and drawing packages, and development tool and control modules.

The result was extraordinary growth in Windows 3.0 applications. In 1989, fewer than 1,000 applications were available for Windows. By 1996, that number was more than 30,000, with a developer community estimated at 50,000 programmers.[6]

As in other format wars, like the Betamax-versus-VHS battle in the VCR industry, the decisive element was not about technology or even about the lack of basic offerings in one format rather than another. It was about mindshare. The average Windows customer uses the same three software packages—word processor, graphics, and spreadsheet—that are available on the competitive operating systems. But end users and MIS directors choose Windows for the option of using the other 29,997 packages, many of which are not available for the Macintosh, or O/S2, or UNIX. The customer might never exercise the options presented by greater selection, but, in 1990, the recipe for a winning business design for Windows hinged on realizing the importance of meeting this customer priority. Once momentum is established in one direction, it is very difficult to reverse. How many Betamax titles are in a Blockbuster Video store today? How many Macintosh titles will CompUSA stock in the year 2000?

In the late 1980s, Gates's methodical and painstaking strategic moves with Windows met the challenge of introducing a new technology into a mass market. They produced the critical alignment of Microsoft's business design with existing customer priorities. The business design was in place.

The launch on May 22, 1990, was spectacular and unprecedented. More than 100 ISVs launched their own Windows products, and 50 PC OEMs enthusiastically announced that Windows would be installed and running on all of their systems. Microsoft spent more than $12 million on marketing, which spurred retail sales of almost 11,000 shrink-wrap copies per day during the first few months. Eight years after the promise of VisiOn, and 6 years after the comparable technology of the Macintosh burst onto the market, the real GUI revolution began—and on Bill Gates's terms. By 1994, the worldwide installed base of Windows exceeded 100 million—not merely surpassing the original penetration of DOS, but opening up the market to new populations of first-time computer users. Windows 95 accounted for more than $1 billion in revenues in 1996.[7]

APPLICATIONS: THE WINDOWS REVOLUTION

With Windows rapidly becoming the standard operating system for PCs, Gates looked for an opportunity to leverage this position into the next major opportunity space for Microsoft. He saw it in the desktop applications market. Each PC ran only one operating system, but the market for applications was enormous. Gates set out to expand the value capture of his Windows standard by attacking this attractive space.

Within the desktop market, the personal productivity applications providers had the strongest positions. The advent of spreadsheets, word processing, and presentation software had made PCs useful in the corporate world, and the leaders, such as Lotus 1-2-3, Wordperfect, and Harvard Graphics, had strong products and loyal customers. Despite the strength of these incumbents, Microsoft designated this space as its next major opportunity.

Microsoft drew on its experience in other standards battles as it developed an attack plan. Establishing individual profit-and-loss centers for each product line, Gates established an aggressive win-at-all-costs mindset in his organization. Gates even personally led the charge by joining in sales calls at the incumbents' biggest accounts. Taking advantage of the rapid adoption of Windows 3.0, product development focused on reducing the costs of switching to new applications. By ensuring file compatibility and similar command structures, users could "upgrade" to Excel, to Word, or to

Powerpoint as they were upgrading their operating system from DOS to Windows. Many customers, excited by the Windows format but frustrated by Wordperfect's and Lotus's lack of a Windows version, saw the move to Microsoft applications as an easy decision. Appealing to the same customer priority that made Windows appealing—ease of use— Microsoft made upgrades simple and established helplines to support users during file conversion.

Microsoft also applied the lessons about pricing that it had learned in previous battles. At the same time that it was pushing on the compatibility and ease of use of its Windows-based applications, it also changed the pricing paradigm that had ruled the market for the previous decade. In the retail channel, instead of pricing each application individually, Microsoft began to offer bundled suites *and* lower prices. The $495-per-application price point disappeared. Suddenly, users could buy bundled "upgrades" for a fraction of that price. For large corporate users, Microsoft initiated concurrent licenses that reflected the number of users at any one time rather than forcing them to buy a copy for each desktop. Corporate buyers loved it.

This combination of differentiation and value capture strategy created a tidal wave of momentum for Microsoft's applications business. Aggressive pricing can be a profit-destroying tactic, but Microsoft understood the narrow window within which it could wrest leadership of the market from the incumbents. If Microsoft could establish a leading position, its standards-based design would allow it to consolidate that position. By owning the standards in the operating systems *and* the top applications, Microsoft could consistently outdesign its rivals by continuously updating and changing its products as a differentiated barrier against imitators. Doing so also raises the switching costs involved in retraining personnel, systems costs, and file conversion.

Microsoft owns the desktop productivity and software market, pulling in $6 billion of the $7 billion available in revenues. In the major applications markets, its flagship Office product owns an 85 percent market share, and that number increases with every upgrade cycle.

Microsoft's economics are characterized by an increasing return to scale. A standards business is just like a telephone network—the more people use it, the more valuable it is. As Microsoft products become more ubiquitous, their total value increases. Because the marginal cost for a software product is negligible, the more it sells, the more profit it makes—and the greater the value the market attaches to its business. Microsoft's long-term profit-centric thinking proclaims: Invest today, profit tomorrow, in order to invest again (Exhibit 13.3).

EXHIBIT 13.3 *Microsoft Business Design Reinvention*

	1975	*1981*	*1990*	*1995*	*1999*
Customer Selection	• Programmers	• Programmers • PC manufacturers	• Programmers • PC manufacturers • Mac users • PC users	• Programmers • PC manufacturers • Mac users • PC users • Network users	
Value Capture	• Software sales	• Software sales • Installed base	• Installed base	• Installed base • Increasing returns to scale	
Differentiation/ Strategic Control	• Create the standard	• Create the standard	• Create the standard • Programs that utilize full capabilities of operating system	• Create the standard • Brand • OEM and application developer relationship	
Scope	• Languages	• Desktop software	• Desktop software • Bundled software	• Desktop software • Bundled software • Communication • Network • Exchange	

THE CURRENT BATTLEGROUND: ENTERPRISE COMPUTING AND THE ELECTRONIC HOME

Having achieved success in the desktop world, Microsoft has turned its sights to two profit zones that represent huge potential value growth in the next 5 years: (1) networked computing in large corporations, and (2) the convergence of voice, video, and data within the consumer's home. In addition, Microsoft has recognized the emergence of a competing paradigm—the Internet—and has built an effective response designed to ensure its leadership in both the office and the home. Each of these sectors places Microsoft in new competitive arenas and stretches its business beyond previous limits.

ENTERPRISE COMPUTING: WINDOWS NT

As the PC has become a more powerful tool within corporations, it is now possible for networks of PCs to compete for the computer functions that had traditionally been the domain of large mainframes and minicomputers. Microsoft has recognized this opportunity (in fact, it went a long way to create it) and has invested aggressively to position Windows NT as the standard vehicle through which networked PCs will compete with the legacy systems.

In its first battle for the networked computing standard, Microsoft took on Novell, the incumbent leader in PC-network operating systems. When Microsoft entered the market in 1991 with Windows NT, the product did not offer as much functionality as Novell's Netware, and it faltered in the face of Novell's strong reputation. Novell maintained a commanding 70 percent market share in 1994.

Repeating the pattern used in previous efforts to create a de facto standard, Gates would not be dissuaded by a first-generation failure. When Windows NT 3.5 was introduced in 1994, Microsoft employed its proven standards-building techniques to ensure the success of its product. To gain mindshare from Novell, Microsoft launched an aggressive marketing effort that set NT as a viable alternative in the minds of customers. NT 3.5 met customers' priorities of speed and of easy administration and setup. It lowered barriers to switching: (1) by allowing NT servers to provide access to Netware servers; (2) by providing utilities to easily convert Netware user accounts to NT; and (3) by sharply undercutting Novell on price. By 1995, Microsoft had nearly 20 percent of the server market, and Novell's share had slipped to 43 percent.

In its newest version, NT 4.0, Microsoft has increased its focus on customer priorities, providing a Windows 95 style interface for setup and administration, and a protected application environment that adds reliability. Not only do these improvements position NT to further outdistance Novell, but they also provide a solid platform on which to attack the broader enterprise computing market. NT is now a robust platform on which to build client-server applications, and it provides the price and performance that make it a compelling alternative for companies of all sizes. By working with leading enterprise applications developers like SAP, and by developing Microsoft enterprise applications like BackOffice, Microsoft has begun to present a viable, economically advantaged alternative to traditional systems.

Microsoft recognizes that, although the market for enterprise computing is an enormous opportunity, the requirements in this space are quite different from those in the desktop world. No longer can ease of use be completely built into the product. Enterprise solutions require substantial on-the-ground technical support, something that Microsoft has never before needed. Instead of building an expensive infrastructure from scratch (something that could take two or three quarters to accomplish), Gates first convinced Digital Equipment (DEC) and then Hewlett Packard to train their service organizations to support NT.

Microsoft is a long way from replicating the leadership position that it has established on the desktop, but its enterprise strategy has all the hallmarks of establishing a standards-based business design. Incumbents, beware!

The Electronic Home

If the corporation is a deep, well-defined pool of profit that Microsoft can see and pursue, the electronic home is an enormous profit pool that is just now forming. As traditionally disparate media of voice, video, and data begin to converge because of technology and deregulation, large changes in consumer behavior are anticipated. How we watch television, how we access our finances, how we shop, how we communicate with each other, how we get our news—all may change as new devices and technologies are wired into our lives. The spending that this could unlock across hundreds of millions of households around the world could create an enormous profit zone for companies with the right business designs.

Microsoft has methodically begun to lay the groundwork for creating the standard in this space. By first understanding how customer priorities may change and the applications that they might find most valuable, Microsoft has created or acquired early leadership positions in online services, including classified advertising, information services, commerce and retailing, and local content management.

It has also begun to position its Windows CE operating system as the preferred platform for a new generation of convergence devices that could replace TVs, PCs, or both. The recent acquisition of WebTV, and Microsoft's $1 billion investment in Comcast, illustrate Gates's orientation toward establishing the rules before the game unfolds. Rather than fighting for a standard in an established market, Microsoft aims to already be in place as the standard when the market finally develops.

Managing the Paradigm Shift: The Internet

The Internet has already begun to transform the computing world. With rapid induction into corporations and steadily increasing penetration of homes, Internet computing is rapidly becoming a critical element of *both* environments. Microsoft's response to the Internet illustrates the adaptive power of Gates's organization.

Just as with applications, Microsoft was a late entrant to the Internet game. However, once in the game, Microsoft has reused the genetic code from the BASIC, DOS, and Windows business designs.

Many observers saw the Internet as a potential threat to Microsoft's leadership. In classic form, Gates responded to the uncertainty posed by the Internet by hedging his bets and leveraging his core businesses for an all-out assault into new territory. Though massively committed to the desktop, he wanted to cover the possibility that the Internet may surpass it in strategic significance.

At first, the Internet game looked as though it was over before Microsoft would even step up to bat. By the time Microsoft decided to become the Internet leader, Netscape had built a sizable lead—on the order of 80 percent market share of Internet browsers. But anyone who has read this chapter knows that Microsoft has responded to similar challenges in the applications world and is capable of similar moves to chip away at Netscape's position. First, just as he had defended against VisiOn, Gates began to recapture mindshare. On the fifty-fourth anniversary of Pearl Harbor, he staged a major press conference at which he assured the world that Microsoft was well positioned to exploit the technologies of the Internet. Next, he used two of the strategies that had helped Microsoft win the GUI war—effective distribution and a low upfront pricing strategy. Purchasers were guaranteed that Microsoft's Web browser would be loaded on most computers, and Microsoft's ability to provide seamless compatibility with the most popular applications—MS Office— would give Microsoft's browser the differentiation needed to trigger adoption by most Windows users.

When Microsoft began to upgrade Windows 3.1 to Windows 95, it included its Web browser, Microsoft Explorer, in the package. This strategy for releasing its Internet browser was basically a combination of the effective distribution and low upfront pricing strategies that Microsoft had employed when it sought to set Windows as the standard operating system. By using the Windows upgrade as a platform for launching Explorer, Microsoft had the ideal distribution system to ensure that Explorer made it onto every Windows 95 machine. Furthermore, by packaging it as an add-on to the operating system, Microsoft charged nothing to the consumer, thus utilizing the lowest upfront pricing strategy possible. Finally, Gates locked up distribution relationships with the leading online providers— America On-Line (AOL), Compuserve, and others—to accelerate penetration.

It worked. Users of Netscape have begun moving to Explorer. Netscape's browser market share fell to 70 percent in March of 1997 (from roughly 80 percent in September of 1996), and, over the same period, Microsoft increased its share from less than 10 percent to 28 percent. An example of the changeover: Chevron, an early Netscape user, has converted to Explorer. The major reasons cited for the decision were Chevron's dependence on the Windows operating system and future product directions.[8]

As in many previous market cycles, Gates is moving rapidly to create the next de facto standard. Using the advantage of scale, he is devoting huge resources to his Internet program: for Microsoft Explorer 1.0, he used 3 programmers; for version 2.0, he used 20; for version 4.0, he is using 700! Realizing the importance of this standard in both the corporate and the home markets, Gates is leaving nothing to chance in creating it.

Microsoft has been a tremendous innovator over its history, but that innovation has been about business design, not about technology. Microsoft didn't invent any of its key technologies. It adapted existing technology to the needs of the market in ingenious ways, and it embedded that technology in a standards-based business design that created strategic value for Microsoft and enormous value for shareholders.

Perhaps the perfect counterpoint to Microsoft's success has been the failure of Apple Computer (see Exhibit 13.4). Apple had brilliant product innovation. It understood ease of use as a customer priority well before the rest of the market. It repeatedly set the standard for technical excellence in the market. Unfortunately, that technology was embedded in a flawed business design. Apple tried to create a standard by keeping everything proprietary to itself. It tried to own the standard by literally owning all of the key elements. This tactic fundamentally limited the ability of other market players to help Apple establish the standard.

A standard is something that drives an entire industry. Microsoft recognized early the importance of investing to recruit other market players—customers, competitors, channels—in creating the kind of momentum that creates that standard. It was prepared to pay the price required to create the standard, and is now enjoying the returns, even as it worries about how to create the standards that will define the *next* half-decade of the computing and convergence world.

EXHIBIT 13.4   *Microsoft vs. Apple: Market Value Growth*

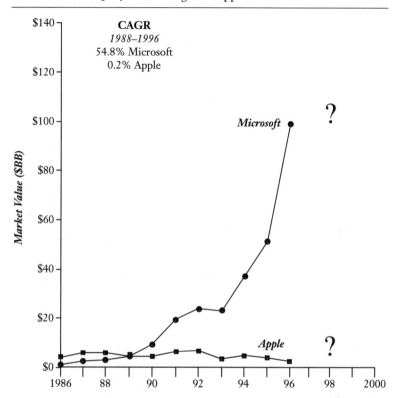

BUILDING A CREATE-THE-STANDARD BUSINESS DESIGN
Pilot's Checklist

☑ *Have I done a deal with* every *major OEM?*

☑ *Have I* maximized *investment in applications developer marketing and support to maximize the value of my technology to the customer?*

☑ *Have I* minimized *price and switching costs for the customer?*

☑ *Have I developed a core suite of applications and services to add value to the standard?*

☑ *Have I developed a blueprint for versions 2.0, 3.0, and 4.0, to keep adding value for* all *my customers?*
—End-users
—Applications developers
—OEMs

PART THREE

The Profit Zone Handbook

FOURTEEN

HOW BUSINESS DESIGN INNOVATION CREATES THE PROFIT ZONE

PERHAPS THE single most striking observation about the reinventors' achievements in business design is how different they are—different from each other, and different from their peers.

The success logic that drives Coke's business design is completely different from the logic that drives GE's. Thermo Electron and Schwab are worlds apart. So, too, are Microsoft and Disney.

Reinvention is about the customer and profitability, but ultimately it is about creativity, about designing a business model that is unique.

Perhaps the most important benefit of studying any reinventors and how they discover or create the profit zone in their industries is grasping how the creative process works in business (how business designs change every 5 years), what discipline (in customer and profit thinking) it requires, and how extraordinary its outcomes can be.

INNOVATION IN BUSINESS DESIGN DRIVES VALUE GROWTH

In the age of market share, companies sought to create and maintain a sustainable competitive advantage. Today, other than patents and protected markets, there is no such thing as long-term sustainable competitive advantage. But there is sustained value growth—over a decade or two, or even longer.

Creating sustained value growth requires reinventing the business design as frequently as every 5 years. The reinventors profiled in Part Two have shown that this is not only possible but can lead to extraordinary outcomes. Note the causality in Exhibits 14.1 and 14.2. Coke's changes in its business design (from franchise bottler model, to U.S. bottler management, to international value chain manager) increased its asset intensity but drove significant improvements in its other financial characteristics (return on sales, profit growth, and strategic control/profit protection). Those changes in the company's financial parameters drove increases in the company's valuation; its market value–sales ratio rose from 0.7 in 1980 to 7.0 in 1996 (see Exhibit 14.2). Together, these factors have created sustained value growth for Coca-Cola and have made it one of the most highly valued companies in the world.

The same causal mechanism is at work in every reinventor's company: business design innovation drives financial improvement, which drives increased valuation, which drives value growth. This pattern of value growth and increasing valuation is so consistent among the reinventors that it is easy to take this kind of performance improvement for granted. It is useful to put the reinventors' track record in context by comparing it to the S&P500 and to the value growth performance of a portfolio of the major market share leaders of the early 1980s (see Exhibit 14.3).

However we juxtapose the data, the rewards of effective business design creativity are quite extraordinary.

THE PARADOX OF RISING PROFIT MARGINS

Classic strategy theory taught us that margins always go down, not up. The combined effect of commoditization, increasing competition, product obsolescence, and customer power always drives margins downward.

EXHIBIT 14.1 *Coca-Cola's Reinventions*

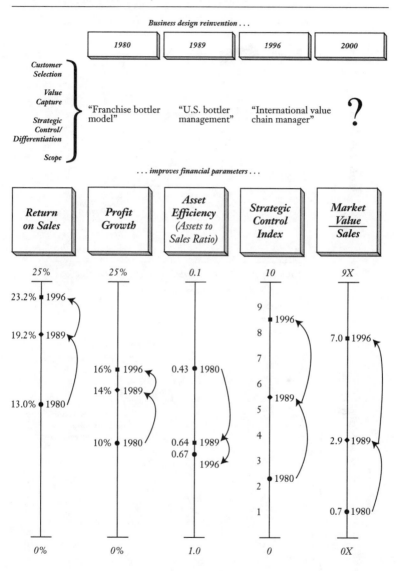

EXHIBIT 14.2   *Coca-Cola's Increased Valuation*

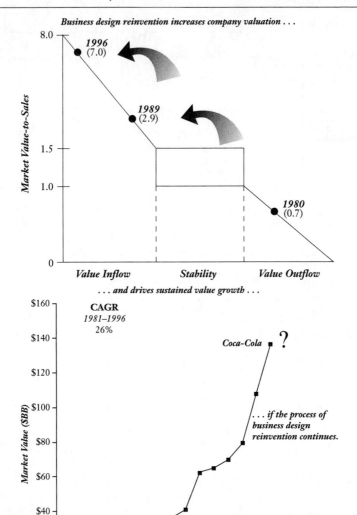

Business design reinvention increases company valuation . . .

. . . and drives sustained value growth . . .

Source: Compustat.

EXHIBIT 14.3   *The Nine Reinventors vs. the S&P500*
and Market Share Leaders

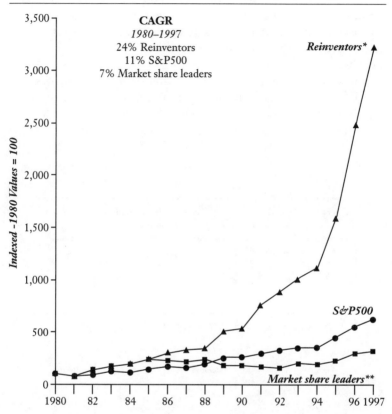

*Reinventors without Microsoft and Intel have a 20 percent compound annual growth rate.

**Market share leaders include American Airlines, Bethlehem Steel, Digital Equipment, Ford, GM, IBM, Kmart, Sears, United Airlines, and U.S. Steel.

These factors have, if anything, intensified in the past decade. There are more competitors per category and the competition is global. Information flows faster, competitive imitation is more rapid, and customers are growing ever more powerful because of the choices and information available to them. Profit margins are under greater pressure than ever and, if anything, should be falling more quickly.

Not so with the reinventors. The power of effective business design reinvention is perhaps best reflected in the pattern of profit margin behavior they have created (see Exhibit 14.4). They are not declining, nor even constant; they are rising in every case.

EXHIBIT 14.4 *The Reinventors' Return on Sales*

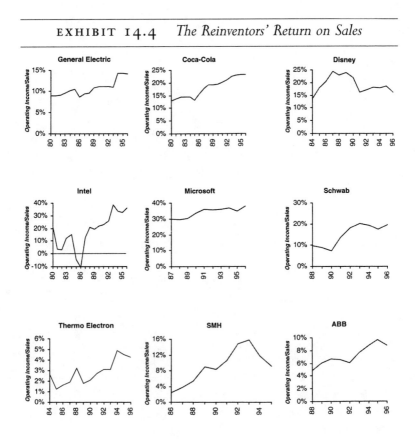

Harder to quantify, but almost as important, is the nature of the revenue mix on which those profit margins are based. In most cases, the business designs have been recrafted in such a way that the ratio of recurring revenue (as opposed to transactional revenue) is increasing. Think of Schwab's assets fees, or ABB's long-term maintenance contracts, or GE's service contract revenues, or Microsoft's upgrade revenues. In every case, business design innovation is improving not only customer relevance, but also the sustained profit performance of the company.

MAJOR MISTAKES

It would be a mistake to take the reinventors' value growth performance for granted. It would also be a mistake to think that the smooth performance curve is the result of a smooth and error-free process. Quite the contrary. Business design innovation requires major nonincremental moves. Making such moves inevitably leads to major errors.

The experience of every one of the ten reinventors in Part Two includes such major missteps. GE and Kidder Peabody. Intel and the Pentium flaw. New Coke. The operational nightmares of Schwab's service system for the financial planners. Every release 1.0 of any Microsoft product. Swatch's ventures in telecommunication products. EuroDisney.

The list could be extended for pages, and could be the subject matter for an entire book. The key point is that there is no great creativity without great errors, and the reinventors experienced more than their fair share.

TARGET FIXATION

Major mistakes, however, come in two varieties. Those mentioned above are examples of new ideas or business design moves that failed. The second variety of major mistake is staying fixated on yesterday's opportunity and business design, never risking a change in course. This type of management error is analogous to "target fixation," a phenomenon observed in military aviators of the pre-laser era.

In the days before laser-guided target acquisition and destruction, traditional attack pilots were experts at dive bombing. The maneuver was fairly simple. Pilots climbed to 20,000 feet, rolled the wing over, dropped the nose of the plane, and commenced a steep dive in the direction of the target. Then, while screaming straight down toward the ground at a speed of 500 knots, the pilot would visually acquire the target and align the bombsight with both the target and the bull's-eye of the sight. As long as the alignment remained perfect, the airplane would stay on track, like an arrow aimed directly at the target. Meanwhile, 1,000 feet clicked off the altimeter every few seconds. Like many processes, dive bombing looked straightforward, but a lot was going on, especially if someone was shooting at the plane.

One of the biggest risks to a dive-bombing aviator was called "target fixation." The pilot could get so focused on keeping the sight on the target, to ensure an accurate drop, that he or she forgot the altitude and flew the plane right into the ground—excellent micromanagement of the current measurement ("Are we on target?"), but no connection to the broader reality.

Target fixation is a common management issue. To focus or simplify tasks, management chooses a process, a metric, and a target. For example, market share, revenue growth, cost position, and time to market (or to reject) are chosen as targets. The data are tracked and graphed. Midcourse corrections aimed at continuous improvement are introduced, and the system takes over. A very efficient process—when it works. The reckoning comes when the business is at the brink of failure and everyone realizes that they have been fixated on the wrong metric and target. Crash!

Why does the crash occur? Targets and metrics are generally perceived as good management practice. Management gets fixated on:

- *Market share of yesterday's product opportunity or yesterday's business design, when the profit zone has moved to services.*
- *Revenue growth in a commoditized no-profit industry segment.*
- *Reducing manufacturing unit costs, when value is created for the customer elsewhere in the value chain.*
- *Fast time to market with the wrong product.*

- *Service that misses the target defined by the customer's priorities and systems economics.*
- *Statistical quality control charts that in no way define quality in the eyes of the customer.*

In simple terms, management is trying to perfect yesterday's business design. The opportunity has passed them by, yet they believe that if they can only get a little bigger or do a little better, they can still win. They are fighting yesterday's war. The battle meanwhile has moved on to an opportunity space redefined by new customer priorities and competitive business designs, where the old measures, processes, and company cultures that are controlling the organization are often obsolete.

In today's world of instant communication, rapidly evolving markets, and short business design cycles, avoiding target fixation and leading the company to new opportunities may be a reinventor's single most important role.

Target fixation helps us understand why so many market share leaders went wrong by fixating on market share. The real issue was defining the profit zone, inventing a new business design, and creating market value. In the past 5 years, there has been a large-scale shift in metrics as more and more companies realize that evolving markets require new business designs aimed at profit and value, not just share.

Meanwhile, the reinventors are not at all comfortable in the current mode. In fact, they're worried. Their concern is how long the "market value" phase will last, and what the next phase will be. Characterized by a strong distaste for unnecessary risk, they have no interest in experiencing the kind of decade-long derailment that the traditional market share leaders suffered. They're worrying about what the next shift will be.

Sitting as we are in the middle of the market value phase, it's hard to visualize what the next phase might be. Knowledge value creation? Employee allegiance? Customer commitment? Customer commitment *and* proprietary information flow?

We don't know yet. But that is why it's so important to open the company's collective mind and be on the lookout for what the next metrics revolution will be. We must avoid the extraordinarily high risk of target fixation. Understanding the fundamentals of business design innovation is perhaps the best preparation for an uncertain future.

The unit that follows is a practitioner's manual for innovation in business design. The questions and exercises it contains are designed to challenge and enable your organization to keep ahead, not just abreast, of changing customer priorities, and to create the next profit zone in your industry. Its purpose is to enable your organization to create a trajectory of sustained value growth.

FIFTEEN

THE PROFIT ZONE
HANDBOOK

THE PROFIT ZONE has detailed a new way of thinking about business. Part One laid out the basic ideas of customer-centric and profit-centric thinking, describing the new strategic concepts necessary to succeed in business today. Part Two illustrated how business leaders have used these concepts over time to become successful. This final section of Part Three brings together all of the ideas of the book and allows the reader to apply them to his or her own company.

Because good business design thinking is a learned skill, guidance is given here in the form of questions. These pages are not to be skimmed quickly. Spend a few quiet hours working through these ideas. Those hours may be the most valuable learning time you'll have all year. You can work through this chapter by yourself or with a team. Having other managers to brainstorm with may make the questions easier to answer and the tools more valuable to use.

MOVING YOUR COMPANY INTO
THE PROFIT ZONE

This handbook has been arranged to help you move your company into the profit zone. The process involves addressing a sequence of twelve questions:

1. *Who are my customers?*
2. *How are their priorities changing?*
3. *Who should be my customer?*

4.   *How can I add value to the customer?*
5.   *How can I become the customer's first choice?*
6.   *What is my profit model?*
7.   *What is my current business design?*
8.   *Who are my* real *competitors?*
9.   *What is my toughest competitors' business design?*
10. *What is my* next *business design?*
11. *What is my strategic control point?*
12. *What is my company worth?*

This Handbook helps you to answer each of these questions by working through a series of exercises.

By answering these questions, you will be equipped to beat your competitors to the profit zone. You will learn the techniques that are necessary to modify your business design and stay within the profit zone as it moves. You will have at your disposal a tool kit filled with techniques that will allow you to reduce the risk of making mistakes and will coach you in identifying your customers' priorities, finding the profit zone within your industry, designing the right business model, and preserving your company's strategic control over its profitability.

Answer each of the questions in light of your experience in your company. Use the techniques identified, and don't hesitate to amplify them with your own ideas. Move forward with confidence. You will be headed toward the profit zone.

1. WHO ARE MY CUSTOMERS?

Throughout the book, we have seen that understanding your customers is the first key to successful business design. A company that lacks customer information is running blindly. Effective business design requires an understanding of many aspects of the customer base.

Many managers believe they know who their customers are because, every day, they see customers in their stores or see customers' names on invoices. However, identifying customers really means being able to categorize them into distinct groups whose behavior can be analyzed accurately. You may separate your customers by age, geography, industry, length of relationship, reason for purchase, frequency of purchase, purchase criteria, or other demographic attributes. You should also try to segment your customers into different groups—for instance, by behavior or by priority. By moving beyond classic customer segmentation, you may find that your groups of customers are very different from each other and from your impressions of them. In the space below, list your major customer groups.

Major Customer Groups

1. _____

2. _____

3. _____

4. _____

5. _____

As a model, look at Coca-Cola's major customer groups. Many individuals might list consumers as Coke's major customer group. Coke's actual list might look something like this:

Coke's Major Customer Groups
1. *Consumers*
2. *Fountain and Vending Customers*
3. *Anchor Bottlers*
4. *National Chains*

One of your most important responsibilities regarding your customers is to understand their priorities. You may need an in-depth market analysis to understand what is most important to your customers. But, through observation and logical thinking, you begin the process of deciphering the priorities that are guiding your customers' behavior. Both in and beyond your market, customers are constantly expressing their preferences. Your answers to the following two sets of questions will help you to find out what is most important to your customers.

Figuring out your customers' priorities in your industry.
* *Name three products or services in your industry that have become popular over the past 2 years.*

Why did customers like them?
What were the underlying reasons for the products' value?
Did they save money? Reduce hassle? Offer security?

Figuring out your customers' priorities in other industries.
- *The customers who buy from you also buy many products and services in other markets. Repeat the above exercise but substitute an unrelated market or industry where your customers are actively engaged. What preferences do they express in that market?*

Your customers will have two sets of needs, those that are spoken and those that are silent or unspoken. It is not difficult to recognize the spoken needs—typically, they are the needs that most of the businesses in an industry try to meet. What is more difficult is identifying your customers' silent needs. To find an ever-shifting profit zone, you will have to do that.

One way to discover what your customers' silent or unspoken priorities are is to consider the entire economic system in which your customers operate. Too often, managers focus solely on the transactions that occur between their company and their customers. This tunnel vision blocks a realistic view of what customers are looking for. Do your customers see you as merely one niche occupant, in one area of their lives or businesses? Is that how you see yourself in relation to your customers? Is that image or relationship the one you want for your business?

Systems economics attempts to quantify the complete economic picture of a particular product or service by modeling out all of the associated costs and revenues. Systems economics is about more than just profitability; it captures all the drivers and variables that affect profitability. Systems economics can take the form of a very complex financial model, or can quickly be used to get a thumbnail sketch of profitability. By thinking about your customers from a systems economics perspective, you will be better able to understand their unspoken needs.

Try the following questions.
- *Imagine yourself as the CEO of each of your five most important customers (or as a head of household in your five most important demographic groups).*

What would your overall objectives be?

What major concerns would you have?

How could a supplier help you toward your goals? How is the supplier currently hindering you?

2. HOW ARE THEIR PRIORITIES CHANGING?

Customers' needs are not static. People and their environments change, creating new customer priorities and, thus, new opportunities for businesses to serve them. The list below gives you several examples of companies that have benefited from changing customer priorities.

Customer Priority Shifts			Example Beneficiary
1. Product functionality	⇒	Price	Autodesk
2. Product/Service	⇒	Solution	GE, Disney, ABB, Hewlett-Packard
3. Availability	⇒	Broadest assortment	Home Depot
4. Product functionality	⇒	Product quality	Toyota
5. Lowest price	⇒	Lowest price and time saving	Wal-Mart
6. Lowest price	⇒	Fair price and time saving	Auto-by-Tel
7. Lowest price	⇒	Lowest system cost	GE
8. Product functionality	⇒	Fast delivery	Dell Computer
9. Solution	⇒	Outsourcing	EDS
10. Product functionality, relationship	⇒	Low-cost, low-hassle	Staples

Understanding customer priority shifts, and responding to them quickly, led to extraordinary financial success for the example companies. Also, consider how changing customer priorities in the coffee industry (a priority shift away from price to quality, leading to a shift from grocery retail brands to specialty coffee stores) allowed Starbuck's to prosper.

Apply this thinking to your own market. Using the information you cited for the products that have succeeded in your industry, fill in the following spaces:

Recent Shifts in Our Industry

1993 *Customer Priorities*	*1998* *Customer Priorities*
1. _____	_____
2. _____	_____
3. _____	_____

Look at the other industries where your customers operate. Do you see any trends that may soon appear in your market? If customers are trying to save time in one of those areas, aren't they likely to value saved time in yours? What advantages can you introduce now, or in the near future, to anticipate your customers' preferences or needs?

Predictable Shifts in Our Industry

1998 *Customer Priorities*	*2002* *Customer Priorities*
1. _____	_____
2. _____	_____
3. _____	_____

3. Who *Should* Be My Customer?

Once you understand who your current customers are, what their current priorities are, and how their priorities are changing, think about how you might expand the boundaries of your customer set. Are there new groups who would value what you do? Can you jump a step along the value chain and serve your customers' customers? Can you step in the other direction and become a supplier to other companies like your own? Creative customer selection has been a crucial element of the reinventors' success.

Consider the following list of the customers of the reinventors. Note that each of the reinventors serves *not just* the group that is the apparent customer, but other customer sets as well.

INNOVATION IN CUSTOMER SELECTION
WHO IS THE MOST IMPORTANT CUSTOMER?

	Not Just	But
ABB	Industrial buyers	Acquired engineering firms
Coca-Cola	Consumers	Anchor bottlers
Disney	Children	Families
GE	Purchasing agents	Solutions seekers
Intel	OEMs	End users
Microsoft	Consumers	Applications developers, OEMs
Schwab	Investors	Financial planners Regional banks Regional brokers
Swatch	Consumers	Watch manufacturers, Watch distributors
Thermo Electron	Industrial buyers	Investors Entrepreneurial talent in the company

Innovative customer selection was critical to value creation for each of the reinventors.

Percy Barnevik identified power companies and local governments as the key members of ABB's customer set, but recognized that his industry had another large group with unmet needs—the local engineering companies that competed with ABB. Those companies needed a strong brand and distribution system—things ABB could provide. So, rather than compete with them for local projects, Barnevik brought them into the ABB network and made them his most important customers.

Roberto Goizueta realized that Coca-Cola had always thought of consumers as its target customers, when, in fact, *bottlers* were the buyers of Coca-Cola's syrup and controlled the commercial availability of Coke beverages. He reoriented the company to see bottlers as the key customers in the system and began organizational reform that led to Coca-Cola's low-cost distribution system. Goizueta was able to think about multiple sets of customers for Coke. Moreover, he was able to consider different types of customers in each set. (See the exhibit on page 297.)

With these examples in mind, try the following exercise:

Who Are Your Key Customers Today?	*In an Effort to Expand Your Customer Field of Vision, What Other Groups/Industry Players Could You Cultivate?*
1. _____	1. _____
2. _____	2. _____
3. _____	3. _____
4. _____	4. _____
5. _____	5. _____

What are the priorities of these groups/industry players?

1. _____
2. _____
3. _____

What might you offer that they would value?

1. _____
2. _____
3. _____

Which ones are most likely to be potential customers?

1. _____
2. _____
3. _____

	Bottler	**Grocer**	**Fountain**	**Vending**	**Consumer**
Type 1	• Local franchise	• Convenience store	• Convenience store	• Hotel chains	• Taste
Type 2	• Regional	• Local grocer	• Restaurants	• Office buildings	• Price
Type 3	• Large, sophisticated, business-driven	• Large, regional chains	• National chains	• Local organizations	• Availability

If you are having trouble answering these questions, you may not be spending enough time talking with your customers, prospects, or new customer sets. Over the past month, how much time have you spent with your five most important customers? Were your conversations polite exchanges, or substantive discussions about your customers' most pressing priorities? Only the latter type of discussions will allow you to understand your customers' key issues and priorities well enough to build a customer-relevant and customer-compelling business design.

Fill in the following worksheet as a way of gauging the amount of time you spend with your customers and the nature of that time.

Customer Interactions Worksheet

	My Five Most Important Customers	*Time Spent with Them in the Past Month*	*Nature of Conversation or Interaction*
1.	_____	_____	_____
2.	_____	_____	_____
3.	_____	_____	_____
4.	_____	_____	_____
5.	_____	_____	_____

4. How Can I Add Value to the Customer?

By now, you have an understanding of who your current customers are, which groups are potential customers, and what their priorities, both spoken and silent, might be. Next, you must understand exactly how you will create value for these customers.

A business earns no profit when customers are willing to pay only the total cost of a product. Each company must ask itself: "What special benefit of our product will compel customers to pay us a premium?" The answer will always say, in some form: "Customers will pay us a premium if we meet their priorities, which are X, Y, and Z."

Your first step is to analyze your customers' priorities. Next, ask how you can meet those priorities more effectively than your competitors.

- *Which priorities are your competitors satisfying?*
- *Which priorities might you be able to serve better than your competitors can?*
- *Which priorities might you satisfy at a lower cost than your competitors are charging?*
- *How large a premium will your customers pay to have each of their priorities met?*
- *Which set of priorities can you serve simultaneously in order to provide the most value for your customers?*

The answers to these questions will provide your company with a blueprint for adding more value to customers than your competitors are providing.

In his first business design innovation—the value-added discount brokerage—Charles Schwab thought through each of the above questions. He saw that traditional brokerage houses met the priorities of customers who needed large amounts of advice and guidance. Schwab also recognized that those houses lagged in technological investments and that the traditional large roster of brokers raised costs. He decided that his company would serve customers who valued easy, inexpensive access to the markets and who expected good service but were satisfied with easy-to-provide information. Having chosen those target priorities, Schwab built a business around a very low-cost infrastructure and a customer-sensitive employee group. He found a way to add more value to his chosen customers than his competitors did, or could.

Think about your own customer set. What's most important to them? How can you significantly improve the value you provide to them?

_____

_____

_____

_____

5. How Can I Become the Customer's First Choice?

Each customer priority has a relative importance, and customers award a conscious or unconscious score to suppliers, based on how well each priority is met. The winning supplier's business design is the one that scores highest on the customer's most important priorities.

A winning profile might look like this:

Customer Priorities	My Score	My Best Competitor's Score
Priority #1 _____	10	6
Priority #2 _____	8	7
Priority #3 _____	7	6

Note that the difference is greatest on the highest priority item, the highest absolute score is achieved on the highest priority item, and "My Score" is higher than the best competitor on each one of the top three priorities.

Now consider your own case. Who is your most important customer? What are that customer's top three priorities? How do you score? How does your best competitor score?

Customer Priorities	My Score	My Best Competitor's Score
Priority #1 _____		
Priority #2 _____		
Priority #3 _____		

6. WHAT IS MY PROFIT MODEL?

How does my organization make a profit? A business design that adds value to the customer but is not *designed* to create high profitability is an incomplete—and in many cases, a fatally defective—business design.

Thinking explicitly about profitability wasn't important in the age of market share. ("Achieve high market share and the profit will follow.") Today, it is critical. High market share no longer guarantees high profits. Furthermore, high profit happens in so many different ways that it becomes important for an organization to have a clear and *shared* understanding of what its profit model is.

As detailed in Chapter 3, high profit happens in *different* ways. Eleven of these ways were discussed in Chapter 3. The Appendix to Chapter 3 summarizes twenty-two profit models.

Do any of these models apply to your business? Does more than one apply? Which ones?

My profit model(s):

1. _____

2. _____

3. _____

In many cases, a business will take advantage of two or three profit models. Disney's profitability, for example, is a function of the blockbuster model (number 6 from Appendix to Chapter 3) and the profit multiplier model (number 7). ABB's profit models include specialization profit (number 9) and customer solutions profit (number 1).

Coca-Cola's profitability is driven by three profit models: multi-component profit—vending, fountain (number 3), brand profit—premium over unbranded beverages (number 12), and relative market share profit—dominant share positions in international markets (number 20).

It is likely that your business derives its profitability from two or more profit models. If none of the profit models in the Appendix to Chapter 3 applies to your business, you may have to develop your own. First, ask: "How does high profit happen in my business? Who is the most profitable company in my business, and why?"

_____

_____

_____

_____

Is there a picture that captures how profitability works in your business? Can you sketch it? What is on the X-axis? Time? Scale? How do the different pieces of your business relate to one another?

Now, describe the profit model that drives your business:

_____

_____

_____

_____

Whether your profit model is one of those discussed in the Appendix to Chapter 3 or one that you've developed, ask the next question: "Does everybody in my organization understand our profit model? Does the organization align its actions to create the conditions that will achieve high profitability? Do we make decisions and allocate resources based on this understanding?"

7. What Is My Current Business Design?

After you have translated your customers' priorities into profit, you will need to design a business model for your company that is consistent with the profit zone in your industry. A company's business design is composed of four strategic elements: (1) customer selection, (2) value capture, (3) strategic control, and (4) scope. The table below profiles these four strategic dimensions of business design.

Dimension	Key Issue	Key Questions
1. *Customer Selection*	Which customers do I want to serve?	To which customers can I add real value? Which customers will *allow* me to profit? Which customers do I *not* want to serve?
2. *Value Capture*	How do I make a profit?	How do I capture, as profit, a portion of the value I created for customers? What is my profit model?
3. *Differentiation/ Strategic Control*	How do I protect my profit stream?	Why do my chosen customers buy from me? What makes my value proposition unique/differentiated vs. other competitors'? What strategic control points can counterbalance customer or competitor power?

Dimension	Key Issue	Key Questions
4. Scope	What activities do I perform?	What products, services, and solutions do I want to sell? Which activities or functions do I want to perform in-house? Which ones do I want to subcontract, outsource, or work with a business partner to provide?

If the business design is to succeed, its elements must (1) be aligned with customers' most important priorities and (2) be tested for consistency to ensure that the business design functions as a coherent and mutually reinforcing whole.

Alongside the dimensions listed below, describe your company's current business design. Fill in as much of the information as you can. The questions listed in the table above will help you shape your responses.

My Company's Business Design

Customer Selection _____

Value Capture _____

Strategic _____
Control   _____
              _____
              _____
              _____

Scope   _____
              _____
              _____
              _____

Keep this business design in mind as you move to the next activity.

Do these have to be the elements of your company's business design? Have you considered other options that you may want to substitute? Does your customer set consist of only one segment of customers, or are there two or more? Do you currently focus on all your customer segments? Is that wise? Have you ever considered downstream customers? In the following chart, what options are relevant for your company?

EXAMPLES OF BUSINESS DESIGN OPTIONS

					Others	
Customer Selection	All segments	Segment one	Segment two	Down-stream customers	___	___
Value Capture	Revenue per unit	Licensing fees	Service revenue	Solutions revenue	___	___
Strategic Control	Brand	Low cost	Two-year lead	Customer relationship	___	___
Scope	Broad line	Narrow line	Fully integrated	Virtual	___	___

A company's business design includes operating dimensions (purchasing, manufacturing, etc.) and organizational dimensions, in addition to the dimensions shown here (customer selection, value capture, strategic control, and scope). Operating and organizational dimensions are described in greater detail in Appendix 1.

8. Who Are My *Real* Competitors?

How can you know whether these are the right strategic elements for your business design? Start by comparing your business design to those of your competitors. Traditionally, competitors are identified as "companies that do what we do." However, your true competitors are any companies that share your customers and/or your scope. Your competitors may be in industries that are different from yours. They may provide a completely different set of products and services. Today, your company must draw a very broad competitive radar screen to capture all the different business designs that compete for your customers' attention, budget, and allegiance. Perform the following activity to identify *all* of your competitors.

1. *Draw a blank radar screen of four concentric circles:*

2. *Populate the inner circle with your direct competitors and put your indirect competitors in the outer circles. See the example on page 306 of how the steel industry might look.*

3. *Now, shift your perspective. Step into your customers' shoes. Look at the world through your customers' eyes. What companies do your customers regard as their best options?*

4. *What companies are not competitors yet, but could be in the next year or two? List them at the very edge of the outer circle.*

If you find it hard to fill out the circles with confidence, consult your customers or the securities analysts who follow your company. Ask them to identify the companies they regard as your competitors. Their choices may be more objective than yours. A few thoughtful resources can help you to get to the right answers more quickly than you could on your own.

9. What Are My Toughest Competitors' Business Designs?

After going through this process, ask yourself: "Who are my two most dangerous competitors (most customer-relevant, most resource-efficient)?" When you have identified these competitors, ask yourself, "How do their business designs compare to mine?"

	My Business Design	Competitor A	Competitor B
Customer Selection	_____	_____	_____
	_____	_____	_____
	_____	_____	_____
	_____	_____	_____
Value Capture	_____	_____	_____
	_____	_____	_____
	_____	_____	_____
	_____	_____	_____
Strategic Control	_____	_____	_____
	_____	_____	_____
	_____	_____	_____
	_____	_____	_____
Scope	_____	_____	_____
	_____	_____	_____
	_____	_____	_____
	_____	_____	_____
Other Dimensions	_____	_____	_____
	_____	_____	_____
	_____	_____	_____
	_____	_____	_____

Do you _know_ what your toughest competitors' business designs are? Exactly how do they differ from yours? For what reasons are they different? Do the differences give you any useful ideas? Look at the examples that appeared earlier in the book. (See Exhibits 7.3 and 10.2.) You can see dramatic distinctions between business designs within the manufacturing, entertainment, and beverage industries.

Knowing the difference between your business design and your best competitors' business designs is helpful because it allows you to understand the value flows within your industry. With this understanding, you will be better able to create value for your customers and respond to their changing needs and priorities.

10. What Is My *Next* Business Design?

When was the last time that your business design changed? For what reasons did it change? More importantly, how well does it match or not match your customers' priorities? This is the key question for any executive to ask about his or her business—and the question that most executives are afraid to ask. A business design that is not aligned with customer priorities will soon move to a state of value outflow. A business design that is well aligned with customers' priorities will be in a state of value inflow until those priorities change.

How should you change your business design in the future, when your customers' priorities change? Use the following space to help you with your predictions.

My Business Design

	1998	2001
Customer Selection	_____	_____
	_____	_____
	_____	_____
	_____	_____
Value Capture	_____	_____
	_____	_____
	_____	_____
	_____	_____
Strategic Control	_____	_____
	_____	_____
	_____	_____
	_____	_____
Scope	_____	_____
	_____	_____
	_____	_____

11. WHAT IS MY STRATEGIC CONTROL POINT?

One of the most important elements of your business design is strategic control. After you have envisioned how your company will need to change as your customers' priorities change, you will be ready to identify the strategic control point in your industry. Recall

EXHIBIT 15.2 *Strategic Control Point Index*

Profit-Protecting Power	Index	Strategic Control Point	Example(s)
High	10	Own the standard	Microsoft, Oracle
	9	Manage the value chain	Intel, Coke
	8	String of superdominant positions	Coke, internationally
	7	Own the customer relationship	GE, EDS
Medium	6	Brand, copyright	Countless
	5	Two-year product development lead	Intel
Low	4	One-year product development lead	Few
	3	Commodity with 10 to 20 percent cost advantage	Nucor, SW Air
None	2	Commodity with cost parity	Countless
	1	Commodity with cost disadvantage	Countless

from Chapter 3 that the purpose of a strategic control point is to protect the profit stream that the business design has created. A business design without a strategic control point is like a ship with a hole in its hull.

There are many types of strategic control points: brand, patent, copyright, 2-year product development lead, 20 percent cost advantage, control of distribution, control of supply, owning customer information flow, a unique organizational culture, value chain control, and others. Each one is designed to keep a company in the profit zone and to prevent others from stealing away the profitability.

Review the strategic control point index shown in Exhibit 3.4, repeated here.

Where would your company be situated on a strategic control point index? Where would your competitors be placed? What can you do to increase your company's strategic control index? How would your profitability increase if you increased your degree of strategic control?

These questions need thoughtful answers when you are designing the next business model for your company. Each of the reinventors considered the same questions en route to a business design.

Bill Gates's de facto standards in the PC world have created, sustained, and protected profitability for Microsoft. Intel has built a system of strategic control points, including a 2-year lead, a brand that consumers demand, and value chain management. Michael Eisner recognized the threat created by Ovitz's strategic control over movie studios, and wrested control from CAA to Disney. The reinventors are highly focused on understanding and creating strategic control. It drives their ability to create value.

12. What Is My Company Worth?

What is my profit model? What is my strategic control point or points? These are two of the most important questions in business today. They determine how profitable we will be, and how long that profitability might last. They determine whether we will succeed or fail in creating value growth. They are two components of a single model that can help us estimate what our company's stock price valuation will be.

The model shown in Exhibit 15.3 identifies the key components of shareholder value growth: return on sales, expected profit growth, asset efficiency, and strategic control. These four elements determine what your company is worth.

Contrast the cases of Intel, Allied Signal, and US Steel. Intel has 38 percent margins, 24 percent profit growth, assets to sales of 0.7 and a 2-year product lead combined with a strong brand and

EXHIBIT 15.3   *How Much Is My Company Worth?*

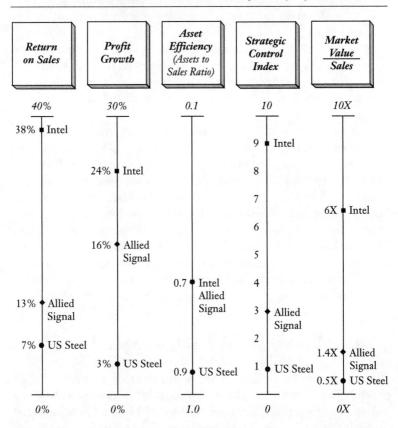

Note: Return on Sales=EBIT/Sales; Profit Growth=projected earnings growth via Value Line & analyst reports; Asset Efficiency=(Assets – Cash & Equivalents – Accounts Payable)/Sales; Market Value/Sales=(Shares Outstanding × Share Price)/Sales.

Source: Compustat, Value Line, Company Reports, CDI Estimates.

powerful value chain management giving it a strategic control index (SCI) of 9. Its market value-to-revenue ratio is 6.

Allied Signal has 13 percent margins, 16 percent profit growth, asset intensity of 0.7, and an SCI of 3. With these characteristics, its market value-to-revenue ratio is 1.4.

US Steel has 7 percent margins, 3 percent profit growth, assets to sales of 0.9, and an SCI of 1. Its market value-to-revenue ratio is 0.5.

These companies occupy their positions on the model because of their respective business designs.

Evaluate your own business design. What is its return on sales, expected 3-year profit growth, assets-to-sales ratio, and SCI? Put your company on the model. How does it compare? Now consider how those variables will change when you move your company to its next-generation business design.

	My Business Design Today	My Business Design Tomorrow
Return on sales		
3-year profit growth		
Assets-to-sales ratio		
SCI		

The reinventors profiled in Part Two have all done an extraordinary job of innovative, customer-relevant, and highly profitable business design. They started with the customer and worked their way back. They invented and reinvented their business design every 5 to 7 years to stay in step with changing customer priorities, and to stay one step ahead of their competitors. They have designed businesses that have produced high margins, high profit growth, low asset intensity, and high strategic control. Their business design reinvention created $700 billion of value growth from 1980 to 1996.

As you think about what *your* company's next business design should be, take advantage of the smart business design thinking that went before you. You'll save yourself time, energy, and risk. You'll significantly increase the probability of creating best-in-industry customer ratings and 20 percent value growth (in up markets and down) for your organization.

CONCLUSION

Each of the reinventors profiled in Part Two has been extraordinarily successful at using carefully chosen tactics to create exceptional profit growth for his company. Middle managers, like those in Chapter 5, have shown that these techniques can be used by anyone at any level in any business. By using these techniques, you will be able to create value for your customers and capture value for your business. You will be able to move your company into the profit zone.

APPENDIX 1

BUSINESS DESIGN

THIS APPENDIX provides a detailed description of the strategic, operating, and organizational dimensions of a company's business design. It presents a template that can be used to profile a company's business design and those of its competitors. (The dimensions and options described in the template are for illustration only. They all have to be customized to your own specific business situation.) See Exhibits A1.1 and A1.2.

Exhibit A1.3 contrasts the business design choices of a very traditional company with those of a very innovative one. Company A's business design (shaded area) is that of a classic manufacturer. It supports a full line of products and serves all customer types. This vertically integrated manufacturer has an adversarial relationship with its suppliers, and performs all R&D in-house. On the organizational side, Company A has a very hierarchical structure, which strongly focuses on doing things "the way they have always been done." Compensation is not strongly tied to company performance.

By contrast, Company B's business design choices (black circles) mark it as an innovative and responsive firm. It has elected to serve distinct customer segments with a tailored product line. Because Company B has cultivated long-term relationships with its customers, its value capture comes from after-sale revenues and even from equity. Its manufacturing operations are less asset-intensive because Company B has chosen to outsource certain activities that are done more cost effectively by others. In Company B, employees work in small profit centers that have significant customer contact, and compensation is a function of the profit centers' results.

As a result of these differences in their business designs, Company A and Company B have created very different outcomes in terms of financial performance and company valuation. See Exhibit A1.4.

These types of differences in business design and related value performance can be found across industries as diverse as manufacturing, steel, air travel, retailing, and pharmaceuticals.

Appendix 2 further explores the relationship between business design and market value.

Appendix 1

EXHIBIT A1.1	*Business Design*

Dimensions	Key Questions
Fundamental Assumptions	How are customers changing? What are customers' priorities? What are the profit drivers for the business?
Strategic Dimensions:	
Customer Selection	To which customers can I add real value? Which customers will allow me to profit? Which customers do I not want to serve?
Value Capture	How do I recapture a portion of the value created for customers as profit? What is my profit model?
Differentiation/ Strategic Control	Why do my chosen customers buy from me? What makes my value proposition unique/differentiated vs. my competitors? What strategic control points can counterbalance customer power?
Scope	What products/services do I want to sell? Which support activities do I want to perform in-house? Which ones do I want to subcontract or outsource?
Operating Dimensions:	
Purchasing System	How do I buy? Transactional or long-term relationship? Antagonistic or partnership?
Manufacturing/ Operating System	How much do I manufacture versus subcontract? Are my manufacturing/ service delivery economics based primarily on fixed or variable costs? Do I need state-of-the-art or ninetieth-percentile process technology?
Capital Intensity	Do I choose a capital-intensive, high-fixed-cost operating system? Or a less capital-intensive, flexible approach?
R&D/Product Development System	Internal or outsourced? Focused on process or product? Focused on astute project selection? Speed of development?
Go-to-Market Mechanism	Direct sales force? Low-cost distribution? Account management? Licensing? Hybrid?
Organizational Dimensions:	
Organizational Configuration	Centralized or decentralized? Pyramid or network? Functional, business, or matrixed? Internal promotion or external hiring?

EXHIBIT A1.2   *Choices, Not Givens: An Example Template*

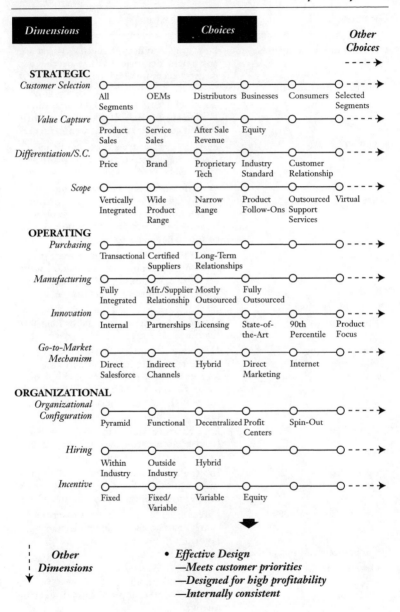

* *Effective Design*
  —*Meets customer priorities*
  —*Designed for high profitability*
  —*Internally consistent*

EXHIBIT A1.3   *Company A vs. Company B*

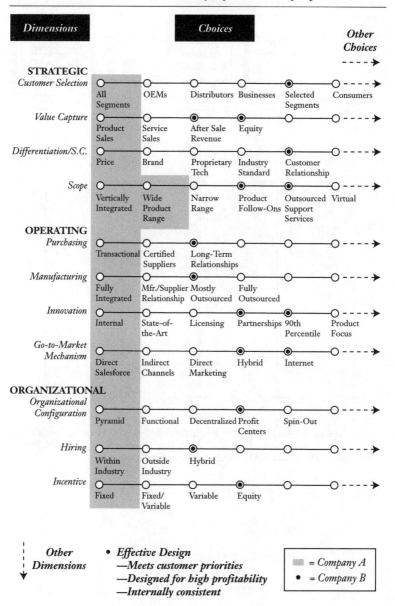

Dimensions		Choices				Other Choices

STRATEGIC

Customer Selection
All Segments — OEMs — Distributors — Businesses — ⊙Selected Segments — Consumers

Value Capture
Product Sales — Service Sales — ⊙After Sale Revenue — ⊙Equity

Differentiation/S.C.
Price — Brand — Proprietary Tech — Industry Standard — ⊙Customer Relationship

Scope
Vertically Integrated — Wide Product Range — Narrow Range — ⊙Product Follow-Ons — ⊙Outsourced Support Services — Virtual

OPERATING

Purchasing
Transactional — Certified Suppliers — ⊙Long-Term Relationships

Manufacturing
Fully Integrated — Mfr./Supplier Relationship — ⊙Mostly Outsourced — Fully Outsourced

Innovation
Internal — State-of-the-Art — Licensing — ⊙Partnerships — ⊙90th Percentile — Product Focus

Go-to-Market Mechanism
Direct Salesforce — Indirect Channels — Direct Marketing — ⊙Hybrid — Internet

ORGANIZATIONAL

Organizational Configuration
Pyramid — Functional — Decentralized — ⊙Profit Centers — Spin-Out

Hiring
Within Industry — Outside Industry — ⊙Hybrid

Incentive
Fixed — Fixed/Variable — Variable — ⊙Equity

Other Dimensions

- **Effective Design**
  —*Meets customer priorities*
  —*Designed for high profitability*
  —*Internally consistent*

▨ = Company A
● = Company B

EXHIBIT A1.4 *Value of Company A vs. Company B*

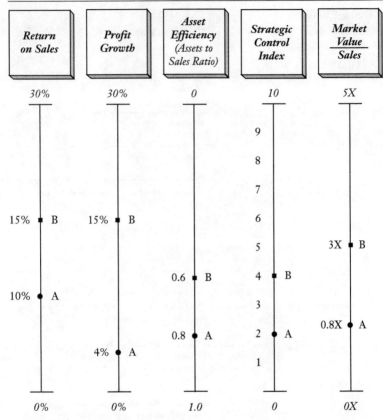

Note: Return on Sales = EBIT/Sales; Profit Growth = projected earnings growth via Value Line; Asset Efficiency = (Assets − Cash & Equivalents − Accounts Payable)/Sales; Market Value/Sales = (Shares Outstanding × Share Price)/Sales.

APPENDIX 2

BUSINESS DESIGN AND MARKET VALUE

FOUR CRITICAL elements determine a company's market value: (1) return on sales, (2) profit growth, (3) asset efficiency, and (4) strategic control.

Return on sales refers to the earnings of a company as a percentage of its sales. Profit growth reflects the estimated profit growth of a company over the next 3 to 5 years.

A company's asset efficiency is determined by its ratio of assets to sales. The lower the asset efficiency (the higher the asset/sales ratio), the greater the drag on the company's profit engine. Even the most powerful profit engine can be overshadowed by a business design that is unnecessarily asset-intensive. Asset intensity absorbs the profit and leaves no free cash flow for the investors.

The strategic control point is the mechanism that a company uses to protect the profit stream that its business design has created. As mentioned in Chapter 3, a business design without a strategic control point is like a ship with a hole in its hull. It will sink much sooner than it has to.

These four elements are determined by a company's business design. Certain business designs provide a high return on sales, high profit growth, high asset efficiency, and a high degree of strategic control. Business designs that produce a high level of performance in each of these categories will have a higher valuation than those that are low in these respects. The value charts in this appendix show the relationship among different business designs within an industry, how these business designs compare on the metrics discussed, and the resulting value that the market places on the business designs. (See Exhibits A2.1, A2.2, A2.3, and A2.4.)

EXHIBIT A2.1   *Steel Industry: Nucor vs. U.S. Steel vs. LTV, 1996*

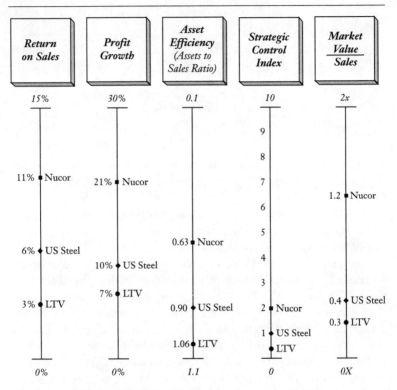

Note: Return on Sales = EBIT/Sales; Profit Growth = projected earnings growth via Value Line & analyst reports; Asset Efficiency = (Assets − Cash & Equivalents − Accounts Payable)/Sales; Market Value/Sales = (Shares Outstanding × Share Price)/Sales.

Over the past two decades, value has migrated in the steel industry from large, asset-intensive, integrated mills such as those of U.S. Steel and LTV, to asset-efficient minimills such as those of Nucor. The value chart for the steel industry puts Nucor's market value-to-sales ratio at 1.2, three times higher than U.S. Steel's business design and four times higher than LTV's. Return on sales, overall, is lower in the steel industry than in some other industries. By comparing business designs within an industry, the value chart provides readers with an understanding of how these metrics affect the valuation of different business designs within the steel industry.

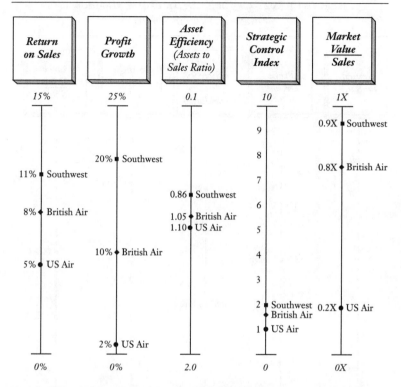

Return on Sales	Profit Growth	Asset Efficiency (Assets to Sales Ratio)	Strategic Control Index	Market Value Sales

Note: Return on Sales = EBIT/Sales; Profit Growth = projected earnings growth via Value Line & analyst reports; Asset Efficiency = (Assets − Cash & Equivalents − Accounts Payable)/Sales; Market Value/Sales = (Shares Outstanding × Share Price)/Sales.

Source: Compustat, Value Line, Company Reports, CDI Estimates.

The value chart for the airline industry reveals the value differential created by the point-to-point business design of Southwest versus the hub-and-spoke business design of US Air. The hub-and-spoke business design created value for many years for many airline companies. Today, Southwest's market value-to-sales ratio is over four times that of US Air. Southwest has a return on sales of 11 percent, US Air is at 5.0 percent. Southwest has an estimated profit growth of 20 percent; US Air is at 2 percent. Southwest has an asset efficiency metric of 0.86, and US Air is over 1; and US Air's strategic control is significantly below Southwest's. British Air's overseas travel business design is between US Air and Southwest on all metrics. Thus, British Air falls between Southwest and US Air on its market value-to-sales ratio.

EXHIBIT A2.3 *Software Industry: Microsoft vs. Oracle vs. Novell, 1996*

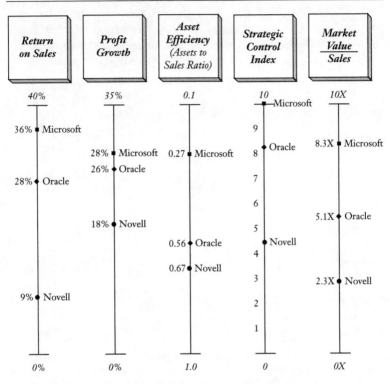

Note: Return on Sales = EBIT/Sales; Profit Growth = projected earnings growth via Value Line & analyst reports; Asset Efficiency = (Assets – Cash & Equivalents – Accounts Payable)/Sales; Market Value/Sales = (Shares Outstanding × Share Price)/Sales.

Source: Compustat, Value Line, Company Reports, CDI Estimates.

In the software industry, there are also significant differences among companies, although the order of magnitude may be different. Software companies have higher return on sales figures, higher profit growth estimates, and greater asset efficiency compared to other industries, but, in relation to each other, the company with the highest return on sales, highest estimated profit growth, greatest asset efficiency, and highest strategic control will have the highest market value-to-sales ratio. Microsoft, Oracle, and Novell demonstrate the differences in business design performance and therefore the differences in valuation.

EXHIBIT A2.4   *Microprocessors: Intel vs. Texas Instruments vs. AMD, 1996*

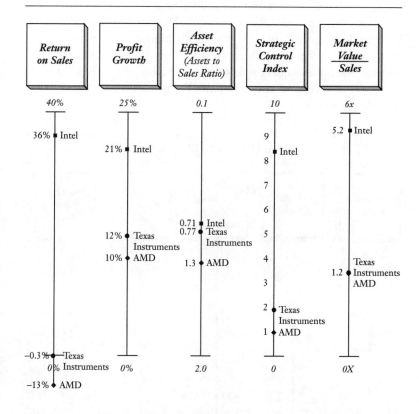

Note: Return on Sales = EBIT/Sales; Profit Growth = projected earnings growth via Value Line & analyst reports; Asset Efficiency = (Assets − Cash & Equivalents − Accounts Payable)/Sales; Market Value/Sales = (Shares Outstanding × Share Price)/Sales.

Source: Compustat, Value Line, Company Reports, CDI Estimates.

Intel, Texas Instruments, and Advanced Micro Devices (AMD) all produce microprocessors, yet they all have very different business designs. Intel's business design gives it the highest return on sales, and the greatest profit growth, asset efficiency, and strategic control. Texas Instruments and AMD have business designs that impact their metrics and give them a significantly lower market value-to-sales ratio than Intel.

Appendix 2

CHANGING BUSINESS DESIGNS

A company's business design must be reinvented over and over again in order to remain customer-relevant and to be capable of producing high levels of profitability. Over time, a company can improve its return on sales, profit growth prospects, asset efficiency, and strategic control. As it does so, its market value-to-sales ratio will increase.

A look at several of the reinventors' companies over time shows how this works.

EXHIBIT A2.5 *Disney*

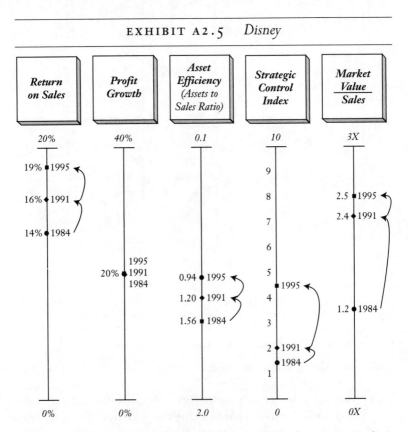

Note: Return on Sales = EBIT/Sales; Profit Growth = projected earnings growth via Value Line; Asset Efficiency = (Assets − Cash & Equivalents − Accounts Payable)/Sales; Market Value/Sales = (Shares Outstanding × Share Price)/Sales.

Source: Compustat, Value Line, Company Reports, CDI Estimates.

From 1984 to 1995, Disney improved its return on sales, its asset efficiency and strategic control (Exhibit A2.5).

A company ready for a change in business design will begin moving down the scale, as is the case with Disney. From 1984 to 1991, Disney moved up in all respects except profit growth. In turn, its market value-to-sales ratio doubled. From 1991 to 1995, Disney increased its return on sales, maintained its profit growth, and decreased its asset intensity. Its market value-to-sales ratio went from 2.4 to 2.5.

EXHIBIT A2.6 *Microsoft*

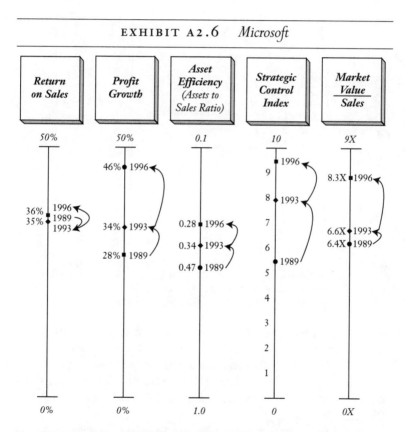

Note: Return on Sales = EBIT/Sales; Profit Growth = projected earnings growth via Value Line; Asset Efficiency = (Assets − Cash & Equivalents − Accounts Payable)/Sales; Market Value/Sales = (Shares Outstanding × Share Price)/Sales.

Source: Compustat, Value Line, Company Reports, CDI Estimates.

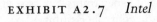

EXHIBIT A2.7   *Intel*

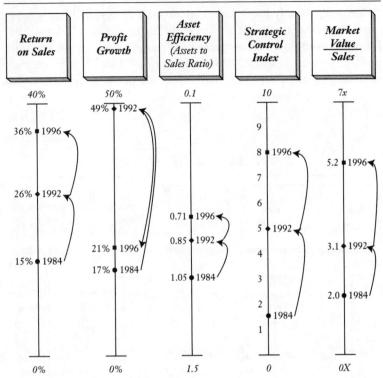

Note: Return on Sales = EBIT/Sales; Profit Growth = projected earnings growth via Value Line; Asset Efficiency = (Assets − Cash & Equivalents − Accounts Payable)/Sales; Market Value/Sales = (Shares Outstanding × Share Price)/Sales.

Source: Compustat, Value Line, Company Reports, CDI Estimates.

Microsoft has maintained a fairly constant return on sales over time, yet its profitability, asset efficiency, and strategic control have increased. As a result, Microsoft's market value-to-sales ratio went from 6.4 in 1989 to 8.3 in 1996 (Exhibit A2.6). Intel has had similar results, except for a decrease in profit growth rate from 1992 to 1996 (Exhibit A2.7).

These value charts explain how market value happens and how value is generated for a company. A company can determine its worth relative to its competitors along these four metrics. As a company changes its business design over time, so that it increases its return on sales, profits, asset efficiency, and strategic control point, it can increase its value.

Notes

CHAPTER 4

1. *The Cincinnati Enquirer*, January 26, 1997.

CHAPTER 6

1–2. Swatch history is from an interview with Nicolas Hayek and SMH/Swatch documents and publications.
3. Interview with Hayek.
4. *Harvard Business Review*: "Message and Muscle, An Interview with Swatch Titan Nicolas Hayek," by William Taylor, March–April, 1993. SMH publicity document, "The History of SMH Group." From *El-Wekalah* (Mideast & Africa), "Swatchology," by Monal Seidan, October 1995.
5. From interview with Hayek.
6. From *Harvard Business Review*: "Message and Muscle."
7. *Id.*
8. From interview with Raman Handa.
9. From *SwissBusiness*, "Medal-Winning Suppliers," by Colin Farmer, February–March 1996. From *Inside Media*, "Nike and Swatch Map Games," May 15, 1996.

CHAPTER 7

1. From interview with Mark Rowland, president, Rowland & Co.
2. From interview with Tom Pirko, managing partner, Bevmark Inc., LLC.
3. Mark Pendergrast, *For God, Country, and Coca-Cola* (New York: Macmillan, 1993), p. 74.
4. Pendergrast, p. 310.
5. Porter, Michael, Coca-Cola versus Pepsi-Cola, HBS Publishing, Case Study N9-389-170, 1989.
6. *Fortune* Magazine, October 28, 1996, p. 84.

7. Pendergrast, p. 339.
8. Pendergrast, p. 343.
9. Pendergrast, pp. 337–339.
10. From interview with Rowland.
11. From interview with Pirko.

CHAPTER 8

1. Schwab history: From *Fortune* Magazine, "How Schwab Wins Investors," by Terence P. Pare, June 1, 1992; *Los Angeles Times*, "Word of Honor," by Richard Lee Colvin, April 30, 1996; *Business Week*, "The Schwab Revolution," December 19, 1994; and various other sources.
2. From *Fortune* Magazine, "How Schwab Wins Investors," by Terence P. Pare, June 1, 1992.
3. *Business Week*, December 19, 1994.
4. From interview with Dan Leemon, executive vice president of business strategy, Charles Schwab & Co.
5. From interview with Mike Kabarec.
6. From interview with Mike Davis.
7. From interview with Greg Lathrop.
8. From interview with Craig Litman.
9. From interview with Charles Schwab.

CHAPTER 9

1. *Forbes*, April 16, 1990.
2. Burgelman and Cogan, *Intel Corp. (A): The DRAM Decision*, HBS Publishing, Case Study, January 1989.
3. Brandenburger, Krishna, and Sinha, *Intel and Licensing in the Semiconductor Industry*, HBS Publishing, Case Study 190133, February 1990.
4. *Business Week*, June 1, 1992.
5. *Fortune* Magazine, February 22, 1993.

CHAPTER 10

1. From Joe Flower, *Prince of the Magic Kingdom* (New York: Wiley, 1991), p. 156.
2. From Ron Grover, *The Disney Touch* (Chicago: Irwin, 1997), p. 55.
3. Grover, p. 83.
4. Grover, p. 101.
5. Grover, p. 104.

6. Grover, p. 132.
7. National Association of Theater Owners.
8. Grover, p. 61.

CHAPTER 11

1. From interview with Hatsopoulos, March 26, 1997.
2. *Id.*
3. Paul Knight, NatWest Securities, Analyst Report, January 1997, p. 10.
4. From interview with Hatsopoulos, March 26, 1997.
5. *Daedalus* (American Academy of Arts and Sciences), "A Perpetual Idea Machine, Thermo Electron, Managing Innovation," March 22, 1996.
6. *Id.*
7. *Id.*
8. From interview with Hatsopoulos, March 26, 1997.
9. PR Newswire, January 22, 1997.

CHAPTER 12

1. From interview with Barnevik.
2. A. Basak, ABN AMRO HOARE GOVETT, Analyst Report, June 11, 1996, p. 7.
3. *Sloan Management Review*, September 22, 1993.
4. From interview with Barnevik.

CHAPTER 13

1. Stephen Manes and Paul Andrews, *Gates* (New York: Touchstone Books, 1994).
2. Manes and Andrews, pp. 125–128.
3. Paul Carroll, *Big Blues: The Unmaking of IBM* (New York: Crown, 1994).
4. James Wallace and Jim Erickson, *Hard Drive: Bill Gates and the Making of the Microsoft Empire* (New York: Wiley, 1992).
5. Wallace and Erickson, pp. 256–257.
6. Wallace and Erickson, p. 360.
7. Analyst reports.
8. Analyst reports.

Acknowledgments

THE PROFIT Zone describes a mindset that can be an extremely powerful tool in setting a company's strategic course. Learning from the experiences and successes of a set of forward-looking business leaders, readers will gain the ability to understand and respond to the evolving business landscape by creating business design responses that lead to sustained, superior profitability.

The approach to strategic thinking that we develop throughout this book is built on the foundation that we laid in our earlier book, *Value Migration*, in which we described a phenomenon of market, industry, and company dynamics that has occurred across dozens of economic sectors. The old rules were breaking down. The traditional measurements of success were no longer valid. Long-time market leaders were falling, and new innovative competitors, operating with new economic assumptions, were capturing significant value for their shareholders. Based on the observations that we and our partners have made in the course of the work we have done for our clients, we articulated a framework for diagnosing value migration within a market, for recognizing the pattern of migration in order to anticipate its outcome, and for creating an organizational capability for detecting and responding to migration when it occurs.

The Profit Zone builds on *Value Migration* by focusing on the question of response: How can you create sustainable profitability and shareholder value growth in a world where value migration continually changes the rules of the game? *Value Migration* detailed numerous examples of new competitors who upset the apple cart with entrepreneurial energy and the advantage of a clean slate, but we recognized that most companies are, to some extent, incumbents. With assets, with customers, with cultures that have enjoyed success, the most relevant examples involve a company that is able to reinvent itself in the face of value migration. We have therefore focused *The Profit Zone* on a series of reinventors—individuals who have been able to lead their organizations through the wrenching business design changes that are necessary to keep a company in the profit zone. The challenges of reinvention are substantial. The list of reinventors is not long. That is what makes their lessons so valuable.

The ideas and examples in this book are drawn from the casework that we have done for our clients since founding Corporate Decisions, Inc. (CDI) in 1983. (CDI merged into Mercer Management Consulting in 1997.) When we founded CDI, the consulting field was dominated by an inside-out approach to strategy that focused on cost and total quality management. Their successors in management theory—time-based competition and business process reengineering—continued this inside-out theme of improving the competitiveness of a business by making it better at what it does. Although these techniques—which persist today—are valuable, they are self-limiting. We have taken a different approach. We believe that the true key to sustainable value growth lies in developing a strategic understanding of the customer. With this understanding as a compass, a company can successfully position itself in the profit zone.

This book is the product of the same organizational and intellectual energy that produces insights for CDI's clients. We would like to thank those clients who have inspired us to develop a deeper understanding of profitability by asking us tough questions—questions like those at the beginning of each chapter in the book. Through that constant challenge, we have identified the reinventors and begun to characterize their actions. Several clients also served as reviewers of sections of the manuscript throughout its development. We thank them for their valuable feedback on the relevance of these concepts to the strategic situations that they face.

The detailed understanding and insights of several of the reinventors presented in this book were gathered during direct interviews. We wish to thank those leaders who participated by revealing the challenges of customer-centric thinking, of organizational inertia, and of strategic leadership. Their feedback was extremely helpful in developing the central theses and frameworks of our overall approach.

We would like to thank Bob Andelman, who contributed much to the process of writing *The Profit Zone*. Bob conducted several of the interviews that provided first-person perspective, developed a more accessible prose, and offered a number of his own insights.

We would also like to thank John Mahaney at Crown Business for his coaching, encouragement, guidance, and feedback as the manuscript developed. His ideas shaped the approach we took, the level of insight and specificity required, and the balance between framework and example. He helped us focus on the most important concepts and themes.

Acknowledgments

Our partners—Kevin Mundt, Bill Stevenson, Ted Moser, Kirk Grosel, John Kania, Charlie Hoban, and Rick Wise—were essential to the development of this material. Our understanding of profitability is based on the intellectual leadership that they showed on specific projects. The talented professionals who make up CDI are lucky to have the leadership of this group. Rick Wise and Ted Moser were especially helpful in furthering the development of our concepts. They challenged us to provide a structure that allows the material to be most useful to a broad audience. Charlie Hoban's editing skills and insights on structure were also extremely valuable as we moved from roughly articulated frameworks to a polished and cohesive manuscript.

Finally, we would like to thank the entire team at CDI who shared their research, their ideas, and their enthusiasm. Special thanks go to the team led by Martin Stein and including Harriet Winter, Steve Sibley, Dave Monaco, Eric Emmons, Richard DeSilva, Nirav Dagli, and Steve Glick. They gathered the research material on the reinventors, from which the book was constructed. Their thoroughness, insight, and energy were critical to getting the project off the ground. Martin Stein, Harriet Winter, and Steve Sibley deserve special thanks for their efforts in manuscript development and their support of the editing process.

Index

Index

Charles Schwab & Company (*cont.*):
  product-centric approach, 154
  profit-centric concerns, 173
  SchwabLife Insurance Services,
    171–172
  ShareLink Investment Services PLC,
    172
  value-added discounter model,
    156–157, 169, 298–299
  value creation, 171
Cisco, 39
citizen, 115–116
Clean Air Act, 226
Clozaril Patient Management System,
  104–107
Coca-Cola:
  acquisitions, 146, 149
  business design, case illustration:
    asset intensity, 52, 146
    bottler relationship, changes in,
      140–143, 145, 296
    customer analysis, 138
    customer selection, 142, 149, 295
    earnings, 150
    future directions, 150–152
    generally, 5, 10, 25, 39–40, 54, 56–57
    high-profit zones, 143–144
    historical background, 138–139
    international business, 147, 150
    manage-the-value-chain, 139,
      144–146
    scope, 142, 149
    strategic control, 53, 142, 149
    value capture, 142, 149
  earnings, 150
  major customer groups, 291
  market share leadership, 141
  market value growth, 137
  multicomponent profit, 301
  Pepsi *vs.*, 142
  value growth, 280–282
Coca-Cola Enterprises (CCE), 146, 151
Comcast, 272
Commodore, 259
communication:
  continuous, 29
  with customers, 25–26, 29
  investment, in watchmaking business
    design, 116
  see also dialogue, with customers
Compaq, 183, 188–189, 261
competition:
  analysis of, 300–301, 305–307
  in automobile industry, 31, 39
  business designs of, 307–309
  global, 6
  impact of, 6
  no-profit zones and, 6–7
  as partners, 161
  2-year lead over, 59
  value growth and, 279–280
  in watchmaking industry, 38

Compuserve, 273
Computervision, 56
consumer electronics industry, 5, 59
copyright, as strategic control point, 52
Cox, Carrie Smith, 104–107
CP/M operating system, 260
create-the-standard business design,
  254–276
Creative Artists Agency (CAA), 199–200,
  311
customer(s):
  analysis of, 23–24, 29–30, 50–51,
    290–293
  continuity, 37–38
  direct contact with, 43–44
  field of vision, 28–29
  Interactions Worksheet, 297
  need/priorities of, 21, 23–25, 30,
    293–294, 299–300
  power of, 6–7, 17, 52
  profitability profile, 50–51
  profit models and, *see* profit-centric
    business design
  relationship with, 98–99, 167–168
  relevance of, 33, 44
  role of, historical perspective, 17
  satisfaction, 17–18
  value-added, 27–28, 298–299
customer-centric business design, 22,
  30–32
customer-centric environment, 9, 15
customer-centric thinking, 17–21
customer development/customer solutions
  profit model:
  checklist for, 90
  General Electric case illustration,
    73–87
  overview, 37–38, 57
customer selection: *see* case illustrations
  in competitor analysis, 308
  components of, 294–298, 302
  current/future business designs, 309
  defined, 10–12, 29, 65
  options, examples of, 304
cycle profit, 67

Davis, John, 153
Davis, Mike, 160
decision-making process, 13, 27–28
de facto standard profit model, 46–47, 62,
  311
Dell, 70, 188, 261
dialogue with customers, importance of, 22,
  29, 83
Digital Equipment (DEC), 3–4, 28, 271
Digital Research, CP/M operating
  system, 260
Disney, Walt, 198
Disney Company, *see* Walt Disney
  Company
Disney Store, 207–210
distribution, as strategic control point, 52

Index

Index

Index

The Profit Zone tells how profits happen. Read these other books by coauthors Adrian J. Slywotzky and David J. Morrison to discover how you can make *sure* profits happen:

How Digital Is Your Business?
0-609-60770-7.
$25.00 hardcover
(Canada: $38.00)

Profit Patterns
0-8129-3118-1.
$27.50 hardcover
(Canada: $39.95)

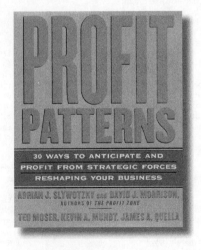